A NOTE ABOUT THE PRESENTATION OF RECIPES

1. Quantities of ingredients have been expressed in standard measurements which are simple to do in the average kitchen around the world. Measurements are given in teaspoons, tablespoons, cups, litres, grams (g), kilograms (kg), millimetres (mm), centimetres (cm), and metres (m) as well as quarts, ounces (oz), pounds (lb), inches, and feet.

    The difference between measuring cups internationally is minimal. When measuring liquids use a clear glass or plastic cup with appropriate markings.

    All volume measurements (e.g. spoon, cup, litre, quart, or any portion of these) are always level measurements.

2. An ingredient is measured after it has been prepared to the state which is described in the list of ingredients. For example, an ingredient may appear in a recipe as:

    1 teaspoon fresh garlic, very finely chopped

    Therefore, measure 1 teaspoonful of fresh garlic which has already been peeled and very finely chopped.

    Or, if a recipe calls for 1 cup of grated beet root (where the beet root has already been cooked and peeled), it will appear as:

    1 cup beet root (cooked and peeled), grated

3. Servings are given in sizes considered generally appropriate when at least two other courses are included in the meal.

4. Quantities of accompanying items in particular, are listed to the nearest reasonable measurement which represents the accumulative quantity recommended for individual servings and extra portions if appropriate. This often applies to sauces and garnishes.

BASIC CONVERSION GUIDE

	METRIC	IMPERIAL
Dry Measures	28 g	1 oz
	1 kg	2.2 lb
Liquid Measures	30 ml	1 fl oz
	250 ml	8 fl oz or 1 cup
Length	2.5 cm	1 inch
	1 m	40 inches
Liquid and	5 ml	1 teaspoon
Volume Measures	15 ml	1 tablespoon
	1 litre	$4^1/_4$ cups
		or $1^2/_3$ pints
		or $^4/_5$ quart

OTHER HELPFUL EQUIVALENTS

	3 teaspoons	1 tablespoon
	4 tablespoons	$^1/_4$ cup
	16 tablespoons	1 cup
Metric	1000 g	1 kg
	1000 ml	1 litre
	10 mm	1 cm
	100 cm	1 m
Imperial	16 oz	1 lb
	8 fl oz	1 cup
	$2^1/_2$ cups	1 pint
	5 cups	1 quart
	2 pints	1 quart
	12 inches	1 foot

from THE
AMBASSADOR'S
TABLE

Margaret H. Dickenson

from THE
AMBASSADOR'S
TABLE

BLUEPRINTS FOR CREATIVE ENTERTAINING

Photographs *by* Luca Invernizzi Tettoni

RANDOM HOUSE OF CANADA

from THE AMBASSADOR'S TABLE

Publisher
SHIRLEY HEW

Project Editor
CHRISTINE CHUA

Art Director
TUCK LOONG

Production Manager
ANTHONEY CHUA

Colour separation
Colourscan Overseas Co Pte Ltd

Printed by
KHL Printing Co Pte Ltd

© 1996 Times Editions Pte Ltd

Canadian Cataloguing in Publication Data

Dickenson, Margaret
        From the ambassador's table

Includes index.
ISBN 0-679-30875-X

1. Entertaining.   2. Cookery.   3. Menus.
I. Title.

TX731.D522 1997   642'.4   C97-930753-8

ACKNOWLEDGEMENTS

I dedicate this book to my dear husband, Larry, and our daughters, Tonya and Christa.

My greatest appreciation is extended to those who particularly encouraged me in this project. They include Renée Zecha, Helen Vanwel, Jean and Kent Harding, Roy McKechnie, Josh Josphson, Jennifer Grange, Alison Fryer, Bahia Jaafar, Michel Chalhoub, Jon Richards, Detlef Skrobanek, Heinz von Holzen, Bob McRae, Howard and Marilyn Campbell, Marianne Pereira, and Mervin Pereira. We are grateful for the loan of some tableware items from our friends in the management teams of the Grand Hyatt, Regent Four Seasons, Shangri-La, and Sari Pan Pacific hotels in Jakarta, Indonesia.

Without the faith in me shown by Shirley Hew of Times Editions this book would not have got beyond my computer. It was a pleasure for Larry and myself to work with a very sensitive and committed team — Christine Chua, Tuck Loong, and Luca Tettoni.

Many Indonesians, as well as residents of Indonesia, have supported this project. They include Jenni Gunawan, Sukmawati Widjaja, Steve Sondakh, Herman Djuhar, Bambang Sumantri, Joseph Chuang, Husodo Angkosubroto, Ian Campbell, and Xaverius Nursalim.

Our dedicated staff at the Official Residence of the Canadian Ambassador in Jakarta deserve special recognition. Their eagerness to learn and their never failing devotion have been remarkable. I would like to convey my very special thanks to Suyono, Darti, Rusli, and Shakun.

CONTENTS

INTRODUCTION

PERSONAL BACKGROUND AND ENTERTAINING PHILOSOPHY

After 28 years in the Canadian Foreign Service and hundreds of requests, I have decided to record and share my very personal know-how for successful entertaining. This is not just another cookbook, or a book on entertaining. *From the Ambassador's Table* reflects a personal life enriched by human relationships, a strong interest in food, and a hearty appreciation of culture. It is a confession of an unconventional strategy for a total look when entertaining, influenced by a life continually seasoned by new experiences and adjustments. It is a testimony of how our family has not only happily adapted to life in many exotic places, but has indeed thrived, benefiting enormously from a rich pageant of diverse cultures.

I grew up on a farm in Northern Ontario, Canada. From a very young age, my responsibilities ranged from milking cows and working in vegetable gardens to doing household tasks. My family roots are Ukrainian. Cabbage rolls, pirozhki, home-made bread, and warm hospitality were always abundant in our home. Food was highly valued, religiously respected, and certainly never wasted. I began to cook at the age of six. My fascination for creative cooking was stimulated by easy access to a variety of fresh farm produce.

My romance with food continued at the University of Guelph where I received a degree in Foods and Nutrition. I also met Larry, my husband-to-be, the first morning of life on campus. We were married three years later. Immediately upon graduation, we began an incredible international odyssey. Over the years, our experiences have been enhanced by two daughters, Tonya and Christa, who never failed to be positive, active, and contributing participants in so many aspects of this adventure.

Our first foreign posting was to Vienna, Austria with accreditation to Hungary and Rumania, followed by a temporary assignment to Belgrade, Yugoslavia. Other assignments include: Moscow, in the former USSR; the European Union, Brussels; Cairo, Egypt; Seoul, South Korea; Kuwait with accreditation to Oman, the United Arab Emirates, Bahrain, and Qatar; Jakarta, Indonesia; plus two assignments in Ottawa, Canada. Larry has been Canada's Ambassador on our last two postings.

Over these 28 years, our focus on personalized entertaining and my love for developing unique recipes have flourished with exposure to different peoples and cultures. The repertoire of original dishes which has evolved reflects subtle influences drawn from our varied postings. Many recipes and menus represent a creative fusion of international cultures and tastes.

A degree in Foods and Nutrition has been an enormous asset in providing professional confidence to my food preparation as well as to our entertaining. In addition to a knowledge of food, its qualities, and how it behaves, I understand the value of sound culinary techniques and standards.

The recipes and style of presentation contained in this book also reflect a happy rural childhood and an affinity with nature. Flowers, leaves, berries, animals, frost, pools, grass, straw, baskets, parcels, and other such items become part of my presentation. In addition, my rural background has taught me to be practical, resourceful, and conscious of the nutritional and economical value of food.

I have found that it is best to choose foods which are healthy, easily available, and reasonable in price even when entertaining. "Smart eating" has become a way of life in our home. Fats, cream, and sugar are used with discretion. Evaporated or low-fat evaporated milk can be substituted for cream, and light versions of sour cream and mayonnaise may be used.

My recipes allow much of the food preparation to be done in advance, or in stages. It has only been during our last two posts that we have had any assistance when entertaining, so it has been necessary for me to develop a set of blueprints for easy entertaining that work effectively whether a host/hostess entertains with or without help.

Although virtually all recipes could be classified as gourmet, most allow for great flexibility in culinary skills and interpretation. I have taught gourmet cooking professionally at college level and have participated in gourmet cuisine television programmes. In addition, it has been necessary for me to teach unskilled embassy residence staff, for them to acquire talents, hopefully enabling them to produce some of the finest cuisine which guests have ever eaten, and to do much of the planning, organization, and orchestration of events. This has not been a particularly complex process, because my blueprints work. Of course, commitment and patience are important factors in any training and learning experience.

For many years and in several different countries, Larry and I have been active in the international gourmet club, La Chaine des Rotisseurs, where detail and the total entertaining package are also priorities in the club's philosophy. As *conseiller gastronomique* of the club in Jakarta, I have enjoyed advising food and beverage managers and personnel of five-star hotels on Chaine des Rotisseurs' dinners.

Our family, always anxious to understand and to be a part of an ever changing international environment, has also developed a passion for the art and antiques of different countries. Regardless of our location, we arrange our collection of diverse art objects in a manner which maintains intimate ties with past experiences. Through our collection, the spirit of those experiences quickly captivates guests. When the first hors d'oeuvre appears, probably presented in a turtle shaped bread or some other tempting manner, guests generally recognize that a sense of communication is being established through the food as well. This is where my concept of a personalized and a total look of successful entertaining begins. Successful entertaining is the skill of establishing effective communication between host/hostess and guests, among guests, and also between guests, the food, and surroundings.

HOW TO DO IT ALL

We have often been told that the way guests are received and entertained in our home leaves them with the satisfaction of having had a very personalized and artistic experience. Many guests depart with the enthusiasm to duplicate the experience themselves when they entertain. Regardless of our international location, appeals have been made for me to write a book on how to do it all.

This book is designed for those who delight in decorative and unique gourmet cuisine but who are too busy, or feel they do not have the resources, talents, or confidence to organize a complete event. Entertaining should be easy and enjoyable. Anyone can do it; and any personal effort is generally well appreciated.

Blueprints for Creative Entertaining is also designed for the experienced cook and professionals in the hospitality industry who are interested in seeing how others do it. As a coffee table book, this book should appeal to those interested in different cultures and travel, or to the curious who wonder how it all happens at an Ambassador's table.

Margaret and Larry Dickenson

CONCEPT OF PERSONALIZED ENTERTAINING

Entertaining successfully can perhaps be best measured by the extent to which guests feel relaxed, happy, and particularly satisfied. Guests become enthusiastically animated by attractive decoration and decor, as well as by exciting cuisine served with a bit of flair or pizzazz. A personalized style of entertaining is appreciated and not quickly forgotten by guests. The real secret is for the host/hostess to entertain in a certain "do-able" style, with the least amount of energy and stress, and with the resources available. A style needs to be developed by the host/hostess where he/she is comfortably in control of the total situation so that the event is relaxing for everyone.

BLUEPRINTS

Strategic thinking, planning, and organizing allows the host/hostess to be in control of the event and to have confidence when entertaining. More time can be spent with guests. It is essential to use a checklist and to plan in writing.

IMMEDIATE DECISIONS

Occasion? New Year's, birthday, family gathering, business or social function, introduction to newcomers, or just a get-together of friends. Events are often more interesting when linked to a particular occasion or theme. Frequently I create a seasonal or ethnic theme with relevant food, containers, textiles, decorations, music, and personal attire.

Guests? Friends, family, colleagues, business or social contacts. A guest list should be carefully planned so that the event will be an enjoyable and rewarding experience for all. We have found that combining people from different backgrounds and professions can generate the most stimulating of social events.

Type of Event? Informal or formal dinner, lunch, drinks, buffet (even a kitchen buffet), cocktail reception, barbecue, picnic. At this stage, it is important to identify what is to be achieved, the number of guests, and what resources are available, including space.

These blueprints apply regardless of the type or size of the event. A host and/or hostess could probably comfortably arrange an informal lunch or dinner for 8, or drinks for 12 to 16 without considering extra help. For large and/or more formal events, outside help may be required.

Time? Often only the starting time of an event needs to be determined. However, it is advisable to designate both a starting and a finishing time for occasions which are to be limited in length.

Place? Garden, dining room, living room, terrace, throughout the house, kitchen, park. Guests can be entertained in different locations during the course of an event (e.g. drinks in the garden or sun room, dinner in the dining room, coffee in the living room or on the patio).

Dress Code? Generally accepted universal dress codes include:
- *Very Casual:* comfortable or sporty clothing, jeans, shorts
- *Casual:* no tie for men, more relaxed clothing
- *Informal:* ties and jackets for men, dresses or suits for women (In correct protocol terms, "informal" means "not formal", that is to say "not black tie". "Informal" does not mean "casual".)
- *Black Tie/Formal:* Tuxedos or white dinner jackets with a bow tie and cummerbund for men, long or cocktail dresses for women
- *White Tie:* Tails for men, long dresses or gowns for women (White Tie events are very rare.)
- *Special Attire:* e.g. beach wear, costumes, ethnic dress, the 1950s

INVITING GUESTS

How guests are invited varies with local customs and traditions as well as the nature of the event. Generally accepted techniques include:
- Particularly for larger events, sending invitation cards directly to guests with all necessary details including an RSVP (i.e. Reply please) or a Regrets Only (i.e. Reply only if unable to attend) notice.
- Contacting guests (by telephone or in person) first to see if they would be available, and then sending invitation cards to tentative and committed guests with an RSVP or PM (i.e. *Pour Memoire*, translating as "to remind") notice respectively.
- Contacting targeted guests only by telephone or in person, without sending invitation cards.

Regardless of how guests are invited, certain essential information must be communicated to the guests:
1. Name of host and/or hostess
2. Name of the invited guest(s)
3. Nature of function
4. Occasion (optional)
5. Place and address of event
6. Starting time, or time interval designated for event
7. Dress code

The day before the event, the host/hostess may wish to call guests who have accepted the invitation to reconfirm their attendance.

MENU PLANNING

The menu depends on the type of event, occasion, guests, place, time, and available resources.

Ideally, a menu should capture the guests' attention. Elements in a menu can definitely charm, surprise, and convince guests that the host/hostess has created the event personally for each individual guest. Initial attention is captured by the presentation of the food, its colours, and shapes as well as the type of food and perhaps its aroma. An appreciation of flavours, textures, and temperature comes with tasting.

All menus should be planned and organized in writing, from the first hors d'oeuvre to the last chocolate or liqueur. Once basic decisions are made, it is essential to consider other details. Well planned menus are usually constructed according to basic procedures. My blueprints for menu planning are as follows:

First, decide on principal elements of a basic menu in the following order:
- principal main course dish
- appetizer or soup or salad (according to preference)
- dessert

If desired, add other courses to expand the basic menu:
- hors d'oeuvres
- appetizer, soup, or salad (depending on which one of the three choices has already been selected)
- sorbet
- chocolates and other little sweets

Add accompanying elements:
- sauces
- vegetables
- pasta, rice, or potatoes
- breads

Continue to adjust and enhance the complete menu, focusing on specifics:
- variety and harmony of flavours, textures, colours, and shapes of elements in each course, as well as in the entire menu

- no (or limited) repetition of the same food element as well as of the same preparation, presentation, or serving techniques
- not all courses served at the same temperature
- different courses served in different types of dishes or containers, and of different heights, shapes, sizes, and materials
- arrangement of food on serving pieces
- garnishes and decoration
- possibility of a flambé
- possibility of a dish to be served personally to guests by the host/hostess

Other Tips for Menu Planning
- Be confident about the choice of food, and its quality.
- Take advantage of products in season and those available (i.e. "Get what you want out of what you have.").
- Create a checklist of universally appealing items which may be included in a menu. (My list includes: fresh herb and salad leaves, salmon, caviar, crêpes, pastry, meringue, a variety of edible containers, flora and fauna shapes, coulis, frosted effect, flambé, tall containers, tulip napkins, and dishes personally served by host/hostess.)
- Offer guests the opportunity to touch and handle food (e.g. edible decoration and edible containers).
- Don't be afraid to repeat menus if the guest list is different, or if recipes are presented differently and for different courses.
- Be aware of possible dietary restrictions. (I am always prepared with ideas and/or a few ready-to-serve alternatives, in response to such last minute announcements.) Guests may be vegetarians, allergic to shellfish, certain nuts, or other particular foods; they may not eat pork or red meats.

WINE SELECTION

The traditional advice is to serve red wine with dark meats, and white wine with white meats and fish. However, often light red wines or fuller bodied white wines are served with dark flesh poultry or fish (e.g. salmon) as well as with veal, pork, and lighter coloured meats. Sauces and the final menu should also be considered when selecting wine for an event. Champagne is usually served with dessert. Champagne may be served as well with hors d'oeuvres for very special occasions, immediately upon the arrival of guests. Finer sparkling white wines are an alternative to champagne, if budgets are limited.

STYLE OF SERVICE FOR EACH COURSE

This is influenced by the type of event, the number of guests, resources available, and the degree of formality. There are many options:
- Prepared trays placed on the table for self service.
- Prepared trays offered individually to those seated at the table (from his/her left). Individuals serve themselves, or are assisted by servers.
- Individual one portion size plates, prepared in and served from the kitchen to each person.
- Individual one portion size plates, prepared personally by the host/hostess at the table from large trays placed in front of him/her, and served to others directly.
- Very casual service of passing filled trays/bowls from one person to another.

Although the type of event helps determine the basic style of service, often a combination of styles is used. For example, during a buffet event, the principal part of the meal is offered to guests from trays arranged on a table for self service. However, a soup or dessert may be prepared in single portions and served to guests individually.

At sit-down events, not only may soup be presented in personal portions to guests, but also appetizers, salads, and/or desserts may be prepared in the kitchen and served individually. Frequently, even the main course appears at the table on single dinner plates already carefully arranged by the kitchen for each person.

The great advantage of served plates is that the kitchen has complete control over the guest's plate including artistic arrangement. Better control also exists over the total quantity of food prepared, particularly if seconds are not offered. This is an important consideration when resources – time, energy, finances – are limited.

Food served on trays to those seated at the table is often a popular option. (This is done by servers or the host/hostess.) Preparing and serving trays may be quicker than offering individually arranged plates. Tray service also allows individuals to make their own choices according to taste and appetite. However, more abundant quantities of food are required, and the artistry of a plate may be compromised.

In my search for the most effective technique when serving the main course, I have developed an option which has proven very successful for all sizes of sit-down dinners. In the kitchen, accompaniments and decoration are arranged on heated individual plates, leaving a vacant area for the principal item and sauce. As the partially prepared individual plates are placed in front of the first guests, a tray of the main dish follows immediately, as does the sauce. These elements may be served, passed, or simply placed on the table. Guests delight in the attractive composition of the plates, and in the invitation to complete the presentation by personally choosing the other elements. Service is quick, effective, and artistic. If desired, a second serving of the main dish and sauce may be offered.

FOOD PRESENTATION

Presentation is crucial. Ample patience and time should be devoted to planning how food can be presented in an irresistibly tempting manner, with the least amount of energy and stress. Remember that "We eat with our eyes"! The choice of serving piece, the arrangement of food in or on the serving piece, and the food decoration can transform any recipe into gourmet fare.

Decide how each tray, bowl, and plate of food should look in its final presentation. Make sketches. Decide on the container, arrangement of food, and the decoration.

Use a variety of serving pieces or other imaginative containers as interesting alternatives to traditional tableware. Creativity may be demonstrated through the use of novel baskets, boxes, or anything that could possibly hold food. It may be necessary to fit these containers with plates or bowls of appropriate sizes or line them with leaves or paper doilies. Ingenious containers may be created from fruit, vegetables, bread, pastry, meringue, and crêpes.

In general, avoid crowding when arranging food on serving pieces. Food is more tempting when it appears fresh and is allowed to "breathe". Elements on a plate need to be appreciated. Individual servings arranged on oversized plates are refreshing.

Food can also be made irresistible when accessorized with the appropriate garnishes or decoration. These may include: fresh edible flowers or sprigs of herbs; various flora, fauna, or other shapes made of fruit, vegetables, pastry, chocolate, meringue, pasta, and other edible materials; frosting with egg white and sugar crystals; dusting with cocoa powder, instant coffee crystals, icing sugar, or peppercorns. Many imaginative options exist. Non-edible items should never be presented with food. Among the few exceptions are: paper doilies, decorative ribbons or mini umbrellas, and paper hats on exposed bones.

Placing individual plates on larger plates lined with a paper doily often helps to frame the food more artistically. The doily also prevents the top plate from sliding, particularly if the doily is held in position with a well hidden piece of tape.

TABLE SETTINGS

For sit-down events, including sit-down buffets, it is necessary to arrange the table(s) with a table setting for each guest. A correctly set table is not only attractive, but is comfortable and convenient for guests. (For buffet occasions, the strategic arrangement of plates, cutlery, and glasses assists guests in proceeding in a logical manner along the line.)

Table Settings for Sit-Down Events
Cutlery
For sit-down events, knives and spoons are placed to the right of the plate while forks are placed to the left. Knives are arranged with the blades facing inward towards the plate. In general, cutlery is arranged in the order of intended use with the first items to be used placed the furthest

distance from the plate. Guests use cutlery starting with the outside pieces and work their way towards the plate during the meal. The bottom of the cutlery arranged on both the right and left sides of the plate should be in a straight horizontal line. This line may also include the bottom of the dinner plate and the bottom edge of the napkin depending on how the napkin is folded and if it is placed to the left of the cutlery.

Dessert cutlery is placed horizontally above the plate. If a fork and spoon are required for dessert, place the fork horizontally, directly above the plate, with the handle to the left; place the spoon immediately above the fork, also in a horizontal position, with its handle on the right.

If a butter knife is required, place it either directly above or on the bread and butter plate in a horizontal position with the handle on the right and the blade facing towards or into the bread and butter plate.

When place settings are more complicated, guests follow the lead given by the host/hostess as he/she picks up cutlery. Guests traditionally do not begin a course until the host and/or hostess have started, or have invited guests to begin.

Coffee spoons and teaspoons are offered to guests when coffee and tea are served, and if spoons are required by guests. A cup is placed on its saucer with the handle of the cup always pointing to the three o'clock position relative to the guest. The spoon is arranged on the saucer, behind the cup, with the handle of the spoon parallel to the handle of the cup.

Glasses and Cups
All glassware is arranged directly above the cutlery to the right of the plate. Glassware is also arranged in order of use, with the glass to be used first placed closest to the reach of the right hand. This is usually a white wine glass as white wine is often served with the first course; however, it could be a red wine glass, or it could be a water glass if no wine is served. If a second wine is served, the glass is placed to the left of the first, closer to the dessert cutlery. Water and champagne glasses are set behind and a little to the left of the first two wine glasses. (A table is more attractive if glasses are not arranged in perfect horizontal

or vertical lines. Horizontal and vertical line deviations when arranging glassware add charm to a table setting, making it appear less rigid.) If only one wine is served, the water glass is placed to the left of the wine glass. If a champagne glass is required, it is set behind and between the wine and water glasses.

At occasions where tea or coffee is served with the food at the table, such as at breakfast or a sit-down tea party, the cup is also placed above the cutlery to the right of the plate. If juice or water is served at the table as well, the glass may be placed to the left of the cup.

Napkins

Most frequently, the napkin is placed to the left of the plate, just beyond and parallel to the cutlery. If it is folded in the traditional rectangular way, the folded edge should face the plate with the bottom left corner open to facilitate unfolding the napkin and arranging it on one's lap. Napkins may be folded in a variety of ways, and placed in other positions (e.g. directly on the central plate, or on the bread and butter plate).

Salt Cellars and Pepper Shakers

Ideally, all guests should be in easy reach of salt and pepper. This means a maximum of four guests per set of salt and pepper.

Place Cards

Required or not? Place cards are only used for sit-down occasions (including sit-down buffets), but they are not essential. Sometimes the host/hostess simply directs guests to their designated places at the table, without the use of place cards and/or a seating plan board.

To clearly indicate the individual seating of guests at the table(s), place cards are arranged in a centre front position directly above the place setting. For some sit-down occasions, a diagram of the seating plan (or a seating plan board) is also prepared, illustrating the seating arrangement at the table(s). The diagram or seating plan board is viewed by guests as they approach the dining area in order to assist them in finding their places.

Modifications for Sit-Down Buffet Events

Some modifications are usually made at sit-down buffets. The table(s) are set as they would be for a sit-down occasion, but with plates or bowls arranged on the buffet table immediately preceding the food which is to be placed on or in them. Bread and butter plates may be placed at individual settings on the tables, if there is sufficient space. It is more elegant to serve wine to guests at the table. However, if staff is limited or not available, it may be more convenient for guests to collect filled glasses of wine at the buffet table before they are seated. In that case, only filled water glasses would be arranged on the table in the position of the second glass, above the cutlery.

Arrangement of Plates, Cutlery, and Glasses for Buffet Events

Plates are stacked at the head of the buffet table. When it is not a sit-down buffet, securely rolled napkins, each containing a fork and knife, follow the plates. The food is arranged directly after the plates and napkins along the length of the table with salt, pepper, and filled glasses of wine or water placed at the end of the line. It is best to arrange a separate dessert table, with suitable cutlery and extra napkins, in another area. At times, a separate space or small table for coffee and tea may also prove convenient.

In general, when possible, it is strongly advisable to arrange (on the same table) dishes or other items (with appropriate cutlery if necessary) immediately before food or drink which is to be placed on or in them. This arrangement is crucial in maintaining an orderly flow of guests along the buffet line; otherwise, guests may access the buffet table at some random spot, and perhaps create an awkward situation.

SEATING PLANS

For more casual or buffet events where there may be a free-seating arrangement, the host/hostess should guide the most prominent guests to particular places at tables when it is a sit-down buffet, or to the choice seating areas when guests are to set plates on their laps.

At many sit-down events (including sit-down buffets), seating plans are prepared assigning guests to designated places at the table(s). To assist guests in locating their seats, often place cards and/or a seating plan board are also prepared. It is not difficult to arrange an appropriate seating plan.

Seating Plans With All Guests at One Table
With Host and Hostess Both Present at One Rectangular Table

The host and hostess may be seated: (i) one at either end of the table, or (ii) across from one another at the centre of the table. Guests are normally seated in order of professional status; however, when a party is to honour someone in particular, he or she (along with his or her partner) becomes the principal guest. The principal female guest is seated to the right of the host, with the second most prominent female guest to the left of the host. The principal male guest is seated to the right of the hostess, and the second most prominent male guest to her left. The third and fourth most prominent female and male guests are seated next to the principal and second most prominent male and female guests respectively; and the process continues. Guests of less profile are seated in the middle of the table (or at the ends, if the host and hostess are seated at the central position, across from one another).

In the final composition of the table, individuals of one gender are only seated beside those of the opposite gender, if there is an equal number of men and women. If the numbers are not equal, compromises must be made. Also at a rectangular table where there is an equal number of male and female guests, the host and hostess cannot always sit directly across from one another or one at either end of the table, and still maintain the male-female alternating seating arrangement. This is true when there are 8, 12, 16, 20, or 24 places at the table.

With Host and Hostess Both Present at One Round Table

The host and hostess are seated across the table from each other. Guests are seated around the host and hostess as outlined above as when they are at one rectangular table.

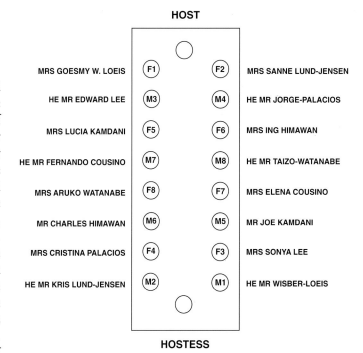

SEATING PLAN FOR SIT-DOWN EVENT WITH HOST AND HOSTESS BOTH PRESENT AT ONE RECTANGULAR TABLE

HOST

MRS GOESMY W. LOEIS	F1	F2	MRS SANNE LUND-JENSEN
HE MR EDWARD LEE	M3	M4	HE MR JORGE-PALACIOS
MRS LUCIA KAMDANI	F5	F6	MRS ING HIMAWAN
HE MR FERNANDO COUSINO	M7	M8	HE MR TAIZO-WATANABE
MRS ARUKO WATANABE	F8	F7	MRS ELENA COUSINO
MR CHARLES HIMAWAN	M6	M5	MR JOE KAMDANI
MRS CRISTINA PALACIOS	F4	F3	MRS SONYA LEE
HE MR KRIS LUND-JENSEN	M2	M1	HE MR WISBER-LOEIS

HOSTESS

With Only a Host or Hostess Present at a Mixed Gender Event

The principal guest may be of the same or of the opposite gender of the host/hostess. Whether the table is rectangular or round, to keep conversation more animated at the entire table, it is advisable that the principal guest be seated across from the host/hostess, becoming in effect the missing hostess/host or a co-host/co-hostess. Guests of opposite gender are seated around the host/hostess and principal guest in descending order of prominence (as outlined above), with men and women seated in alternating positions at the table, to the extent possible.

*With Only a Host or Hostess Present at
a One Gender Event*

In this case, it is also advisable that the principal guest becomes in effect like a co-host/co-hostess, seated across from the host/hostess. The second most prominent guest is seated to the right of the host/hostess, and the third most prominent guest to the right of the principal guest. The fourth is placed to the left of the host/hostess, and the fifth to the left of the principal guest. The seating procedure continues in this manner until all the guests have been given specific places at the table.

**SEATING PLAN FOR SIT-DOWN
ONE GENDER EVENT WITH
ONLY A HOST OR HOSTESS PRESENT**

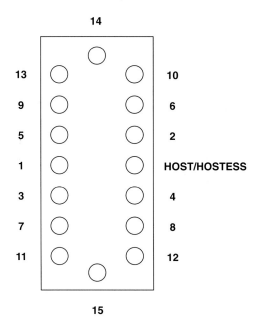

Seating Plans With Two or More Tables
With Host and Hostess Both Present

It is usually recommended that the host and hostess be seated at separate tables with the most prominent female and male guests seated to their right, and the second most prominent female and male guests to their left. The rest of the formula is similar to that outlined above, alternating male and female guests to the extent possible.

With Only a Host or Hostess Present

In this situation, it is advisable that the principal guest be seated across from the host/hostess, becoming in effect the missing hostess/host or a co-host/co-hostess. Guests of opposite gender are seated around the host/hostess and principal guest in descending order of prominence as outlined above, with men and women seated in alternating positions at the table, to the extent possible. Guests of greater prominence are seated at the host/hostess's table. The remaining guests are seated at the other tables according to the host/hostess's instinct as to which seating arrangements would probably produce the most effective groupings.

TABLE CENTREPIECES AND DECORATION

For table centrepieces, cut flowers beautifully arranged in magnificent bouquets are always exquisite. Other options also exist. A browse through one's home may result in the discovery of novelty boxes, baskets, containers, or a variety of collectibles which could become the basis for, or focus of, fabulous centrepieces and decorations at little or perhaps no cost. I find this approach amazingly helpful in developing a theme for an event. Often a few fresh flowers or leaves fitted into floral water tubes can be cleverly added to a combination of objects, creating a very original and attractive table arrangement. There are dozens of other decorative materials, such as interesting textiles, shells, fruits, vegetables, ribbons, and bows.

Touches of decoration can be similarly added to other entertaining areas. Guests feel particularly welcomed when the area just outside the front door or entrance has also been thoughtfully decorated. Remember that "First impressions count"! Baskets of flowers and fruit, dried branches, wreaths, and candles are easy decorations for both interiors and exteriors.

Ten of My Favourite Decorating Tips
1. Open novelty boxes filled with almost anything from flowers or fruit (fresh, dried, or a novelty type), to Christmas balls and ribbons
2. Attractive baskets filled in a similar manner

3. Artistic bird cages decorated with a few branches and flowers
4. A collection of co-ordinating candlesticks of different heights
5. Figurines, sculptures, or simply fruit and vegetables, arranged on interesting pieces of draped textiles
6. Coffee beans, peppercorns, or cloves placed in unique clear glass containers (e.g. boxes, jars, bowls), and arranged with flowers, fruit, or other objects of interest
7. Clusters of Frosted Grapes
8. Bouquets of Seaweed Chrysanthemums
9. Dried branches decorated with a multitude of possible items from single blossoms or festive balls to Frosted Grapes or Seaweed Chrysanthemums
10. Flowers (dried or fresh) arranged inside a "wall" of bark, grass, or cinnamon sticks

Lemons on cloves lend a decorative touch to a side table

ADDING TO THE TOTAL LOOK
Music?
Yes or no? The type of music is determined by the occasion and the ambience desired. Recorded music is the usual choice, however, a pianist or small musical group can make an event particularly memorable. Music students and non-professionals often are delighted with an invitation to perform. However, it is advisable to verify the talent level of potential performers prior to making a commitment.

Lighting
Special lighting adds charm particularly to evening or night-time events. Lighting may include candles, strings of lights, spot lighting, torches, lanterns, and illuminated pumpkins.

If candles are arranged on a dinner table, they should be lit. Candles are not lit during daylight hours; the only exception may be in a darkened room at Christmas.

Lit candles, as well as most special lighting effects, must be arranged with care and away from flammable materials.

Clothing and Accessories of Host/Hostess
The choice of clothing and accessories of the host/hostess also represents a part of the total look when entertaining. The attractive appearance of the host/hostess usually impresses guests and assures them that they have been invited to a well planned and organized event.

ITEMS AND SERVICES TO BE PROCURED
Checklist
- Invitation cards, guest book
- Food, beverages, ice
- Tableware, glasses, silverware, serving trays
- Pots, pans, other special items for food preparation and service
- Barbecue, fuel
- Tables, chairs
- Table linens and napkins
- Flowers, candles, other decorations
- Place cards, seating plan board
- Ground coverings, platforms, canopy
- Special lighting (e.g. string lights, spotlights, torches, lanterns)
- Visual and sound effects (e.g. PA system)
- Entertainment
- Extra staff
- Camera

Quantity
Careful calculations are important at this stage. Counting saves resources and reduces stress. Final quantities

procured should also include a reasonable margin of "extras". When calculating quantities of food, careful examination of the menu as a whole assists in estimating the quantities required of individual items.

Means of Procurement
Goods and services are often purchased or rented. Required items may also be fabricated by the host/hostess, borrowed, or procured on an exchange agreement.

Extra Help
Additional help may be required for preparation, serving and/or clean-up. Several options exist:
- Hiring professionals who offer the required services
- Requesting assistance from a willing spouse and/or family members
- Hiring non-professionals (e.g. one's own children and/or their friends, neighbourhood baby sitters, cleaning women, or students)

If well chosen, a person can be trained to do exactly what suits the host/hostess's needs. Regardless of the source, it is best to hire the same help when entertaining, so that time spent on training is reduced.

PLANNING WORK SCHEDULES

Food Preparation Schedule
To facilitate food preparation when entertaining, it is always advisable to keep on hand a certain inventory of favourite basic items or ingredients which have already been prepared. Such items should be appropriately stored either in the refrigerator, freezer, or cool dry cupboard. My list includes a variety of salad dressings, cooked sauces, fillings, pastry, pastas, ice cream, breads and flavoured butters, as well as a supply of crêpe mixture, pesto, toasted almonds, and other basics. A limited quantity of prepared hors d'oeuvres and sweets also relieve preparation responsibilities when entertaining.

When a menu is planned, serious consideration must be given to the time and energy available for the necessary food preparation. A schedule for food preparation outlines the completion of tasks so that most items on the menu are basically completed hours before the event, some items are completed the previous day, and others are done well in advance. A written schedule may be designed as follows:

Advance Preparations:
Day: Items: (Person(s) Responsible:)*
Day Prior to Event Preparations:
Time: Items: (Person(s) Responsible:)*
Day of Event Preparations:
Hour: Items: (Person(s) Responsible:)*
Last Minute and During Event Preparations:
Hour and Minutes: Items: (Person(s) Responsible:)*

(*When food preparation involves more than one person, it is best to assign specific tasks to each individual.)

It is amazing what one person can comfortably and enjoyably do when a written schedule has been organized. In drawing up a schedule for food preparation, it is imperative to work with the final detailed menu and to be aware of the fact that other setting-up tasks must be done. After the food preparation schedule has been drafted, it may become clearer if extra assistance is required, or if the menu should be modified.

Flexibility, a positive attitude, and creativity are great assets when food is being prepared. Items may need to be adapted, substituted, or eliminated. If a crisis seems to be looming during the preparation of a particular recipe, ingenuity on the part of the kitchen may not only make the product salvageable but may lead to a new recipe or creation. Remaining calm and collected is a great advantage. As a general rule, a host/hostess should never apologize for irregularities, or make any negative comments pertaining to the food or any other element of the event. Often such actions only draw attention to some detail which may have gone unnoticed.

Setting-Up Schedule
Tables should always be arranged well in advance of an event. It is best to set tables and to organize tableware, cutlery, and glasses a day before. If this is not possible, the task should then be done as far in advance of the guests' arrival as possible. Attention can then be focused on other preparations.

For the same reason, trays and serving pieces, flowers, and decoration should also be organized the previous day or well in advance of the event.

Time must be devoted to other details which may include arranging the bar, lighting, special equipment, and final decorations. Furniture may also need to be rearranged.

ETIQUETTE FOR SERVICE OF FOOD AND BEVERAGES

In general, food service should not be delayed because of absent guests, especially at the risk of frustrating those who have arrived on time. It is most comfortable for all when late arrivals are warmly and graciously received by the host/hostess and allowed to fit into the event at its current stage.

Service of Drinks and Hors d'Oeuvres

Drinks are offered immediately upon the arrival of the first guest(s). When at least some guests have arrived and the serving of hors d'oeuvres begins, the most prominent female guest present at the time is the first to be offered an hors d'oeuvre. Hors d'oeuvres are then served to those around her, regardless of gender. (The only exception is when a man of very high status is the principal guest and is without a female partner.) If the event is male only, then similarly the most prominent male guest is first offered an hors d'oeuvre.

Apple Swan and Frosted Grapes on drinks tray

Order of Service for Sit-Down Events

During mixed gender events, the most prominent guest and his/her partner are asked to lead the flow of guests to the dining room. Female guests are always served first, in order of priority with the hostess being served last, and immediately before the male guests are served. Male guests are also served in the same manner with the host served last. At single gender events, service is done according to order of priority of guests, with the host/hostess served last.

For each course, when everyone has been served, the host/hostess should invite guests to begin their food, or he/she should begin as a signal for others to start. Often guests watch as the host/hostess takes the lead for each course to verify the cutlery to be used, and perhaps the technique of using it. The host/hostess should be the last to complete each course.

Order of Service for Buffet Events

At more formal buffet occasions, the most prominent guests, usually in couples, are invited first to the buffet table, with the principal woman leading. Again, the only exception is when a man of very high status is the principal guest and is without a female partner. Sometimes female guests as a group are invited to precede male guests; however, this is not necessary and risks being boring.

At a sit-down buffet, there may be an arranged seating plan with place cards on the table (and perhaps a seating plan board as well). If there is a free-seating arrangement, the host/hostess should guide the most prominent guests to particular places at tables or to the choice seating areas.

During buffet events while guests are seated, the principal guests and women should take priority if food or beverages are served or if items are removed. Also during the event, the host/hostess should strategically move guests from one area to another, encouraging more interaction and making the event more stimulating. This is more easily done when guests are dining with plates on their laps.

It is best to invite the principal guest(s) and women to the dessert buffet first, but this is not absolutely necessary if other guests are ready for dessert sooner and are eager to begin.

Service of Coffee, Chocolates, and Liqueurs

When the meal is completed and guests have left the table, coffee or tea is offered first to the principal guest(s). Those guests standing/seated in closest proximity to the principal guest(s) are served next, with women taking priority if comfortably possible. Liqueurs, chocolates, and other items should also be served in a similar fashion. Sometimes to avoid any break in conversation, coffee, tea, and finishing touches may be served at the table. This is particularly relevant to working lunches or dinners.

ORCHESTRATION OF ACTUAL EVENT

Attention given to logistics ensures better control and a smooth flowing event. Discipline and patience are required to think through the complete event, regardless of its size. This step should not be overlooked. It is indeed beneficial to quickly visualize every step in relative detail, to make appropriate decisions and preparations. It avoids last minute decision making, unanticipated situations, and complications. Thinking through an event does not necessarily need to be done at a desk.

With the schedules for food preparation and set-up already prepared, it is prudent for the host/hostess to think in terms of how an event should actually unfold.

Food and Beverage Service

To become familiar and comfortable with the serving routine for a particular event, the service of food and beverages for each course should be reviewed regardless of the event. Who does what, when, and how? For a sit-down affair such as a dinner, it is always helpful to play act the service of the complete dinner for just a few "guestless" places. This is particularly essential when using outside help for the first time. It should include the serving of all courses with their accompaniments and beverages as well as the removal of dishes and appropriate items between courses. It is essential to review the order in which individuals are to be served. During a sit-down event, all plates (prepared or empty) are placed in front of a person from his/her left side and removed from the right. Trays of food are offered from the person's left. Water, wine, and other beverages are served from the person's right.

Details To Be Verified Before Arrival of Guests

- Serving time established and co-ordinated with kitchen activities
- Food waiting for last minute details
- Thought given to possible alternatives for guests with dietary restrictions
- Equipment ready for final food preparation
- Last check of dishes and serving pieces required for each course
- Hors d'oeuvre trays out (possibly accompanied by a small attractive dish to collect olive pits, shrimp tails, etc.)
- Drink trays and bar ready; juice, white wine, champagne, and beer chilled; red wine at room temperature or slightly chilled (and perhaps a sufficient number of bottles opened and "breathing"); ice and other requirements prepared
- Coffee and liqueur trays prepared
- Cocktail napkins handy for drinks, hors d'oeuvres, chocolates
- Guest book out
- Space and hangers available for coats; area prepared for boots or possibly shoes
- Sufficient soap, towels, and tissue arranged in guest bathroom
- Music playing
- Lighting on
- Ashtrays arranged (if smoking is allowed)
- Payment handy for hired staff
- Vases on hand for possible gifts of cut flowers

Details To Be Verified During Event

- Before principal food service begins, perhaps discreet confirmation that all guests have no dietary restrictions (particularly if an item on the menu is often associated with allergies or religious beliefs)
- Plates and dishes appropriately heated or chilled
- Water and wine transferred to dining room for service
- Water glasses filled
- Candles on dinner table lit before guests are invited to the table
- Seating plan board (if used) on display near dining area
- Most prominent guests and/or women invited to dining area first

- Food ready, as and when required
- Each plate correctly prepared and garnished
- Extra drops of spilt sauce or other bits removed from prepared plates and trays before being served
- Host/hostess facilitating effective conversation by introducing subjects, encouraging dialogue, and engaging guests
- "Noise level" of conversation attained and maintained. (The success of an event is often directly related to the noise level of the conversation.)
- Before dessert (and only if smoking is to be allowed at the table), small ashtrays placed on dining table
- Before dessert is served, removal from the table of salt, pepper, bread and butter plates and knives, couteau (knife) bars, and any other equipment not required for dessert
- Choice of regular or decaffeinated coffee offered
- Major clean-up procedures by host/hostess in kitchen delayed until all guests have departed
- Discreet farewells made to guests departing early

Details To Be Verified Immediately After Departure of Guests
- Candles extinguished and/or special lighting turned off
- Ashtrays emptied
- Appropriate equipment turned off and checked
- Remaining food and opened wine properly stored
- Necessary clean-up initiated
- Appropriate items retrieved from exterior
- Adequate water in any flower arrangements received
- Perishable garbage removed
- Help paid

Final Follow-Up
The appropriate follow-up should be done the day after the event, or as soon as possible. This list may include:
- Further organization of some remaining food
- Cleaning and storing dishes, glasses, flatware, and other equipment

- Restoring furniture to original position
- Returning borrowed or rented equipment
- Settling outstanding bills
- Making calls to thank guests who have thoughtfully sent or brought a gift
- Vacuuming and cleaning
- Grooming and watering flower arrangements
- Making additional notes regarding the occasion to record, perfect, and modify the menu, procedures, and other details (The notes may also include the final guest list, theme, decorations, flowers, music, and attire worn by host and/or hostess.)

MENUS

The menus presented in this book reflect sensitivity to the global community in which we live. They represent my personal fusion of international cuisines. Religion as well as dietary and ethnic preferences play an important role in my menu planning. Variety in a single menu not only makes for an exciting culinary experience but is essential when personal tastes and dietary restrictions of guests are unknown to the host/hostess. The menus are created with those recipes which we have found to be continually appealing to guests around the world. They may be successfully produced in small or large quantities, and are suitable for occasions ranging in size from a few guests to hundreds. Many menus have obvious ethnic themes, but with a unique international interpretation.

Coriander Zucchini Soup (page 121), Chinese Sweet and Sour Fish (page 159), and Frosted Lemon (page 186)

BASIC MENUS

—◦—

When menu planning, I always start with a basic menu of three courses, upon which the final menu is structured. The basic lunch and dinner menus listed here may be used interchangeably (i.e. individual courses or entire menus).

BASIC LUNCH MENUS

Creamed Escargots in Crêpe Purse*
Apricot Garlic Chicken
Chocolate Lattice Fruit Basket

—

Deluxe Beet Wanton Ravioli
Satay Kebab
Decadent Butterscotch Banana Noodle Soup

—

Coeur de Palmier, Avocado, and Watercress Salad
Triple Fettuccine Experience
Caged Frozen Mint Mousse

—

Coriander Zucchini Soup
Chinese Sweet and Sour Fish
Frosted Lemon

—

Blinis and Caviar
Dickenson's Fast-Track Borshch
Apricot Pirozhki in Butterscotch Sauce Supreme

—

Mushroom Salad Intrigue
Indonesian Sweet Blackened Chicken with Kiwi
Ice Cream Parfait

—

Strawberry and Peach Soup Eclipse
Salmon Stroganoff Coulibiac
Sour Cream Blueberry Brûlée

—

Hearty Carrot and Wild Rice Soup
Vegetarian Omelette in Crêpe Bowl
Assorted Ice Cream in Meringue Nest**

BASIC DINNER MENUS

Strawberry Asparagus Salad
Poached Fish Fillets with Crab Meat Mousse
Fruit Pastry Blossom

—

Peppercorn Prawns on Wild Rice
Pesto Beef Steak
Ice Cream Cherry Crêpes

—

Smoked Salmon with Fried Capers
Grilled Oriental Lamb Chops
Irresistible Triple Chocolate Cheesecake

—

Mango Soup with Kiwi
Escargot Stuffed Chicken Breast
Fenced Maple Syrup Mousse

—

Beef Carpaccio
Grilled Marinated Salmon
Almond Tiramisu Cup

—

Escargots en Croûte
Tarragon Veal with Roasted Bell Peppers
Peaches and Cream Meringue Combo

—

Mushroom Cappuccino
Herb Pork Farci
Delectable Chocolate Mousse

—

Seafood Mousse Parcel
Roast Chicken with Wild Rice Dressing
Strawberry Peppercorn Duet

*To make crêpe purses, use basic technique outlined in Pancake Sachets (page 77).
For Creamed Escargots see Escargots en Croûte (page 109).

**Commercial meringue nests may be used.

Seafood Mousse Parcel (pages 97–98), Roast Chicken with Wild Rice Dressing (page 143), and Strawberry Peppercorn Duet (page 176)

COMPLETE MENUS

The complete menu for a particular occasion is structured around a basic menu. A host/hostess may modify the basic menu to reflect a particular theme, to take advantage of seasonally available products, or to make simple substitutions of recipes from other basic menus or personal files.

Personalize basic menus by including an hors d'oeuvre. Extend the menu further by adding another course, e.g. appetizer, soup, or salad. Serving chocolates, liqueurs, or other finishing touches draws an occasion to a charming conclusion. Every element on a menu demands planning, resources, and co-ordination of logistics.

My first trick is to do much or most of the preparation in advance, storing items in the freezer, refrigerator, or a cool dry place. In this way, more extravagant menus can be presented by a busy person with a full-time job and other responsibilities. (I know, I have done so.) Because I keep limited quantities of basic items or components for recipes on hand, rarely is there the need to prepare absolutely everything for the final or complete menu. The recipes in this book have been created so that many of them can be prepared, or partially prepared, in advance. Of course, accurately calculating requirements is essential in the efficient expenditure of resources, particularly time.

Finally, presentation is one of the most important elements of a menu. Simple recipes or even purchased items become fine cuisine when served in an outstandingly creative way. When compliments are made, accept them graciously. It is not necessary to explain the simplicity of a recipe.

The examples of complete menus have been taken directly from notes which I keep when entertaining. These are menus which work for us. They are only meant to be a guideline for others. These complete menus have also been designed to reflect themes which offer a range of choices when trying to decide on the total look for an event.

COMPLETE MENUS FOR THEME EVENTS
Creating Successful Theme Parties

1. Build themes around seasons, festivities, and/or resources available.
2. It may be more practical to choose a title for the theme which does not make a total commitment to the theme, particularly in terms of decor, food, and recipes (e.g. Shades of …, Touches of …, Impressions of …, Some Memories of …, Hints of …, Tastes of …, Flavours of …, Excerpts from …).
3. Intertwine favourite recipes with themes, including at least some recipes which reflect or complement the themes.
4. Enhance themes through other creative means such as the choice of an invitation card (or original invitation "device"), tableware and serving pieces, floral arrangements, music, lighting, and clothing.

Note

1. It is not necessary to serve all and/or the same items indicated on the particular menu.
2. Regardless of the event or theme, the hostess (or host) should personally try to present at least some of the hors d'oeuvres or another dish.
3. F1, F2, etc. and M1, M2, etc. refer respectively to female and male guests in order of priority. Similarly, G1, G2, etc. pertain to guests in general. H indicates the host or hostess.

Chocolate Apricot Coins and Oysters (pages 197–198), Meringue Mushrooms (page 207), and Dice and Floral Painted Sugar Cubes (pages 200–201)

DRINKS*
International Flavours and Flair

—⊶⊷—

(Drink Tray Garnish: Mini Tomato Lotus Flowers)
Pancake Sachets with Smoked Salmon
Black Olive Rabbits
Chicken Pears with Apricot Curry Mayonnaise
Bouquet of Petit Seaweed Chrysanthemums
Mini Mushroom Cappuccinos**
Papaya on Basil Carpets
Frosted Grapes
Chocolate Butterflies***

Style of Food Service
Hostess (or host) personally serves food arranged on trays, plates, and in interesting containers. Additional portions of Mushroom Cappuccino are spooned personally by the hostess (or host) into emptied mini cups.

Work Schedule
1. Advance Preparation or Basic Supplies on Hand: Basic Crêpe mixture, Black Olive Rabbits, Chicken Pears, Apricot Curry Mayonnaise, Seaweed Chrysanthemums, Mushroom Cappuccino, Chocolate Butterflies.
2. Day Before: Prepare Frosted Grapes; arrange flowers; select music.
3. Day of Event: Prepare Tomato Lotus Flowers, pancakes, Pancake Sachets, whipped cream (for Mushroom Cappuccinos), Papaya on Basil Carpets; set up trays and seating area; fry Chicken Pears.

*Option Coffee or tea may be served instead of drinks. If people are seated, individual small plates (e.g. bread and butter size) may prove convenient for guests as they are presented with hors d'oeuvres.

**The mini Mushroom Cappuccinos should be served in tiny cups or glasses (e.g. mini Chinese cups, Arabic coffee cups, "shot" glasses, or liqueur glasses).

***Option Other types of chocolate may be served.

Pancake Sachets with Smoked Salmon (page 77), Papaya on Basil Carpets (page 82), and Mini Mushroom Cappuccinos (page 125)

DATE
Thursday, September 2
TIME
17:00
NUMBER OF GUESTS
8
THEME
International Flavours and Flair
DRESS CODE
Informal/lounge suit
PRINCIPAL TABLEWARE
Chinese porcelain
COFFEE TABLE ARRANGEMENT
Floral arrangement in Korean box
ADDING TO THE TOTAL LOOK
Chinese embroidered cocktail napkins, serving box and baskets

LIGHT LUNCH
A Czar's Light Lunch

—

(Drink Tray Decoration: Small Matrushka Doll)
Salmon Stroganoff in Hors d'Oeuvre Cases*

At Table
Blinis and Caviar Garnished with Salad
Ice-cold Vodka

—

Dickenson's Fast-Track Borshch
Dark Bread and Butter

—

Apricot Pirozhki
Butterscotch Sauce Supreme

Probably Not At Table
Coffee
Glasses of Tea from Samovar**
Lemon, Milk, and Dice and Floral Painted Sugar Cubes

—

Chocolate Apricot Coins and Oysters
Meringue Mushrooms

Style of Food Service at Table
Servings of appetizer and dessert are prepared in the kitchen, and served to each individual at the table; host serves vodka at the table; hostess serves the borshch, and additional dessert, at the table.

Work Schedule
1. Advance Preparation or Basic Supplies on Hand: Salmon Stroganoff, pastry hors d'oeuvre cases, Basic Crêpe mixture, Apricot Pirozhki, Butterscotch Sauce Supreme, Dice and Floral Painted Sugar Cubes, Chocolate Apricot Coins and Oysters, Meringue Mushrooms, vodka in freezer.
2. Day Before: Prepare borshch; set table; arrange trays and dishes; do floral arrangements; select appropriate music.
3. Day of Event: Prepare blinis.

*Hors d'oeuvre pastry cases are available commercially or mini pastry cups may be prepared using the recipe for Basic Pastry.

****Optional**

Dickenson's Fast-Track Borshch (page 123)

In keeping with my family's Ukrainian tradition, we were given money instead of wedding gifts when we got married. We decided to set aside the money for a special purchase some day. While in Vienna, I accompanied Larry on one of his Canadian trade promotion trips to Hungary, and we were given a private tour of the Herend china factory outside of Budapest which produced the exquisitely hand painted china for the Austro-Hungarian royal family. At the end of an impressive tour, I asked how an order could be placed. The question seemed to shock our guide, the factory manager, who assured us that such an order was impossible. The only outlets were commercial shops which were not well supplied and where customers would have to take what was available. He explained that the factory was a communist state owned factory which only produced the china. Sales were the responsibility of another company. Insisting that there must be some sort of formula for direct factory purchases, I had him record a rather extensive order for our favourite pattern, "Fleurs de l'Inde" ("Flowers of India"). He promised to pursue this unusual matter. Weeks passed, months went by. We moved temporarily to Belgrade for a few months, then were permanently transferred to Moscow, and still no Herend. By this time, Larry impatiently suggested ordering fine bone china from a Western European country. Ignoring all such suggestions, I continued to send letters of inquiry to the Herend factory in Hungary, always careful to include a copy of the original order. Two full years later, two enormous wooden crates arrived at the embassy in Moscow. Larry was completely taken by surprise. Our Ambassador and his wife were filled with admiration as their own search over many years, in the most exclusive antique and china shops in Europe, only netted them a tea service and a few odd pieces. Indeed, each piece of Herend is a work of art. Happily, there is a sufficient number of place settings so that our two daughters can also enjoy using "Fleurs de l'Inde" in their homes. Perhaps they will recall some of the places and situations around the world where this beautiful china always added a special charm to our home.

DATE
Saturday, January 7

TIME
12:00

NUMBER OF GUESTS
6

THEME
A Czar's Light Lunch

DRESS CODE
Informal

TABLE
Rectangular

SEATING PLAN
(Three facing three)
F1——Host——F2
M2——Hostess——M1

PRINCIPAL TABLEWARE
Herend china

DRINK AREA ARRANGEMENT
Palekh boxes, Herend porcelain objects

TABLE CENTREPIECE
Large covered Herend soup terrine, floral spray in Herend candlestick

COFFEE/TEA AREA ARRANGEMENT
Russian samovar and icons

ADDING TO THE TOTAL LOOK
Bottle of ice-cold vodka on table

ALFRESCO LUNCH

Summer Time

(Drink Tray Garnish: Fresh Garden Flowers)
Salmon Snow Pea Boats
Fresh Vegetable Pieces with Coriander Mayonnaise Dip

At Table
Strawberry and Peach Soup Eclipse

Avocado à la Russe with Shrimp
Garlic Bread

Triple Fettuccine Experience
with Sun Dried Tomatoes and Chicken
Red Bell Pepper Mayonnaise

Frosted Lemon Garnished with Frosted Grapes

Not At Table
Tea with Lemon and Cloves, Sugar

Marzipan Cherries and Mini Carrots

Style of Food Service at Table
Servings of all courses are individually prepared in the kitchen, and presented to each person separately at the table. A bowl of additional Triple Fettuccine Experience is offered at the table, and those who wish extra portions serve themselves.

Work Schedule
1. Advance Preparation or Basic Supplies on Hand: Coriander Mayonnaise, Hollandaise Mayonnaise, Home-made Pasta, Red Bell Pepper Mayonnaise, Lemon Ice Cream, Garlic Butter, Garlic Bread, Marzipan Cherries, Mini Carrots.
2. Day Before: Prepare Almond Strawberry Soup, Champagne Peach Soup, Frosted Lemons, Frosted Grapes; arrange dishes and trays; select appropriate music.
3. Day of Event: Prepare Salmon Snow Pea Boats, fresh vegetable pieces, shrimp, Avocado à La Russe, Triple Fettuccine Experience with Sun Dried Tomatoes and Chicken; set table; do floral arrangements.

Triple Fettuccine Experience with Sun Dried Tomatoes and Chicken (page 149)

*W*e had a lovely garden in Cairo which had several Indian mango trees loaded with maturing fruit. Some months after our arrival, we suddenly realized that the maturing mangos were almost gone but no fruit had passed through our kitchen door. The gardener assured us that only bad ones had fallen from the trees and he had quickly disposed of them so as not to attract insects. By the next season, his game was revealed. Because of their high quality, all the mangos from our garden had been selling for a premium price at the local community market – along with the dozens of seedlings which our gardener carefully nursed in individual pots occupying a large and conspicuous area of the patio. Of course we were given to understand that the seedlings were to replace plants in our own garden; however, the local market was always their final destination.

When the next mango season arrived, I watched the fruit on the trees ripen and was able to retrieve some. I washed them and put them directly into the freezer. I have developed several recipes, such as mango soup, mango mayonnaise sauce, mango sherbet, and ice cream, where frozen mango may be used as effectively as fresh mango.

During the several posts which followed our assignment in Egypt, we learned that the conflict of interest between our gardener's loyalty to us and his entrepreneurial aspirations is not a characteristic limited to Egyptian gardeners. History repeated itself in Korea with the local pears which were huge, round, and deliciously juicy. In Indonesia, we lost our rambutan and mango harvests for one season. Our own memory seems to be short-lived; it always takes us at least until the second season of fruit before we realize that we have already been through this experience.

DATE
Sunday, June 21
TIME
12:30
NUMBER OF GUESTS
4
THEME
Summer Time
DRESS CODE
Summer Casual
TABLE
Round
SEATING PLAN
M
Host   Hostess
F
PRINCIPAL TABLEWARE
Covered wooden chicken
bowls, baskets
TABLE CENTREPIECE
Small garden flowers and
parsley around covered
wooden chicken bowl,
matching individual floral
arrangements
TEA AREA ARRANGEMENT
Glass or crystal containers of
fresh lemons on whole cloves
**ADDING TO THE TOTAL
LOOK**
Coloured Dough Napkin
Rings

FORMAL DINNER
The Beauty of Nature

(Drink Tray Garnish: Apple Swan)
Smoked Oysters in Pita Shells
Chicken Pears with Apricot Curry Mayonnaise

At Table
Escargot Soup in Turtle Bread Bowl
Garlic Butter Carrot Shapes

Strawberry Asparagus Salad
Citrus Peel Dressing and Honey Mustard Mayonnaise

Poached Fish Fillets with Crab Meat Mousse
Tomato Brandy Cream Sauce
Squid Ink Linguini
Doubly Dark Wild Rice
Honey Soya Matchsticks of Zucchini and Carrot
Waffled Toast

Fruit Blossom on Painted Chocolate Stem

Not At Table
Decaffeinated Coffee
Coarse Brown Coffee Sugar Crystals
Whipped Cream Sprinkled with Cinnamon
Tea
Regular and Floral Painted Sugar Cubes
Lemon Slices and Milk

Chocolate Turtles and Nutty Chocolate Eggs
Liqueurs

Style of Food Service at Table
Servings for all courses are individually prepared in the kitchen, and presented to each person separately at the table. Small quantities of sherry arranged in escargot shells are offered to individuals at the table once the soup has been served, thus allowing each person the option of adding a touch of sherry to his/her soup. Butter and Waffled Toast are offered at the table, and at the appropriate times according to the menu. Additional main course, arranged on a single tray, is offered individually to those at the table (from their left side). Before prepared plates of dessert are presented to those at the table, the hostess may decide to personally pipe in chocolate the initials of each person on rim of the plates. The hostess remains in her seated position at the table, and does the piping with a securely closed small plastic bag filled with melted chocolate. (One lower corner of the bag has been cut off to make a fine opening through which the chocolate is piped.)

Work Schedule
1. Advance Preparation or Basic Supplies on Hand: Horseradish Mayonnaise, Chicken Pears, Apricot Curry Mayonnaise, Escargot Soup, Small Turtle Bread Shapes, Garlic Butter, Butter Shapes, Citrus Peel Dressing, Honey Mustard Mayonnaise, Squid Ink Linguini, Pastry Blossoms, White Chocolate Cream (for Fruit Blossoms), Painted Sugar Cubes, Chocolate Turtles, Nutty Chocolate Eggs.
2. Day Before: Prepare egg filling (for Smoked Oysters in Pita Shells), crab meat mousse, Tomato Brandy Cream Sauce, Doubly Dark Wild Rice; set table; arrange trays and dishes; do floral arrangements.
3. Day of Event: Prepare Apple Swan, Smoked Oysters in Pita Shells, Turtle Bread Bowls (hollow out interiors), Asparagus and Strawberry Salad, Fish Bath, Poached Fillet of Fish with Crab Meat Mousse, zucchini and carrot matchsticks, Waffled Toast, Fruit Blossoms (fill), Chocolate Stems; prepare coffee maker; fry Chicken Pears.

DATE
Thursday, April 10

TIME
19:30

NUMBER OF GUESTS
10

THEME
The Beauty of Nature

DRESS CODE
Formal/Black Tie

TABLE
Rectangular

SEATING PLAN
F2—M4—F3—M1
Host   Hostess
F1—M3—F4—M2

PRINCIPAL TABLEWARE
White and gold fine china

TABLE CENTREPIECE
Covered baskets filled with
jade flowers and highlighted
with long stems of fresh small
white orchids, jade fruit,
wooden statues, silver
candlelabras

**COFFEE AREA
ARRANGEMENT**
Large jade floral tree

**ADDING TO THE TOTAL
LOOK**
Classical chamber music,
candles in entertaining areas,
Swan Napkins

Escargot Soup in Turtle Bread Bowl (page 122)

*I*t was always a particular privilege to be invited to a function at the Canadian Ambassador's residence in Moscow. He was a wise, well-seasoned diplomat, one of the great experts on the former Soviet Union. His wife was a wonderfully spirited lady of Latin American origin. She has had an enormous influence on my style of entertaining. She always made an effort for her guests in a very personal way, and always with inimitable style. Although she did not share my particular personal interest in cooking the food herself, she knew how to manage, plan the menu, and order the best from the best. She had a formidable knowledge and command of etiquette. At a formal sit-down lunch for an important dignitary, some doomed guest made the memorably inappropriate decision to light up a cigarette after the first course had just been served. The hostess, ignoring her waiter's bell, chose to clap her hands loudly to catch the head waiter's attention, demanded the table be cleared immediately, and to bring ashtrays followed by dessert. One could call this a lighted light lunch.

A formal place setting with place card

DATE
Tuesday, May 14

TIME
19:00

NUMBER OF GUESTS
10 (of one gender)

THEME
Imagination Reigns*

DRESS CODE
Informal**

TABLE
Rectangular

SEATING PLAN
(Five facing five)
G6—G2—H—G4—G8
G9—G5—G1—G3—G7

PRINCIPAL TABLEWARE
Celadon stoneware from Bali
with flora and fauna motifs

**DRINK AREA
ARRANGEMENT**
Collection of pond green
pottery vases and containers
with fauna motifs

TABLE CENTREPIECE
Large covered turtle bowl
stoneware, matching lattice
lanterns, fresh fruit, grasses,
and simple flowers

**ADDING TO THE TOTAL
LOOK**
Colourful, matching woven
placemats

INFORMAL DINNER
Imagination Reigns

(Drink Tray Garnish: Seaweed
Chrysanthemums)
Pesto Avocado Spread
Grilled Baguette Slices
Peppercorn Prawns with Ginger Mayonnaise

At Table
Smoked Salmon with Fried Capers
Horseradish Mayonnaise
Waffled Toast
Butter Shapes

Mushroom Cappuccino

Escargot Stuffed Chicken Breast in Phyllo
Parcel
Red Bell Pepper Sauce
Spears of Fresh Asparagus

Chocolate Lattice Fruit Basket

Not At Table
Tea and Decaffeinated Coffee
Lemon Slices and Milk
Dice Sugar Cubes

Pineapple Cream Chocolates
Liqueurs

47

Style of Food Service at Table

Appetizer, soup, and dessert are individually prepared in the kitchen, and presented to each person separately at the table. Main course may be prepared on large trays and offered to individual guests (from their left side), allowing them to serve themselves. Or, main course may be arranged on trays or in bowls and placed directly on the table, with guests invited to serve themselves and pass trays on to others. Another formula is to prepare individual servings of main course as well in the kitchen, and present them to those seated at the table. Waffled Toast and Butter Shapes are offered to guests at the table once the smoked salmon has been served. If individual servings of main course have been prepared in the kitchen, additional main course may be arranged on a single tray and offered personally to those at the table.

Work Schedule

1. Advance Preparation or Basic Supplies on Hand: Seaweed Chrysanthemums, Pesto, Garlic Butter, Ginger Mayonnaise, Fried Capers, Horseradish Mayonnaise, Butter Shapes, Mushroom Cappuccino, Chocolate Lattice Baskets, Dice Sugar Cubes, Pineapple Cream Chocolates.
2. Day Before: Prepare Escargot Stuffed Chicken Breast in Phyllo Parcels, Red Bell Pepper Sauce, mashed potato (if necessary for arranging asparagus in a standing position); set table; arrange trays and dishes; do floral arrangements; select music.
3. Day of Event: Prepare Pesto Avocado Spread, Grilled Baguette Slices, Peppercorn Prawns, Waffled Toast, whipped cream, asparagus, Fruit Baskets (fill); paint chocolate flower decoration on plates; prepare coffee maker; bake chicken; sauté prawns.

*Note: A variety of interesting themes may be created, depending on one's imagination and resources available. Identify what collectibles, tableware, textiles, artifacts, art objects, and other resources are on hand or are easily acquired. Build a theme around the results of such finds. Complement the theme with some appropriate food and at least a few related recipes.

**In correct usage an "informal" dress code does not mean casual attire. Rather, it means a dark lounge suit for men and an attractive dress or suit for women.

*I*n many of our posts, we have not been able to find some of the items which I enjoy using. Thankfully, this is not always a serious problem if the item is available in a city which we may be visiting. After the Gulf War in Kuwait, many products were not available. During a trip to Bahrain, I asked Larry to go to a large supply house to purchase escargots. He, considering the request reasonable, asked how much I required. Calculating my future needs carefully while judging the limits of my husband's generosity and patience, I suggested he go equipped with the largest and sturdiest of our suitcases. As anticipated, I received the expected response: "Do you really need that much?" After a short pause, and no response on my part, he continued: "I'm going to look stupid when the bellman puts an empty suitcase in the trunk of the taxi." I quickly convinced him that it really boiled down to a question of ego for him. Did it really matter what the bellman thought? And we were leaving that afternoon, so the bellman might be gone by our next visit. So off Larry went to do the errand. He proudly reappeared about two hours later with a bulging suitcase and one fatigued bellman. He had quite an adventurous outing. Yes, the bellman did think Larry rather peculiar as the bellman threw the empty suitcase in the trunk. But the first surprise came when Larry asked for escargots at the shop and the shopkeeper reached for a can. At this point, Larry opened the suitcase and said "Fill it up!" The astonished merchant had lots of questions of course. Through the combined efforts of the merchant, the taxi driver, and Larry, the escargots were placed in the trunk. At the hotel, the bellman was awaiting Larry's return with all the pizzazz which he confidently reserved for dignitaries and well-heeled clients. As the trunk opened, Larry and the taxi driver anxiously suggested that they help the bellman with the suitcase; however, the overly eager bellman insisted he could manage himself. After a few strategic attempts, he condescended to accept assistance. Of course, the poor bellman was generously tipped, and our guests in Kuwait were able to enjoy my many original escargot recipes.

BUFFET DINNER*
*Accessorized from Indonesia***

(Drink Tray Garnish: Tropical Shells and Flowers)
Satay Kebab with Citrus Peel Dip
Indonesian Garlic Cashew Nuts on Fresh Leaves

Mango Soup with Nutmeg Garnish

Seaweed Chrysanthemums
Salmon Stroganoff Coulibiac***
on a Tropical Sea of Blanched Red Cabbage
Fried Capers and Horseradish Mayonnaise
Coeur de Palmier, Avocado, and Watercress Salad with
Mandarin Oranges
Tomato Lotus Flowers
Herb Vinaigrette
Indonesian Sweet Blackened Chicken with Kiwi
Chelo Rice with Doubly Dark Wild Rice Garnished with
Toasted (Indonesian) Almonds
Pineapple Carrot Salad in Pineapple Bird of Paradise
Frosted Grapes
Coriander Mayonnaise
Garlic Bread

Lemon Ice Cream Crêpes Flambé
Cherry and Ginger Sour Cream Sauces
Chocolate Butterfly Garnish

Java Coffee and Jasmine Tea
Milk and Sugar

Chocolate Turtles
Liqueurs

Style of Food Service at Table

If the event is not a sit-down (at standard tables) buffet, all courses are offered buffet style with hostess or host assisting in serving guests at the buffet table.

Work Schedule

1. Advance Preparation or Basic Supplies on Hand: Oriental Marinade, Citrus Peel Dip, Seaweed Chrysanthemums, Salmon Stroganoff, Fried Capers, Horseradish Mayonnaise, Herb Vinaigrette, Garlic Butter, Toasted Almonds, Coriander Mayonnaise, Garlic Bread, Lemon Ice Cream, Basic Crêpe mixture, Cherry Sauce, Ginger Sour Cream Sauce, Chocolate Butterflies, Chocolate Turtles.
2. Day Before: Prepare Mango Soup, Basic Pastry and Salmon Stroganoff Coulibiac, Doubly Dark Rice, Frosted Grapes, ice cream (cut); set tables (if sit-down buffet); arrange trays and dishes; do floral arrangements; select music.
3. Day of Event: Prepare Satay Kebab, red cabbage, salads, Tomato Lotus Flowers, marinade and glaze for chicken, kiwi, Chelo Rice, Pineapple Bird of Paradise, crêpes; prepare coffee maker; cut chicken; bake Salmon Stroganoff Coulibiac; grill chicken.

*Option If a sit-down buffet is preferred (and possible), tables must be set with sufficient place settings for all those attending. There could be a seating plan or free seating. Soup and dessert may be served at the table, with guests going to the buffet for other courses.

If a wider selection of vegetarian dishes is desired, consider offering Warm Sesame Tofu Salad or Pesto Pasta Salad. Pesto Pasta Salad is a convenient dish to serve when the number of guests and/or appetite sizes are unknown.

**Option Choose an appropriate title to suit personal resources, such as "Dinner Accessorized from Our Most Recent Trip/from Days Gone By/from the Garden". The dress code should be appropriate and reflect the spirit of the theme.

***Option Salmon Stroganoff may be served in pastry cases (appetizer size) rather than encased in the fish pastry of the coulibiac version. Pastry cups are easily made in regular size muffin pans using the Basic Pastry recipe (page 221). Puff pastry cases are often available commercially at pastry counters, or they may be ordered.

DATE
Friday, August 17

TIME
19:30

NUMBER OF GUESTS
30

THEME
Buffet Dinner Accessorized from
Indonesia**

DRESS CODE
Informal/Lounge Suit or Batik**

TABLE
Dining table for buffet of food
(Guests have access only to
available coffee, nesting, end,
garden or other casual tables)*

SEATING PLAN
Free seating*

PRINCIPAL TABLEWARE
"Batik" brown and white china

DRINK AREA ARRANGEMENT
Indonesian decorations
and tropical flowers

TABLE CENTREPIECE
Indonesian artifacts, bird cage,
bowls, baskets, textiles,
tropical flowers and fruit

COFFEE AREA ARRANGEMENT
Indonesian artifacts and textiles

ADDING TO THE TOTAL LOOK
Candles and batik napkins

*D*urian is a fruit which grows wild in the rain forests of some parts of Indonesia and the surrounding region. One durian may weigh as much as 3 kg. It has a thick firm skin of densely packed conical spines. The fruit has a strong smell. One either loves durian or hates it.

Larry refused to allow me to taste durian as it would mean bringing the fruit onto our premises. However, $1^1/_2$ years after our arrival in Indonesia, during an official trip to North Sulawesi, I noticed vendors on the roadside with durians piled like mountains. I explained to the protocol officer accompanying us my great desire to taste durian and my husband's ban on it at our home in Jakarta. Later that evening, after a very long day of official functions, Larry and I jumped into the car designated to us for the visit. We lay back, ready to savour the long drive to our rustic romantic home-stay in the mountains. Immediately, a pungent odour hit us. I realized that my moment of executive decision making had arrived. I didn't want to annoy Larry, however, I could not seem unappreciative of the great efforts of the protocol officers in trying to locate durian in the dark of the night. Here was the opportunity which I had been denied for more than a year. I decided that I would have the durian removed from the trunk and spread on the grass. I would examine the fruit, taste a $^1/_4$ teaspoonful, rave about the flavour, and then generously offer it to our police escort and protocol officers with definite instructions to rid the car of all the durian fragrance by morning. I found that the fruit had a rich glutinous smoothness which resembled nothing else I had experienced. It was neither juicy, nor acidic in nature, nor particularly sweet. It seemed similar to a rich buttery custard which had been highly flavoured with a sweet fragrance.

A faint odour of the durian did linger in the car for the remainder of our visit, despite our attempts to get rid of it. A few months after our first encounter with durian, Larry decided to taste the fruit himself. He loved it!

Fried Capers (*page 214*), Salmon Stroganoff Coulibiac (*page 107*), Coeur de Palmier, Avocado, and Watercress Salad (*page 134*), Tomato Lotus Flowers (*page 208*), and Garlic Bread (*page 225*)

A few months after our arrival in Jakarta, Larry began a bimonthly tradition of hosting a business breakfast at the residence. The breakfasts became exciting occasions as I was able to design all sorts of fascinating breakfast creations and presentations. At the first breakfast, the guest of honour, a regular visitor to the Canadian residence over the years, expressed surprise at the creative menu that was unfolding. Turning to Larry, he inquired about "the cook":

Guest: Does the residence have a new cook?

Larry: Yes.

Guest: Does the cook always travel with you?

Larry: Yes.

Guest: He must be expensive?

Larry: Not salary-wise!

Guest: How long have you had him?

Larry: Since before we graduated from university.

At this point the commercial officer from the embassy could no longer stand the agony of holding back his laughter: "The cook is the Ambassador's wife!"

Above: Lemon Ice Cream Cherry Crêpes Flambé (page 187)
Left: Indonesian Sweet Blackened Chicken with Kiwi (page 148), Pineapple Carrot Salad in Pineapple Bird of Paradise (page 131), and Chelo Rice with Doubly Dark Wild Rice (page 223)

BARBECUE

Touches of a Thousand and One Nights

❦

(Drink Tray Garnish: Small Arabic Coffee Pot)
"Gahwa" (Arabic Cardamon Coffee)*
Lamb Stroganoff in Phyllo Triangles
Strawberries on Basil Carpets

—

Coriander Zucchini Soup in Tulip Napkins

—

Satay Kebab (Chicken, Beef, and Fish)**
Citrus Peel Dip and Coriander Mayonnaise
Grilled Oriental Lamb Chops***
Corn on the Cob
Asparagus and Mixed Cooked Vegetables
Saffron Rice with Oregano
Mini Salad Eggplant with Bell Pepper Rings
Mushroom Salad Intrigue
Black Olives
Herb Vinaigrette
Pita Bread and Hot Garlic Bread
Tahina Sauce

—

Irresistible Triple Chocolate Cheesecake Garnished with
Pistachio Nuts
Butterscotch Sauce Supreme

—

Mint Tea and Turkish Coffee*

—

Ginned Dates
Liqueurs

Style of Service

The soup may be served to guests at the tables, or the guests may collect it from the buffet table. The main part of the meal is served buffet style with hostess or host assisting in serving guests at the buffet table. Dessert is personally cut by hostess or host, and served to guests.

Work Schedule

1. Advance Preparation or Basic Supplies on Hand: Lamb Stroganoff in Phyllo Triangles, Citrus Peel Dip, Coriander Mayonnaise, Oriental Marinade, Herb Vinaigrette, Garlic Butter, Pita Bread, Garlic Bread, Irresistible Triple Chocolate Cheesecake, Butterscotch Sauce Supreme, Ginned Dates.
2. Day Before: Prepare Coriander Zucchini Soup, Tulip Napkins, Satay Kebab (cut pieces), Tahina Sauce; arrange trays and dishes; set up tables and decor (to extent possible); do floral arrangements; select music.
3. Day of Event: Complete table and decor preparations; prepare Strawberries on Basil Carpets, Satay Kebab and lamb chops, saffron rice, vegetables and salads, Arabic Cardamon Coffee; barbecue Satay Kebab and lamb chops.

*Optional To make these coffees, special techniques must be used. Arabic Cardamon Coffee or "Gahwa" is made from cardamon and special Arabic coffee. Arabic "Gahwa" can be various shades of amber brown in colour. As an essential element of a traditional Arabic welcome, it is always poured from elegantly shaped silver, bronze, copper, or even porcelain coffee jugs ("dalla") into very small handleless cups ("fanajeen"). On the other hand, Turkish Coffee is a particularly strong black coffee made from very finely ground coffee beans. Both Arabic "Gahwa" and Turkish Coffee are served in small quantities.

**Optional Any or all of the choices may be offered. According to personal preference, cut pieces into a size suitable for arranging on the skewers. Other dips of choice may be served.

***Optional Grilled Marinated Salmon or Pesto Beef Steaks. (If Pesto Beef Steaks are on the menu, beef should not be included in the Satay Kebab.)

DATE
Saturday, July 26

TIME
19:00

NUMBER OF GUESTS
20

THEME
Touches of a Thousand and One
Nights

DRESS CODE
Gallabiya or Middle Eastern
touches

TABLES
(Arranged indoors or outdoors,
or a combination of both)

4 round tables with 5 place
settings each; or

5 card tables of 4 place settings
each; or

According to personal resources
and preferences

SEATING PLAN
Free seating (with the host and
hostess sitting at different
tables)

PRINCIPAL TABLEWARE
"Kilim" motif china on brass
liners engraved with Egyptian
and Arabic characters

DRINK AREA ARRANGEMENT
Middle Eastern decorations,
kilims and cushions

TABLE CENTREPIECE
Middle Eastern artifacts, textiles,
antique copper and brass objects

COFFEE AREA ARRANGEMENT
Middle Eastern chest, camel
sacks, Arabic coffee pots, coffee
beans, branches of dates

ADDING TO THE TOTAL LOOK
Torches, ethnic lamps, candles in
brass candle sticks, tenting effect

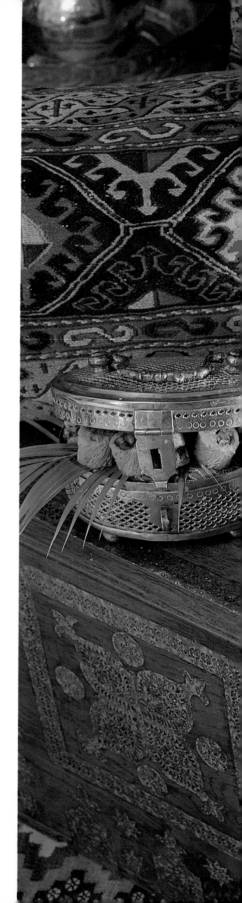

*I*n *Egypt, drama was added to almost every dinner party as the gas bottle for our stove ran*
out of fuel at some appropriately strategic moment – usually while I stood wondering why
the Baked Alaska was not browning after having been in the oven far too long.

Those gas bottles were tricky items. Usually, they were reasonably full and functioned
well, but sometimes they arrived empty or they leaked. One night when Larry was in Canada
on a trade mission, I awoke and sensed the house needed to be checked. In the still of the night,
I cautiously worked my way through the house. A faint whistling sound appeared to be coming
from the back kitchen. Yes, one of the gas bottles was leaking. I didn't know what to do, but
realized something should probably be done quickly. I grabbed the house and garden gate
keys, and ran a block down the street to wake up an Egyptian friend. We rushed back to our
home; he carefully carried the leaking bottle out to the patio, opened the faulty valve, and
released all the gas into the air. This adventure still makes for good dinner conversation,
especially when we are together with our Egyptian friends. Most male guests are enthusiastic
in declaring that they too would respond promptly to such pleas of distress!

Above: Mixed cooked vegetables, mini salad eggplant with bell pepper rings,
Pita Bread (pages 224–225), Tahina Sauce (page 231), and Garlic Butter Shapes (page 216)
Right: Gahwa, Ginned Dates (page 200)

DATE
Saturday December 17

TIME
18:00

NUMBER OF GUESTS
36

THEME
Holiday Season** – A Global
Experience

DRESS CODE
Smart Casual

PRINCIPAL TABLEWARE
Porcelain with Christmas motifs

DRINK AREA ARRANGEMENT
Christmas decorations, candles,
Christmas tree, rocking horse,
reindeer

TABLE CENTREPIECE
Candles, poinsettia, Christmas
baskets, "clove" house, holiday
cookies

ADDING TO THE TOTAL LOOK
Other Christmas decorations,
holiday music, coloured candles
and napkins, dried fruit
and nuts

COCKTAIL RECEPTION*

*Holiday Season** – A Global Experience*

(Drink Tray Garnish: Frosted Grapes and Holly)
Pancake Sachets with Black Caviar
Black Olive Rabbits
Tasty Morsels on Chinese Spoons
(Indonesian Sweet Blackened Chicken)
Creamed Escargots*** in Mini Pastry Cases
Pesto Avocado Spread on Wholewheat Crackers
Prawns in Coconut Jackets with Ginger Mayonnaise
Salmon Snow Pea Boats
Satay Kebab (Beef) with Citrus Peel Dip
Broiled Goat Cheese on Polenta Cake with Garlic Dressing
Apricot Pirozhki in Butterscotch Sauce Supreme
Cream Cheese Strawberries

Optional Expanded Menu
Fenced Maple Syrup Mousse Torte in Chocolate (Wreath)
Frame with Sugar Bow
Coffee Sour Cream Sauce

Coffee and Tea
Whipped Cream Sprinkled with Cinnamon
Milk and Sugar Cube Parcels
Marzipan Sweets
Almond Praline
Dried Fruit and Nuts

Work Schedule

1. Advance Preparation or Basic Supplies on Hand: Basic Crêpe mixture, Black Olive Rabbits, Indonesian Sweet Blackened Chicken, Creamed Escargots, Pesto, Ginger Mayonnaise, Oriental Marinade, Citrus Peel Dip, Polenta Cake, Garlic Dressing, Apricot Pirozhki, Butterscotch Sauce Supreme, Cream Cheese Strawberries, Coffee Sour Cream Sauce, Sugar Cube Parcels, Marzipan Sweets, Almond Praline.

2. Day Before: Prepare Frosted Grapes, beef (cut), Fenced Maple Syrup Mousse Torte; arrange table, dishes, trays, decorations, flowers.

3. Day of Event: Prepare pancakes, Pancake Sachets, Tasty Morsels in Chinese Spoons, Pesto Avocado Spread, Prawns in Coconut Jackets, Salmon Snow Pea Boats, Satay Kebab, goat cheese (cut), Chocolate (Wreath) Frame with Sugar Bow, whipped cream; prepare coffee maker; fry Coconut Prawns; barbecue Satay Kebab; broil Goat Cheese on Polenta Cake.

*Option If desired, the types of hors d'oeuvres served may be limited to only about 6 types, or expanded to include more choices. The suggested menu (calculating about 2 units of each hors d'oeuvre per guest), leaves guests delightfully satisfied, and often convinced that they have had a complete meal.

**Option There are many other possibilities such as Thanksgiving, New Year's, Chinese New Year, St. Valentine's Day, Idul Fitri, Easter, Earth Day, or even a national day. Components of the reception such as decoration, food, dress code, should be co-ordinated to suit the theme.

***See Escargots en Croûte (page 109). Mini pastry cases are available commercially, or may be prepared using the recipe for Basic Pastry (page 221).

I will never forget the day my husband-to-be was introduced to my grandparents and pirozhki. As soon as we arrived, Grandmother was busy boiling a large pot of water. A few minutes later, an enormous bowl of potato and cheese pirozhki well bathed with butter and fried onions appeared before Larry. Of course, my grandparents expected him to consume the pile with great enthusiasm. Not being accustomed to my family's Ukrainian traditions and hospitality – nor to my rather indiscreet sign language – he only gingerly sampled one or two. Grandfather was not impressed! However, Larry soon acquired a great taste for pirozhki (but never for the fried onion garnish!).

Fenced Maple Syrup Mousse Torte in Chocolate (Wreath) Frame (page 193)

RECIPES

Mango Fruit Pastry Blossoms (page 177)

HORS D'OEUVRES

Hors d'oeuvres are one of the most important elements in entertaining. They are served to guests first, and first impressions count. Never underestimate the strategic value of an impressive hors d'oeuvre, personally prepared and served by the host/hostess. One secret of successful entertaining is to convince guests that they are special and that extra energy has been spent to make a personal effort just for them.

Another secret is "to save the nuts" – even if you intend to pass them yourself. Nuts may risk indicating that you have not taken that extra step to create something special for guests. However, nuts freshly roasted or fried and seasoned in your kitchen are certain to be a real treat. These I serve arranged in small portions on Chinese porcelain spoons.

One tasty hors d'oeuvre made *à la maison* is well worth the effort. A busy person may choose to serve a deli-prepared fish, liver, or vegetable pâte as an hors d'oeuvre. In this case, present the pâte attractively, accompanied by freshly prepared waffled toast shapes placed in a napkin lined basket or decorative box. Guests notice the difference, and delight in the imagination of the kitchen.

I have created versatile hors d'oeuvre recipes suitable for both formal occasions and lighter entertaining. One or two of these hors d'oeuvres are delicious when served with drinks, before lunch or dinner. Hors d'oeuvres may also be offered at morning coffee parties, afternoon teas, evening drinks, or after-the-theatre/game events. It is easy to organize a fabulous cocktail reception by choosing 6 or more types of hors d'oeuvres, and serving them in a definite order to enhance the taste experience of guests. Start with savouries and continue towards sweeter flavours, mix hot and cold items as well as meat, fish, and vegetable dishes, contrast colours and textures. If desired, for these occasions, complete the menu with other treats from Finishing Touches and/or Desserts.

Apricot Pirozhki (page 93)

Seaweed Chrysanthemums

Guests frequently do not realize that Seaweed Chrysanthemums are part of the menu. When guests understand that they are edible, everyone must try at least one, and many come back for seconds and thirds. This recipe for Seaweed Chrysanthemums is a result of our family's Asian experiences. It was in Korea that we developed a great love for seaweed; and in Indonesia, wanton (or eggroll dough) is a familiar element of the local cuisine. Seaweed Chrysanthemums may be made by the dozens and used over several weeks. Also, when there is a sudden need for flowers to grace a luncheon table, I quickly arrange bouquets of Seaweed Chrysanthemums spilling out of baskets or novelty boxes. Guests are astonished by an invitation to eat the table decorations!

Ingredients

10 sheets* seaweed (18 cm x 20 cm or 7 inches x 8 inches)
20 eggroll dough squares (about 10 cm or 4 inches square)
(or see Pirozhki (Ravioli, Wanton) Dough: page 223)
1 egg white
3 cups oil for deep-frying

(Makes 20)

From sheets of seaweed, cut 20 seaweed squares of which each is exactly the same size as eggroll dough squares*. (Scissors are best for this task.)

From remaining pieces of seaweed, cut 20 ribbons; each seaweed ribbon should be 7$^1/_2$ cm or 3 inches long, and 8 mm or $^1/_3$ inch wide. (For each chrysanthemum, there must be one eggroll dough square, one seaweed square, and one seaweed ribbon.)

Lay eggroll dough squares, individually, on a flat surface. Brush exposed surface of each with egg white. Place one seaweed square on top of one eggroll dough square to exactly cover dough, forming a double layer.

Use one double layered square to make each Seaweed Chrysanthemum. Fold a double layered square in half to form a rectangle (half the size of the square), with seaweed on the outside. Seal rectangle closed along the long open side (opposite the fold side) with egg white.

Along and from folded edge, make cuts (3 mm or $^1/_8$ inch apart) towards long sealed edge to within 1 cm or $^1/_3$ inch of sealed edge. (A fringe effect is created at folded edge.)

Roll up rectangle along the long sealed edge, securing the end of the roll in position with egg white.

Wrap the rolled-up end with a seaweed ribbon to form base of chrysanthemum; seal end of seaweed ribbon in place with egg white.

Open out folded and cut (fringed) edge slightly, to form a chrysanthemum.

Deep-fry Seaweed Chrysanthemums, a few at a time, in hot oil until golden brown (25 seconds or longer). Drain on paper towels.

If not to be consumed immediately, arrange chrysanthemums in a single layer on paper towel lined baking trays for a day, allowing them to dry thoroughly. To store, arrange in covered cardboard boxes, and keep in a cool dry place.**

Serve Seaweed Chrysanthemums on their own, or as an edible decoration accompanying other hors d'oeuvres or other dishes.

*If you want to economize on the seaweed, seaweed trimmings from the chrysanthemums which are prepared first may be "patched" into position on other eggroll squares.

**If Seaweed Chrysanthemums lose some of their crispness or flavour during storage, arrange them in a single layer on a baking tray and place in a warm oven (150^{0}C/300^{0}F) for about 30 minutes.

Smoked Oysters in Pita Shells

Few know what to do with smoked oysters other than to serve them on crackers. In this recipe, elements are combined to enhance the smoked flavour while mellowing the distinctive oyster taste. The pita bread also adds a pleasant chewy texture.

Ingredients
30 pieces Mini Pita Bread*, commercial (or pages 224–225)
(diameter: 4 cm or 1¹/₂ inches)**
butter as required
¹/₃ cup Horseradish Mayonnaise (page 232)
1 can smoked oysters, drained*** (can size: 105 g or 4 oz)

Garnish
very small parsley leaves
diced tomato (firm flesh only)

Carrot Egg Filling
3 hard boiled eggs, chopped
¹/₃ cup carrot (cooked, well drained, and cooled), grated
salt to taste
white pepper to taste
pinch to ¹/₃ teaspoon ground nutmeg
1 tablespoon mayonnaise

(Makes 30)

To make Carrot Egg Filling, carefully toss chopped egg and grated carrot together. Season (according to taste) with salt, pepper, and nutmeg. Lightly fold in mayonnaise. (Makes 1 cup Carrot Egg Filling.)

Lay Mini Pita Bread on a clean flat surface. Along the seam at one side, carefully pry or cut each pita bread open, leaving top and bottom sections intact at back.

Butter both (upper and lower) interior walls of each mini pita. Lightly paint inside of lower wall with Horseradish Mayonnaise.

Fill each mini pita with Carrot Egg Filling (1 teaspoon). Allow mini pita to remain slightly opened at front like an oyster shell.

Place a drop of Horseradish Mayonnaise on carrot filling at front opening; add one small smoked oyster*** as if it were peeking out of pita shell.

Garnish individual oysters with a parsley leaf and a small piece of tomato strategically placed at one side of oyster.

Arrange hors d'oeuvres in a single layer in an airtight container. Cover with a lightly dampened paper towel to maintain freshness of bread (or to reduce the original dryness of the pita). Refrigerate until ready to serve.

(Prepare Smoked Oysters in Pita Shells at least 2 hours prior to serving so that filling can set. If desired, they may be prepared 8 hours or more in advance.)

*Option Pastry or other edible cases and bases may be used instead of pita bread. Home-made Mini Pita Bread is not complicated to make.

**Option If mini pita bread are too large, cut them in half. These hors d'oeuvres must only be "one bite" in size, for convenient consumption. Avoid adding too much filling for guests who insist on nibbling an hors d'oeuvre, and who may risk losing some of the filling.

***Normally, there are about 30 small oysters in one can. Large oysters should be cut into appropriate sizes, and arranged so that the cut edges are not facing outwards.

Salmon Snow Pea Boats

Salmon* Snow Pea Boats, besides being tasty, add colour and shape to an hors d'oeuvre tray. Another colour and flavour combination is created when the snow peas are topped with a few pearls of caviar, rather than the salmon.

Ingredients

40 small young snow peas, with ends attached
(length: about 7 cm or 3 inches)

$1/2$ cup cream cheese

$2/3$ teaspoon onion, grated

$1/3$ cup smoked salmon*, cut into small pieces

(Makes 40)

Place snow peas in baking dish, cover with boiling water, and let stand for $1^1/2$ minutes. Drain, dry, and allow snow peas to cool.

Blend cream cheese and onion together.

Carefully open curved edge of snow peas with tip of a small sharp knife. Place a little cream cheese mixture ($1/4$ to $1/2$ teaspoon) inside each pea, along spine.

Top cream cheese filling with flaked salmon* ($1/3$ teaspoon per snow pea), allowing salmon to protrude out of shell. Arrange Salmon Snow Pea Boats in a single layer, in an airtight container. Refrigerate until ready to serve.**

*Options Canned red sockeye salmon may also be used. (Drain salmon; remove and discard bones and skin; break salmon into small flakes.)

Caviar Snow Pea Boats
Arrange a little caviar ($1/8$ teaspoon) on each cream cheese filled snow pea.

Walnut Snow Pea Boats
Top cream cheese filling with chopped walnuts.

**Salmon (or Walnut) Snow Pea Boats may be prepared up to 10 hours before the event. However, if caviar is used, add the caviar to the cream cheese filled snow peas shortly before serving to avoid any discolouration of the cream cheese.

Pancake Sachets

Pancake Sachets are always a great hit. They are a perfect way to greet guests and to set a cordial mood. A variety of fillings may be used including vegetarian types.

Ingredients

12 pancakes (Basic Crêpes: page 221), prepared
(diameter: 12 cm or 4^1/$_2$ inches)

^{1}/$_2$ cup sour cream

1^1/$_2$ tablespoons caviar*

12 stems of fresh coriander or parsley
(length: 12 cm or 4^1/$_2$ inches)

(Makes 12)

To make coriander stems flexible, blanch only the stems (not leaves) by dipping into boiling water for 5 seconds. (If parsley is used, it may be necessary to split heavier stems in a vertical manner.)

Lay pancakes on a flat surface, with the first-cooked side down. Add 1^1/$_2$ teaspoons sour cream to centre of each pancake; make a small depression in the centre of sour cream, and add about ^{1}/$_4$ teaspoon caviar*.

Draw up edges of pancake evenly over sour cream and caviar to form a sachet. Tie pancake sachet closed with one coriander stem, allowing leaves to be displayed like plumes. (It may be necessary to use a double knot.)** Trim stem if necessary.

Place pancake sachets in a single layer, and well separated, in an airtight container. Refrigerate until ready to serve.***

To serve, arrange sachets individually on a serving tray with the coriander ties facing forwards, and with the plume-like leaves projecting gracefully in a horizontal manner.

*Option

Pancake Sachets with Salmon

For each pancake sachet, use ^{1}/$_2$ teaspoon sour cream and ^{1}/$_2$ teaspoon Horseradish Mayonnaise, plus about ^{3}/$_4$ teaspoon chopped smoked salmon (or drained flaked canned red salmon).

**If tops of crêpe sachets seem a little dry, spray very lightly with a mist of warm water.

***Pancake Sachets with Caviar are best served within 1^1/$_2$ hours of being prepared, as caviar may discolour the sour cream. Pancake Sachets with Salmon may be prepared several hours in advance.

Pesto Avocado Spread

This hors d'oeuvre can be made in a few minutes if a little Pesto is on hand. The avocado spread may be served in ramekin dishes, sealed with a layer of sour cream, and crowned with toasted almonds in a daisy petal arrangement. I serve Pesto Avocado Spread with thin $1/2$ cm or $1/5$ inch slices of narrow baguette which have been lightly toasted on a wire rack under a pre-heated broiler for 1 to $1\frac{1}{2}$ minutes (turning once). If appropriate and convenient, guests enjoy serving themselves.

Ingredients

1 to $1\frac{1}{2}$ teaspoons* Pesto (page 226)
1 cup avocado flesh, mashed or puréed
$1/2$ teaspoon dried tarragon leaves
crushed black peppercorns to taste
pinch of salt
$1/3$ to $1/2$ cup thick sour cream
2 tablespoons Toasted Almonds (page 226)

(Makes 4 to 6 servings)

Gradually add only sufficient Pesto* to the avocado purée, allowing mixture to remain thick. Add tarragon, pepper and salt.

Place Pesto Avocado Spread in a small serving bowl (or 2 ramekin dishes). Cover surface completely with a thick layer of sour cream.**

Cover filled bowl with a "hood" of plastic wrap; refrigerate for several hours to set.***

Before serving, decorate sour cream generously with Toasted Almonds.

Serve with small thin slices of unbuttered toast (e.g. 25 to 30 narrow baguette slices, toasted).

*I prepare Pesto and freeze it in ice cube trays, thawing quantities as required.

The amount of Pesto added depends on the consistency of the puréed avocado. The final Pesto Avocado Spread should be quite thick, allowing it to be picked up without dripping and spread with a butter knife. (It may be necessary to remove the surface oil from the pesto and use only the thicker portion of the pesto.)

**The sour cream also prevents discolouration of the avocado spread.

***Pesto Avocado Spread retains its quality for 1 to 2 days, depending on the type of avocado.

Tasty Morsels on Chinese Spoons

(or Witloof Leaves)

One of the most important elements of this hors d'oeuvre is its container. The delicacies which one decides to arrange on the Chinese spoons or witloof (Belgian endive) leaves can be left to the imagination. Begin by opening the refrigerator door to check the "leftovers"! I always keep some remaining pieces of tasty chicken (e.g. Indonesian Sweet Blackened Chicken) in the freezer ready to be arranged on Chinese Spoons. Additions of Honey Mustard Mayonnaise and fresh kiwi are "musts" with poultry.

Ingredients

30 Chinese spoons*
a few lettuce leaves
2/3 cup Honey Mustard Mayonnaise (page 229)
1 to 1 1/2 cups alfalfa sprouts
1 cup chicken (flavourfully cooked**) or smoked poultry
1 fresh kiwi fruit
fresh watercress*** as required

(Makes 30)

Arrange Chinese spoons* separately on a flat surface. Place a little Honey Mustard Mayonnaise (1/4 teaspoon) in bottom of each spoon. Tear lettuce leaves into small pieces suitable in size to line spoons. Secure one piece of lettuce in position on top of mayonnaise in each spoon.

Place another drop of Honey Mustard Mayonnaise on top of lettuce. Add sufficient alfalfa sprouts (1 1/2 teaspoons) to make a loose nest in spoon. Top alfalfa sprouts with a little more Honey Mustard Mayonnaise.

Cut chicken into pieces of suitable size (about 3/4 teaspoon) to fit into alfalfa sprout nest.

Peel kiwi fruit; cut crosswise into 5 slices; cut each slice (like a pie) into 6 pieces.

Garnish chicken in each spoon with a piece of kiwi, using a little Honey Mustard Mayonnaise to secure kiwi in position. Refrigerate until serving time.

(This hors d'oeuvre may be prepared several hours in advance.) To serve, cover trays with a light bed of watercress; arrange filled spoons on watercress.***

*Option If Chinese spoons are not available, the upper tips (about 5 cm or 2 inches) of witloof (Belgian endive) leaves are an option. Vegetable circles may also be prepared and used as a base, by thinly slicing (3 mm or 1/8 inch) certain vegetables (e.g. white or red radish, zucchini, cucumber) in a crosswise manner. Quantities of ingredients need to be adjusted to suit size of leaves or vegetable circles. (Omit the lettuce.)

**Indonesian Sweet Blackened Chicken is recommended for this recipe; Apricot Garlic Chicken is also delicious. If roast chicken is used, it should be well seasoned with salt, pepper, and a little sweet soya sauce.

***Optional The watercress not only makes the spoons appear even more attractive and refreshing, but also protects them and prevents them from sliding.

Garlic Cashew Nuts

These delicious cashew nuts are prepared in a very typically Indonesian way. I often serve them as an hors d'oeuvre arranged as individual servings on Chinese spoons.

Ingredients

15 g or 1/2 oz fresh garlic, peeled whole cloves
1 cup vegetable cooking oil
175 g or 6 oz shelled cashew nuts (i.e. not roasted or fried)
1/4 teaspoon salt

(Makes 375 g or 6 oz, or 1 1/3 cups)

Cut peeled garlic cloves into thin slices (twice as thick as "paper thin"). Set aside.

Heat oil in a medium frying pan or wok over medium heat. Fry cashew nuts in hot oil, stirring constantly until nuts are golden brown. Remove fried nuts from oil with a metal slatted spoon; transfer to paper towels; allow to drain.

In same frying pan or wok, fry sliced garlic, stirring constantly until light golden in colour. Transfer fried garlic to paper towels; allow to drain.

While nuts are still warm, combine with fried garlic; season with salt.

If not using immediately, allow Garlic Cashew Nuts to cool thoroughly. Place in an airtight glass jar; store in a cool dry place.*

*It is best to consume the Garlic Cashew Nuts within a few days. (The garlic may not retain its fresh flavour for an extended period of time.)

Above: Garlic Cashew Nuts
Left: Tasty Morsels on Chinese Spoons

Strawberries on Basil Carpets

Having one's own herb garden is a marvellous asset and source of inspiration. In addition to Pesto, I have come up with another creative use for basil.

Ingredients

1 tablespoon white vinegar

1 1/2 tablespoons sugar

12 fresh medium size strawberries*

24 fresh basil leaves (large and attractive)

1/4 cup thick sour cream

24 Toasted Almonds, slivered (page 226)

(Makes 24)

Combine vinegar and sugar; stir to dissolve sugar.

Remove stems from strawberries. Rinse strawberries under gently running cold water; drain and dry with paper towels. Cut berries in half lengthwise.

Arrange berries in a single layer on a large flat platter. Bathe with sweet vinegar solution. Allow berries to rest in vinegar bath for about 5 minutes, turning frequently. Drain well.

Wash, drain, and dry basil leaves. Arrange on a flat surface with top side of leaves facing up. Trim leaves if necessary.

Place a drop (1/4 teaspoon) of sour cream in centre of each leaf. Place one bathed berry half on leaf with stem end of berry at stem end of leaf. Insert a single sliver of Toasted Almond under berry and into sour cream. Refrigerate to set, and until ready to serve.**

*Option Small pieces of fresh papaya may also be used instead of strawberries.

**This hors d'oeuvre may be prepared up to 6 hours before serving if the cream is thick and the strawberries are well drained. Place the Strawberries on Basil Carpets in an airtight container; arrange them in a single layer, well separated; refrigerate.

For convenience in serving, Strawberries on Basil Carpets may be served on teaspoons. A drop of sour cream placed under the Carpets prevents them from slipping off the spoons.

Chicken Pears

Chicken Pears please the palate with an interesting combination of flavours and textures. I frequently serve Chicken Pears in a doily lined Turtle Bread Box with the lid propped up against the back of the turtle and a few sprigs of parsley tucked under the turtle, accompanied by Apricot Curry Mayonnaise.

Ingredients

Basic Chicken Mixture
250 g or 1/2 lb fresh chicken, minced
1/2 teaspoon curry powder
2 tablespoons almonds, chopped
1/4 cup Toasted Coconut (page 227)
1/4 cup dry breadcrumbs
3/4 teaspoon fresh mint leaves, chopped
1/5 teaspoon ground nutmeg
1 small egg, beaten
1/4 cup Basic Thick White Sauce
(Basic White Sauce: page 232)
salt to taste
white pepper to taste

Pear Shapes
2 to 3 sticks thick spaghetti, uncooked
1/4 cup flour
2 eggs, beaten
1 cup cornflake crumbs
oil for deep-frying as required

Dip
3/4 cup Apricot Curry Mayonnaise (page 231)

(Makes 50)

To prepare the Basic Chicken Mixture, cook chicken in a large ungreased skillet over medium heat; stir constantly and break apart minced chicken as it cooks. Add curry powder; cook thoroughly. Remove from heat; allow to cool.

Place the cooled chicken in a food processor; process for a few seconds until finely chopped.

Transfer the chopped chicken to a large bowl. Add almonds, coconut, breadcrumbs, mint, and nutmeg; mix well with a fork. Stir in one beaten egg; add Basic White Sauce; combine thoroughly. Season with salt and pepper. Adjust flavours if desired.

To make the pear shapes, take about 1 teaspoon of Basic Chicken Mixture; mould into a pear shape. To make a stem, securely plant a piece of spaghetti (8 mm or 1/3 inch long) into the top of each pear shape.

Arrange flour, beaten eggs, and cornflake crumbs in three separate flat bowls.

Roll the pear shapes in flour; then dip them in beaten egg; and finally roll them in cornflake crumbs.*

Deep-fry the Chicken Pears in hot oil until golden brown.

Serve Chicken Pears hot with Apricot Curry Mayonnaise dip.

*Chicken Pears may be frozen at this stage to be used when (and in quantities) desired. Thaw in the refrigerator before frying.

Satay Kebab

Having lived in the Middle East and Asia, we have been well exposed to kebab and satay. From my experience, both these terms translate as almost anything seasoned and threaded on skewers, grilled, and served with a tasty sauce. Citrus Peel Dip has been created using only enough peanut butter to offer an unidentifiable nut flavour and texture. However, a wide variety of dips would be delicious. The recipe may be adapted to serve as a main course dish, especially appropriate for barbecues.

Ingredients

500 g or 1 lb tender beef* (e.g. fillet)
1 recipe Oriental Marinade (page 225)
1 red or green bell pepper
4 rings pineapple (preferably fresh)
30 (approximate) wooden skewers
(length: 12 cm or 5 inches)

Citrus Peel Dip**

1/2 cup coconut milk
1/2 cup sour cream
1/3 cup pineapple jam
1 1/2 tablespoons hoisin sauce
1 to 2 tablespoons lime (or lemon) peel, grated
2 tablespoons peanut butter, creamy and only slightly crunchy
1 tablespoon fresh garlic, crushed
1 teaspoon fresh ginger root, grated
1/4 to 1/2 teaspoon fresh hot red chilli pepper, crushed
salt to taste
crushed black peppercorns to taste

(Makes 8 to 10 servings)

To facilitate cutting, use partially frozen meat*. Cut into cubes (1 cm or 1/2 inch). Arrange pieces in a shallow glass baking dish.

Pour Oriental Marinade over cubes of meat; refrigerate for several hours, turning occasionally.

To prepare Citrus Peel Dip**, mix all dip ingredients together, adding lime peel, chilli pepper, salt and pepper according to taste; refrigerate. (If possible, prepare Citrus Peel Dip at least 1 day in advance, allowing flavours to develop. Makes about 1 1/2 cups of dip.)

Cut bell pepper and pineapple into appropriate size pieces to accompany meat on skewers; set aside. (Makes about 30 pieces of both bell pepper and pineapple.)

Soak wooden skewers in hot water for 10 minutes; drain. (Soaked wooden skewers are more resistant to scorching and burning.)

Drain meat, reserving marinade. Thread each skewer with three pieces of meat, arranging one piece of bell pepper or pineapple between each piece of meat.

Grill skewers of meat to desired degree of doneness***, over hot charcoal or under pre-heated broiler; baste frequently with reserved marinade, and turn regularly to allow for even browning.

Serve Satay Kebab immediately, on large fresh leaves, accompanied by Citrus Peel Dip.

*Options Chicken, lamb, or fish may be used. (Note: Beef previously roasted to a rare or medium rare point of doneness may also be used successfully.)

**Options Coriander Mayonnaise (page 231), or a sauce of choice, including barbecue sauces, may be used. (Coriander Mayonnaise is excellent with all varieties of Satay Kebabs.)

***Chicken and fish must be completely cooked. (Cooked chicken releases a clear liquid when pierced with a fork. The flesh of cooked fish flakes easily with a fork.)

Lamb Stroganoff

In the Middle East, lamb is the traditionally popular meat. This recipe was developed to offer a Middle Eastern version of the beef stroganoff which we have enjoyed since our posting to Russia. Minced lamb produces a stroganoff which can easily be used as a tasty filling for a variety of small hors d'oeuvres (e.g. in Phyllo Triangles, mini pastry shells, or cases). It also makes an appealing filling for Chinese steamed buns. The stroganoff may be divided into convenient portions and frozen, ready to be included in a number of recipes. When time permits, prepare Lamb Stroganoff in Phyllo Triangles, and keep them on hand in the freezer. These triangles are not difficult to make, once a technique has been developed.

Lamb Stroganoff is not only delicious, but also versatile. When creatively combined with pasta, rice, or vegetable waffles, this stroganoff is very successful as an appetizer or as a main course dish for the family.

Ingredients

$^1/_2$ large onion, chopped
$^1/_2$ can mushrooms, sliced (can size: 425 g or 15 oz)
1 tablespoon vegetable oil
$1^1/_2$ teaspoons fresh garlic, crushed
2 teaspoons fresh ginger root, finely chopped
500 g or 1 lb lamb, minced
$1^1/_4$ teaspoons curry powder
$1^1/_2$ teaspoons mint leaves, dried or fresh (chopped)
$1^3/_4$ to 2 cups thick Green Peppercorn Sauce (pages 234–235)
salt to taste
crushed black peppercorns to taste

(Makes $3^1/_4$ to $3^1/_2$ cups)

Over medium high heat, sauté onion and mushrooms with oil, in a large skillet. Cook until golden brown, stirring regularly. Transfer mushroom mixture from skillet to a bowl.

In the same skillet, carefully sauté garlic and ginger for about 2 minutes; add lamb and curry powder. Cook until brown, stirring frequently.

Stir in mushroom mixture, mint, and Green Peppercorn Sauce; heat thoroughly. Season with salt and pepper to taste. Adjust other seasoning if desired.*

*At this stage, the Lamb Stroganoff may be cooled thoroughly; placed in an airtight container; stored, refrigerated, or frozen until required. Use the stroganoff for making a variety of hors d'oeuvres such as Phyllo Triangles, filled mini pastry shells and cases, or as an alternative filling for Crispy Coin Pouches.

Lamb Stroganoff in Phyllo Triangles

Ingredients

10 sheets phyllo pastry, commercial
(size of sheet: 28 cm x 45 cm or 11 inches x 18 inches)
$^1/_3$ to $^1/_2$ cup butter, melted
$^1/_2$ recipe Lamb Stroganoff (see recipe above)
2 egg yolks

(Makes 40)

To prepare Lamb Stroganoff in Phyllo Triangles, carefully separate sheets of phyllo pastry; lay on a flat surface and cover with a damp cloth. Take one sheet, arrange on a cutting board; cut sheet lengthwise into 4 equal strips (7 cm x 45 cm or $2^3/_4$ inches x 18 inches). Brush each strip with melted butter.

Place $1^1/_2$ teaspoons of Lamb Stroganoff filling near bottom right hand corner of each strip; take that corner and fold it upwards (and to the left side) to form a triangle, enclosing filling. (Note: The bottom left corner of strip

maintains its original position, while the bottom edge of original strip is placed exactly along lower left side of strip.) Continue to fold the triangle upwards and then to right side. Repeat the steps (always retaining triangular shape where filling is enclosed) until strip has been completely wrapped into a triangular parcel. Repeat procedure to make more triangular phyllo parcels.

Place Phyllo Triangles, seam side down, on ungreased baking sheets. Paint the exposed surfaces with egg yolk.

Bake Lamb Stroganoff in Phyllo Triangles at 180ºC/ 350ºF until golden brown (about 12 to 15 minutes).* Serve Phyllo Triangles hot.

*At this stage, Phyllo Triangles may be allowed to cool thoroughly. Arrange layers of triangles in an airtight container, separating layers with sheets of wax paper; freeze. When required, thaw frozen Phyllo Triangles in refrigerator. Before serving, place triangles, well separated, on ungreased baking trays; bake for about 6 minutes at 180ºC/350ºF.

Prawns in Coconut Jackets

The very light cornstarch and coconut coating gives the prawns a particularly delicate taste. Regular visitors to our home know that virtually anything dipped in Ginger Mayonnaise is a delicious experience! Prawns in Coconut Jackets may also be served as an appetizer, or in larger quantities as a casual main course dish.

Ingredients

1 kg or 2$\frac{1}{4}$ lb or 32 medium size prawns* (fresh or frozen), unpeeled**
$\frac{1}{2}$ cup cornstarch
$\frac{2}{3}$ teaspoon salt
$\frac{1}{3}$ teaspoon black peppercorns, freshly crushed
2 egg whites, lightly beaten
1$\frac{1}{2}$ cups desiccated coconut
3 cups oil for deep-frying

Garnish
fresh coriander leaves***

Dip
1 cup Ginger Mayonnaise (page 231)

(Makes 32, or about 10 servings)

Peel prawns, leaving tails attached.** Remove veins. Set prawns aside.

Combine cornstarch, salt, and pepper in a flat bowl. Place egg whites and coconut in two other separate flat bowls.

Dust prawns with cornstarch mixture; dip into egg white; roll in coconut.

Heat oil, preferably in a large wok, over medium high heat. Deep-fry prawns, in three batches, until tender and golden (about 7 to 8 minutes). Drain on paper towels.

If desired, garnish with coriander leaves and serve immediately, accompanied by Ginger Mayonnaise.

*Option Large shrimps may also be used.

**Option Peeled uncooked prawns, with or without tails attached, may also be used.

***Optional

Crispy Coin Pouches

The touch of hot chilli adds a subtle zip to this hors d'oeuvre. Often I use different fillings, depending on the occasion, my mood, the availability of ingredients, or what returning guests might have already experienced inside these little pouches *chez nous*. A vegetarian version is created by replacing the crab meat with more cheese or with cooked (and well seasoned) vegetables. Pouches stuffed with Lamb Stroganoff offer a modified samosa experience.

Ingredients

2 eggs, lightly beaten

1 tablespoon milk

$^1/_2$ cup aged white cheddar cheese, grated

$^1/_2$ cup crab meat, flaked (or slivered ham)

$^1/_8$ to $^1/_2$ teaspoon fresh hot red chilli pepper, very finely chopped

$^1/_4$ cup flour

1 cup dry breadcrumbs

20 to 24 pieces Mini Pita Bread, commercial (or pages 224–225) (diameter: 4 cm or 1$^1/_2$ inches)

$^1/_2$ cup oil for frying

Dip

1 cup Ginger Mayonnaise (page 231)

(Makes 20 to 24, or 6 to 8 servings)

Beat egg with milk in a flat bowl; set aside.

To prepare filling*, toss together cheese and crab meat; add sufficient chopped hot chilli pepper to give mixture a little "bite". Set aside.

With tip of a sharp knife, carefully open each Mini Pita Bread, on one side along seam, like a pouch. Add sufficient filling to just fill pouch (about 1 teaspoon**); arrange filling evenly inside pouch, keeping pita bread intact. Press down lightly on surface.

Place flour and breadcrumbs in 2 other separate flat bowls. Dust filled pouches with flour; dip into egg mixture; coat with breadcrumbs. (Ensure that any openings or cracks are closed with coating.)*** Refrigerate at least 50 minutes.

Heat oil in a large skillet over medium heat. Fry pouches, in batches, until crispy and evenly browned on both sides (about 1 minute per side). Drain on paper towels.

Serve Crispy Coin Pouches hot, accompanied by Ginger Mayonnaise as a dip.

*Options A variety of other fillings such as Lamb Stroganoff or a tasty cooked vegetable mixture may be used.

**If using Lamb Stroganoff as the filling, add only about $^1/_2$ teaspoon stroganoff to each pouch. If pita bread of a different size is used, adjust the amount of filling placed in each pouch accordingly.

***If placed in an airtight container and covered closely with plastic wrap, filled pouches may be frozen at this stage for several weeks. Thaw in refrigerator before frying.

Apricot Pirozhki

(illustrated on page 68)

When I was growing up, large bowls of pirozhki was a regular treat on Sundays, holy days, and at all Ukrainian gatherings. Apricot Pirozhki is my own unique version of that childhood ethnic treat.

Ingredients

1 recipe Pirozhki (Ravioli, Wanton) Dough (page 223)

Apricot Filling
75 g or 2$^1/_2$ oz dried apricots, finely chopped
2 teaspoons brown sugar
$^1/_6$ teaspoon ginger powder
1 tablespoon orange flavoured liqueur (or water)

Butter Bath
1 tablespoon butter

*Maple Syrup Glaze**
1 tablespoon butter
1 teaspoon lime (lemon) rind, grated
1 tablespoon maple syrup

(Makes 50)

To prepare apricot filling, place chopped apricots, sugar, ginger, and liqueur in a small heavy saucepan. Cover; place mixture over low medium heat for 3 minutes, stirring frequently, and adding a drop of water, if necessary, to keep it moist. Remove warm mixture from heat. Keep covered; allow apricot filling to cool.

Roll Pirozhki Dough out thinly (just thicker than "paper thin") on a clean surface, or with a pasta roller machine. Using a cookie cutter, cut out small circles of dough (diameter: 3$^1/_2$ cm or 1$^1/_2$ inches). Arrange circles of dough between sheets of plastic wrap to avoid drying. (It is best to cut 6 circles at a time, and to make them into pirozhki.)

To make pirozhki, place a small amount of apricot filling ($^1/_4$ teaspoon) in centre of each circle, fold dough in half over filling, and pinch edges closed.**

To cook, quickly drop pirozhki in a steady stream (but one at a time, to avoid sticking together), into a generous amount of salted boiling water, stirring constantly with a wooden spoon. (The pirozhki should not be crowded while cooking.) Cook at a gentle boil, until pirozhki come to surface of water, float, and dough is cooked (about 5 minutes).

Handling pirozhki with tender care, strain cooked pirozhki immediately; drain well.

Place pirozhki on a large platter; bathe with 1 tablespoon butter.

If not serving immediately, separate pirozhki and allow to cool in a single layer on platter. When cool, promptly cover closely with plastic wrap to prevent edges from drying.

To store pirozhki, arrange in single layers, separated by wax paper, in an airtight container. Refrigerate or freeze*** until required.

Just before serving, place pirozhki in a small heavy saucepan; add only sufficient boiling water to cover them. Bring to a boil. Drain immediately.

To serve, gently turn pirozhki in butter, grated lime rind, and maple syrup.* Place in a small serving dish. Serve immediately, accompanied by cocktail forks or toothpicks.

***Option** For a creamier "dessert type" of hors d'oeuvre, serve Apricot Pirozhki bathed in about $^1/_3$ cup hot Butterscotch Sauce Supreme (page 236), rather than the Maple Syrup Glaze.

**Avoid over-stretching the dough and weakening the skin. Pinch the pirozhki closed very tightly. One broken or opened pirozhki may reduce the quality of the batch.

***Pirozhki may be frozen for up to 2 months. To reheat, place unthawed pirozhki in a heavy saucepan; add only sufficient boiling water to cover them. Bring to a boil. Drain immediately.

APPETIZERS

Appetizers, as the name obviously suggests, must tempt the appetite. The recipes in this book include items that are generally well received, and perceived by guests as being somewhat exotic. They often include caviar, salmon, seafood, crêpes, pastry, escargots, toasted nuts, and tasty unusual sauces. Vegetarian appetizers also deserve attention; they tend to be lighter and are well appreciated as a pleasant change.

Guests are always intrigued when food is presented in edible containers or non-edible ones such as novelty boxes, baskets, or shells. Serve individually prepared portions of appetizers on plates smaller than a dinner plate. This allows them to be fitted into flat baskets (lined with a napkin), or to be placed on larger plates with a doily arranged between the plates to prevent slipping. A single serving of an appetizer also looks luxurious on an oversized plate or in an oversized bowl.

Serving sizes of appetizers are usually substantial without being overwhelming. The appetite is stimulated, somewhat appeased, definitely inspired for what is to come next, but not yet satisfied. Part of the strategy in effective menu planning includes offering portion sizes of each course which do not detract from the balance of the meal.

Peppercorn Prawns on Wild Rice (page 104)

Smoked Salmon with Fried Capers

Traditional smoked salmon is usually a special treat for guests. I like to personalize smoked salmon by presenting it with Fried Capers, Horseradish Mayonnaise, and unbuttered Waffled Toast. A few extra Fried Capers artistically placed on the rims of the plates offer a final touch of decoration and taste.

Ingredients

175 g or 6 oz smoked salmon, thinly sliced
$^1/_3$ cup Fried Capers (page 214)
1 small white onion, cut into very thin rings

Garnish
sprigs of fresh dill
2 lemons, cut into wedges

Dip
$^2/_3$ cup Horseradish Mayonnaise (page 232)

(Makes 4 servings)

To serve smoked salmon, arrange slices on plates or a serving tray.

Arrange Fried Capers and onion slices with salmon. Add fresh dill and lemon wedges, as a garnish. Serve with Horseradish Mayonnaise.

Seafood Mousse Parcels

If desired, the spinach wrapping in this recipe may be omitted. A single large mousse may also be prepared. Sometimes I paint the interiors of Pastry Blossoms with Ginger Mayonnaise, and drop the Seafood Mousse Parcels (with or without the spinach wrapping) into the blossoms. The Seafood Mousse Blossoms are garnished and served.

Ingredients

olive oil as required
125 g or 4 oz fresh young spinach leaves*

Seafood Mousse
250 g or $^1/_2$ lb crab meat, cooked
3 tablespoons Basic White Sauce (page 232),
medium thickness

pinch of cayenne pepper
salt to taste
white pepper to taste
$1^1/_2$ teaspoons unflavoured gelatin
1 tablespoon water (or juice from canned crab or shrimp)
3 tablespoons mayonnaise
$1^1/_2$ tablespoons whipped cream, unsweetened

Garnish
1 cup Watercress Sauce (page 233)
3 tablespoons Ginger Mayonnaise (page 231)
125 g or 4 oz crab meat**, cooked and flaked
red caviar as desired

(Makes 8 spinach wrapped* servings, or $1^1/_2$ cups of Seafood Mousse)

Smoked Salmon with Fried Capers

To make Seafood Mousse Parcels wrapped in spinach*, remove stems from spinach leaves; discard stems. To blanch leaves, bring a generous amount of water to a boil in a medium size pot. Drop leaves into pot, and immediately remove pot from heat. Turn leaves carefully in hot water for about 30 seconds. Drain leaves well in a large sieve; open leaves out flat; pat dry between paper towels. Line 8 small*** ramekin dishes (1/4 cup size) with plastic wrap; very lightly oil plastic wrap. Then line oiled plastic wrap in ramekin dishes with a single layer of blanched spinach leaves, allowing extra parts of leaves to hang over sides of dish; refrigerate.

To prepare Seafood Mousse, purée crab meat in a food processor. Add white sauce and cayenne pepper. Add salt and white pepper according to taste. Transfer crab meat mixture to a bowl.

Sprinkle gelatin over water (or juice from seafood); allow gelatin to soften for 5 minutes; dissolve gelatin thoroughly over hot water. Set aside until mixture begins to cool.

Combine cooling gelatin mixture with mayonnaise; fold into crab meat mixture. Fold in whipped cream. (Makes 1 1/2 cups Seafood Mousse.)

Spoon Seafood Mousse (3 tablespoons) into each lined ramekin dish. If dishes have been lined with spinach, fold any extra hanging spinach leaves over mousse; add more leaves to ensure that mousse is covered completely with a thin layer of spinach.

Cover dishes of mousse with plastic wrap; refrigerate overnight, allowing mousse to set and flavours to develop.

To serve, remove mousse parcels from ramekin dishes by carefully lifting out plastic wrap lining. Turn each mousse parcel upside down on a thin coulis of slightly warm Watercress Sauce (1 1/2 tablespoons); discard plastic wrap. Garnish top of each parcel with a little Ginger Mayonnaise (1 teaspoon); crown with flakes of crab meat; sprinkle crab with pearls of red caviar.

*Option The spinach wrapping may be omitted. In that case, spoon mousse directly into the plastic lined dishes. If desired, more mousse (1 tablespoon) may be added to each dish, making about 6 servings.

**Frozen or canned crab meat may be used; however fresh crab meat is preferable.

***Option If one large mousse (with or without spinach lining) is desired, use a 1 1/2 cup mould. Makes 4 to 6 servings.

Seafood Mousse Parcel in Pastry Blossom

Blinis and Caviar

Blinis and Caviar have become almost a trademark of the Dickenson household, served as an hors d'oeuvre or an appetizer. Blinis and Caviar can be very quick and inexpensive to prepare especially if there is frozen crêpe batter on hand in the freezer, as well as caviar (e.g. lumpfish) and sour cream in the refrigerator. Guests who may have doubted their appreciation for caviar thoroughly enjoy this dish. The blinis and sour cream definitely mellow and enhance the flavour of the caviar. Of course, expensive caviar may be used, but it is not necessary.

Blinis and Caviar are best served with ice-cold vodka, making the dish an authentic "food of the Czars". We always keep a bottle of vodka in the freezer, particularly for this recipe. The vodka does make a difference.

Ingredients

18 blinis (Basic Crêpes: page 221), prepared
(diameter: $7^{1}/_{2}$ cm or 3 inches)
$^{1}/_{2}$ cup sour cream*
$^{1}/_{4}$ cup caviar*

Garnish
2 lemons, cut into wedges
6 sprigs of fresh dill**

(Makes 6 servings)

Prepare blinis (i.e. crêpes); stack in 2 piles on a plate. Place plate of blinis in a plastic bag; refrigerate until time of serving.

Just prior to serving, separate blinis carefully. For individual portions, arrange 3 blinis in a flat position on each of 6 plates, keeping blinis separated.

Place 1 teaspoon sour cream in centre of each bliny. Add $^{1}/_{2}$ teaspoon caviar to sour cream on each bliny.

Garnish plates with lemon wedges and sprigs of fresh dill.

*Adjust quantities according to type of caviar and to taste. If lumpfish caviar is used, drain caviar with a small fine sieve, to remove excess black liquid. Return caviar to jar; refrigerate until required. It is best to do this at least 1 day in advance. (If desired, refrigerate black liquid and use it to make Violet Caviar Pasta.)

**Optional

Beef Carpaccio

Beef Carpaccio is another traditional but wonderful recipe which can be prepared rather quickly. To personalize this recipe, I pipe Dijon mustard in a crisscross manner on top of the beef before adding the mushrooms.

Ingredients

250 g or 9 oz frozen beef fillet (tenderloin)*
175 g or 6 oz fresh mushrooms, thinly sliced
1/3 to 1/2 cup Herb Vinaigrette (page 229)
salt to taste
coarsely cracked black peppercorns to taste

Garnish

12 fresh basil leaves
Dijon mustard to taste
Parmesan cheese to taste

(Makes 6 servings)

Remove frozen beef from freezer; allow to thaw slightly before cutting into paper-thin translucent slices. Arrange slices in a single layer on a wax paper lined tray; cover with plastic wrap. Refrigerate to keep chilled.

Just before serving, toss sliced mushroom with Herb Vinaigrette; season with salt and cracked peppercorns.

To serve Beef Carpaccio, arrange slices of beef in a single overlapping layer on chilled serving plates. Pile seasoned sliced mushrooms in centre (on top of beef). Accent mushrooms with whole fresh basil leaves.

Garnish beef with Dijon mustard, large thick curls of Parmesan cheese, and cracked black peppercorns according to taste.

*Option Other tender cuts of beef, such as rib-eye, may be used. Well marbled beef adds extra flavour.

Avocado à la Russe

⸺

This appetizer is prepared in just a few minutes. It may be served with a variety of toppings such as cooked and seasoned shrimp or crab meat, as well as caviar, or simply Toasted Almonds. I prefer to make individual servings with half an avocado for each person. However, a platter of peeled and sliced avocado may be garnished in a similar manner with Hollandaise Mayonnaise, sour cream, and a choice of topping. Avocado à la Russe served with dry toast and ice-cold vodka is a refreshingly delectable combination.

Ingredients

250 g or $^1/_2$ lb whole shrimps* (fresh or frozen), unpeeled

$^1/_4$ to $^1/_3$ cup Herb Vinaigrette (page 229)

2 avocados, well ripened

$^1/_4$ to $^1/_3$ cup** Hollandaise Mayonnaise (page 231)

$^1/_4$ to $^1/_3$ cup** sour cream

Garnish

small fresh leaves (e.g. red spinach, basil, parsley)

(Makes 4 servings)

Drop unpeeled shrimps* into boiling salted water. Bring water back to a boil; boil gently until shrimps are cooked (about 4 minutes). Drain shrimps; peel, removing heads, tails, veins; rinse and drain well. Bathe shrimps with Herb Vinaigrette; refrigerate, allowing shrimps to marinate for at least 2 hours; turn occasionally.

Cut avocados in half lengthwise; remove stone. Place avocado halves on serving plates with cut side up. If necessary trim bases, so that avocado halves rest in a level and stable position.

Spread Hollandaise Mayonnaise (1 to $1^1/_2$ tablespoons) evenly over flesh of each avocado half. Place sour cream (1 to $1^1/_2$ tablespoons) in central depression, over Hollandaise Mayonnaise.***

Just before serving, crown sour cream with shrimps; drizzle with remaining Herb Vinaigrette marinade*. Garnish appropriately with fresh herb or salad leaves.

*Options Peeled and/or previously cooked shrimp may be used. (Adjust quantities accordingly.)

Other alternatives include:

$^1/_2$ to 1 cup crab meat (cooked and tossed with Herb Vinaigrette)**
$1^1/_2$ to 3 tablespoons black caviar**
2 to 4 tablespoons Toasted Almonds**

Omit the vinaigrette if caviar or Toasted Almonds are used.

**Quantities depend on size of avocados, and personal taste.

***Avocado halves may be prepared to this stage, several hours in advance. Cover with a "tent" of wax paper; refrigerate.

Peppercorn Prawns on Wild Rice

⸺

(illustrated on page 94)

For individual servings of 3 to 5 prawns, I arrange small separate pools of Saffron or Tomato Brandy Cream Sauce, or Ginger Mayonnaise ($1^1/_2$ teaspoons per pool) on heated plates. I sprinkle each mini pool with Doubly Dark Wild Rice, and top with one Peppercorn Prawn.

Ingredients

1 kg or $2^1/_2$ lb or 30 medium size prawns (fresh or frozen), unpeeled

3 tablespoons Garlic Butter (page 223)

salt to taste

freshly (coarsely) crushed black peppercorns to taste

1 recipe Doubly Dark Wild Rice (page 223)

$1^1/_2$ cups Saffron Sauce (pages 232–233)

(Makes 6 to 10 servings)

Avocado à la Russe

Peel prawns, leaving tails attached. Remove veins. Rinse; drain; set aside.

Immediately before serving, melt Garlic Butter in a large heavy skillet over medium heat. Carefully sauté prawns, until cooked (about 4 minutes); season with salt and pepper to taste, be generous with the crushed black peppercorns.

Heat Doubly Dark Wild Rice and Saffron Sauce. Arrange Peppercorn Prawns on Doubly Dark Wild Rice, accompanied by Saffron Sauce. Serve immediately.

Salmon Stroganoff Divine

Salmon Stroganoff Divine is versatile as well as delicious. As an appetizer, Salmon Stroganoff Divine may be served in combination with Basic Pastry, phyllo pastry, crêpes, or pasta. Favourites at our table are Salmon Stroganoff Coulibiac (Salmon Pastry Fish) and crêpe purses filled with the stroganoff. Arranged in mini pastry cups, Salmon Stroganoff Divine may be served as an hors d'oeuvre. Presented with rice or pasta, or as Salmon Stroganoff Coulibiac, it makes an excellent main course dish, particularly for lunches.

Ingredients

2 cans red sockeye salmon (can size: 213 g or 7¹/₂ oz)

1¹/₂ cups* evaporated milk

2 tablespoons butter

2 teaspoons fresh garlic, finely chopped

2 teaspoons fresh ginger, finely chopped

2 tablespoons onion, chopped

1 cup canned whole mushrooms, well drained

1 cup green pepper, diced

¹/₃ cup flour

¹/₂ teaspoon ground nutmeg

¹/₂ teaspoon dried tarragon leaves

pinch of cayenne pepper

salt to taste

¹/₂ teaspoon black peppercorns, crushed

(Makes 4 cups)

Drain juice from canned salmon into a measuring cup; add enough* evaporated milk to make 2 cups of liquid; set milk mixture aside.

Remove and discard bones and skin from drained salmon; break salmon into large flakes; set aside.

To make Salmon Stroganoff Divine, melt butter over medium heat in a large skillet; add garlic, ginger, and onion; sauté for 3 minutes.

Slice mushrooms thinly. Add mushrooms and green pepper to skillet; cook for about 5 minutes. Remove mushroom mixture from skillet; set aside.

In a bowl, whisk flour into milk mixture, blending thoroughly to suspend flour. Sieve suspended flour mixture into skillet over moderate heat, stirring constantly; cook until sauce bubbles and thickens. Add mushroom mixture, nutmeg, tarragon, cayenne pepper, salt, and pepper.**

Very carefully fold salmon into mushroom cream mixture without reducing size of salmon flakes; heat well. Adjust seasoning if necessary.

If Salmon Stroganoff Divine is not served immediately, allow it to cool. Refrigerate or freeze until required.

*Amount may vary depending on the quantity of juice recovered from draining the canned salmon. (Also, if Salmon Stroganoff Divine is to be served over pasta, carefully add extra milk or light cream to make a thinner mixture.)

**If a thinner mixture is desired, add a little extra evaporated milk, 1 tablespoon at a time.

Salmon Stroganoff Coulibiac

(illustrated on pages 52–53)

Salmon Stroganoff Coulibiac or Salmon Pastry Fish is quite original as an appetizer for sit-down occasions. It is also a much appreciated addition to buffet dinners where the host/hostess cuts the fish and serves it personally to individual guests. The pastry sculptured fish is attractive served on a large tray completely surrounded by a sea of thinly frenched green beans (cooked and seasoned), or of finely shredded red cabbage (blanched if desired).

Ingredients

3 recipes Basic Pastry (page 221)

2 egg yolks, beaten

1¹/₂ recipes Salmon Stroganoff Divine (page 106)

¹/₂ maraschino cherry or small tomato

1¹/₂ cups Horseradish Mayonnaise (pages 232)

¹/₂ cup capers, well drained

(Makes 10 to 12 appetizer, or 25 to 35 buffet appetizer, or 6 to 8 main course servings)

If a fish board serving tray* is not available, draw a large whole fish shape (55 cm or 22 inches long and 20 cm or 8 inches wide) on paper. (Fish size and shape should represent appearance of final product desired.) Enlarge drawing by 1¹/₂ cm or ¹/₂ inch on all sides to make a fish shaped pattern; cut out final pattern.

Roll pastry into two large thin sheets (size of each sheet: 58 cm x 23 cm or 23 inches x 9 inches). Using the paper pattern, cut out one fish shape from each sheet of pastry, exactly the size of pattern. (The 2 pastry fish shapes are exactly the same.)

Place one pastry fish shape on an ungreased baking sheet; spread evenly with Salmon Stroganoff filling, 2¹/₂ cm or 1 inch thick, leaving a 1¹/₂ cm or ¹/₂ inch border of pastry exposed around all edges. Bring the pastry border up around the salmon filling on all sides, to resemble a wall around the filling. Very lightly dampen the exposed pastry wall with a little water.

Carefully lay the other fish shaped pastry sheet over the top of the salmon stroganoff to overlap the wall of the pastry sheet containing the Salmon Stroganoff. Press the top pastry sheet against the raised wall of the other pastry sheet, sealing the pastry fish closed.

Using the tip of an inverted teaspoon, and working from the tail of the fish body towards the head, carefully make shallow impressions to resemble scales. On the tail, mark lines in the pastry to resemble those of a tail fin.** (Impressions must not pierce through pastry.)

Just before baking, brush exposed surfaces of the pastry fish evenly and completely with egg yolk.

Bake at 190⁰C/375⁰F until golden brown (about 45 minutes).

Remove from oven; place baking tray with Salmon Stroganoff Coulibiac on wire rack; allow to rest for at least 10 minutes. Using wide metal spatulas and/or a firm long piece of thin cardboard, transfer the Salmon Stroganoff Coulibiac to a large serving tray. Add half a maraschino cherry or small tomato, cut side down, to resemble an eye.

Serve Salmon Stroganoff Coulibiac with Horseradish Mayonnaise and capers.

*__Option__ A fish board with a sculpted head and tail may be available. If so, draw an appropriate fish body shape 1¹/₂ cm or ¹/₂ inch larger on all sides than a shape which would exactly fit on the board between the existing sculpted head and tail. Adjust quantities of pastry and Salmon Stroganoff accordingly.

**The Salmon Stroganoff Coulibiac may be prepared to this stage up to 1 day in advance of the event; cover carefully, but not too closely, with plastic wrap; refrigerate.

Escargots en Croûte

Small ramekin dishes are required for this particular recipe*. Lamb Stroganoff and Salmon Stroganoff Divine en Croûte may also be prepared in a similar manner.

Ingredients

³/₄ recipe Basic Pastry (page 221)
1 egg yolk, beaten

Sautéed Escargots

2 tablespoons butter or margarine
1 to 2 teaspoons fresh garlic, finely chopped
1 to 2 teaspoons fresh ginger root, finely chopped
2 cans escargots, drained
(can size: 115 g or 4 oz drained weight)
¹/₄ teaspoon ground nutmeg
¹/₄ teaspoon ground cinnamon
1 teaspoon fines herbes

Sauce for Escargots

1 tablespoon butter or margarine
1 to 1¹/₂ teaspoons fresh garlic, finely chopped
1 to 1¹/₂ teaspoons fresh ginger root, finely chopped
¹/₂ medium size onion, sliced
2 tablespoons flour
1 cup whole milk
¹/₂ cup evaporated milk
1 large tomato, sliced and cooked
1 tablespoon fresh parsley, chopped
1¹/₂ teaspoons dark beef bouillon cube, very finely crushed
pinch of ground nutmeg
pinch of ground cloves
³/₄ teaspoon salt
¹/₈ teaspoon black peppercorns, crushed
1 tablespoon white wine
1 tablespoon medium dry sherry

(Makes 2²/₃ cups, or 12 servings in ¹/₄ cup size ramekin dishes)

To prepare sautéed escargots, melt butter in a small skillet over medium heat; add garlic and ginger; sauté gently for 3 minutes. Stir in escargots; sauté for 5 minutes; add nutmeg, cinnamon, and fines herbes. Cover, remove from heat, and set aside.

To prepare sauce for escargots, melt butter in a medium size saucepan over medium heat. Add garlic, ginger, and onion; sauté for 5 minutes. Blend in flour. Add whole milk and evaporated milk, stirring constantly until sauce thickens and bubbles. Add tomato, parsley, and crushed bouillon cube to the sauce; blend well. Stir sautéed escargots into sauce. Season with nutmeg, cloves, salt, and pepper; add wine and sherry. Reduce heat to very low, allowing creamed escargot mixture to barely simmer for about 20 minutes; remove from heat. Adjust seasoning.**

Roll out pastry (3 mm or ¹/₈ inch thick) on a lightly floured surface; cut out circles 2¹/₂ cm or 1 inch wider in diameter than top diameter of the small ramekin dishes.

Add a little extra milk to escargot mixture if necessary to ensure a creamy consistency. Fill ramekin dishes three-quarters full with escargot mixture. (If dish is too full, contents may boil out.)

Cover each dish with one circle of pastry; fold excess pastry evenly over top edge of dish, and press bottom edge of pastry against dish to seal tightly. Arrange pastry covered dishes on baking sheets (for convenience in handling); separate dishes well.***

Just before baking, paint surface of pastry with egg yolk. Bake at 200⁰C/400⁰F until pastry is golden brown (12 to 15 minutes). Serve immediately.

*Option Creamed escargots may be used for a variety of other recipes (e.g. in pastry cases, crêpe purses). Add more flour if a thicker mixture is desired.

**At this stage, the escargot mixture may be refrigerated or frozen until required. (Reheat mixture and blend until smooth before placing in ramekin dishes.)

***The dishes may be filled and the pastry dome set in place 2 hours before baking; refrigerate. Remove filled dishes from refrigerator about 10 minutes before baking.

Deluxe Beet Wanton Ravioli

⟡

Beet Wanton Ravioli, garnished with a touch of sour cream and a bit of parsley, is always a special treat.

Ingredients

2 recipes Pirozhki (Ravioli, Wanton) Dough* (page 223),
$^{1}/_{4}$ cup Garlic Butter (page 223)
1 to $1^{1}/_{4}$ cups Citrus Peel Dressing (page 230)
$^{2}/_{3}$ to 1 cup sour cream

Garnish
parsley

Beet Filling
$1^{1}/_{3}$ cups beet root (cooked and peeled), grated
(or 400 g or 14 oz uncooked fresh beets)
$^{1}/_{4}$ cup old cheddar cheese, grated
$1^{1}/_{4}$ teaspoons fresh garlic, finely chopped
1 teaspoon fresh ginger root, finely chopped
$^{1}/_{2}$ teaspoon black peppercorns, coarsely crushed
salt to taste

(Makes 30, or 10 servings)

To prepare beet filling, place grated beets in a sieve; press as much additional juice as possible out of beets. (This process reduces the grated beets to about 1 cup of very dry pulp, plus $^{1}/_{3}$ cup juice. Set juice aside for another recipe such as Borshch.) Combine dry beet pulp (i.e. 1 cup) with cheese, garlic, ginger, pepper, and salt. Set beet filling aside.

Prepare Pirozhki Dough**; roll dough out very thinly. (A pasta roller machine is convenient for this task.) From large sheets of rolled dough, cut out circles of diameter about 8 cm or 3 inches. (Work with a few circles at a time, always keeping dough closely covered with plastic wrap to prevent drying.) Place about $1^{1}/_{2}$ teaspoons beet filling in the centre of each circle; lightly dampen outer edge of circle with a drop of water; fold dough in half over filling; press overlapping edges together and pinch ravioli closed.

(To ensure a secure seal, beet filling must remain away from edge of dough.)

Repeat the process to make more ravioli. Arrange the filled ravioli between sheets of plastic wrap until ready for cooking.

Fill a large deep skillet (or electric fry pan) two-thirds full with salted water; bring water to a boil. Cook ravioli in about 3 or 4 batches, to avoid crowding. Slip ravioli (one at a time to prevent sticking) into boiling water; bring water back to a very gentle boil. Cook ravioli uncovered, until done (about 5 minutes), carefully turning ravioli from time to time, to ensure even cooking. (To turn, use a large slatted spoon or slatted egg turner. The spoon or egg turner should be coated with or made of plastic.)

Carefully lift out cooked ravioli, one by one, onto large flat platters; drain well. Arrange ravioli in a single layer on platters; butter both sides generously with Garlic Butter. (If not serving ravioli immediately, allow to cool and cover with plastic wrap to prevent drying.***)

Heat Citrus Peel Dressing. Serve Deluxe Beet Wanton Ravioli bathed generously with Citrus Peel Dressing (about 1 to $1^{1}/_{2}$ teaspoons per ravioli). Garnish with sour cream (about 2 to 3 teaspoons per serving) and parsley. If desired, offer extra Citrus Peel Dressing and sour cream.

*Option Commercial wanton skins, approximately 10 cm or 4 inches square, may be used. About 20 squares are required for this recipe. If wanton squares are thin and fragile, seal 2 squares together. (Brush one square lightly but completely with a little water; place a second square evenly on top of first; press together.) Use the double layered square as one single square. Therefore, 40 thin wanton squares would be required.

**Option If using commercial wanton squares, arrange a few squares at a time, on a flat surface. Fold each square in half diagonally, lightly creasing dough along fold line; open out square to its original position. (A diagonal crease line should be evident on wanton square.) Add $^{3}/_{4}$ tablespoon beet filling to square, carefully arranging filling to one side of the crease line near the centre of the wanton square. Lightly dampen all outer edges of square; fold dough in half (along crease line) over filling to form a triangle; press overlapping edges together and pinch closed. Allow 2 triangles per serving.

***The Beet Wanton Ravioli may be refrigerated for several days or frozen for up to 1 month. To store, arrange buttered and cooled ravioli in single layers in an airtight container. Separate layers with plastic wrap. To reheat, remove ravioli from refrigerator or freezer, and place directly into a large skillet of boiling water. When water returns to a boil, ravioli are hot. Remove carefully, drain, and continue as outlined.

Broiled Goat Cheese on Polenta Cake

Broiled Goat* Cheese on Polenta Cake is a refreshing change to traditional appetizers. We were first introduced to this wonderful "peasant food" while on a brief posting to the former Yugoslavia. There, it was served as an hors d'oeuvre with goat cheese melted on top of a huge slab of cornmeal cake which was then cut into generous chunks. I have since developed my own lighter version where tomato drizzled with a garlic dressing and garnished with fresh basil definitely enhances the total effect. This is a simple-to-prepare appetizer, particularly if frozen cornmeal cake is on hand.

Ingredients

350 g or 12 oz** goat cheese*
1/2 cup walnuts, chopped

Polenta (Cornmeal) Cake

1 cup yellow cornmeal
1/3 cup flour
2 teaspoons shredded coconut
1/2 teaspoon fresh hot red chilli pepper, finely chopped
1/4 teaspoon ginger powder
1/3 teaspoon salt
1/3 teaspoon baking soda
2 teaspoons baking powder
1 cup whole milk
3 tablespoons yoghurt
1 small egg, slightly beaten
1 1/2 tablespoons maple syrup or maple flavoured syrup
3 tablespoons butter, melted

Garnish

5 medium size ripe tomatoes, cut into wedges
30 fresh medium to large size basil leaves
2 cups Garlic Dressing (page 230), or commercial

(Makes 10 servings of 3 triangles per serving)

Butter 2 baking pans; set aside. (Pan size: about 20 cm or 8 inches square.)

To make the Cornmeal Cake, mix together in a bowl, cornmeal, flour, coconut, chilli pepper, ginger, salt, baking soda, and baking powder. Make a well in the centre; add milk, yoghurt, egg, maple syrup, and butter. Carefully draw dry ingredients into wet ingredients only to just moisten the dry ingredients. (Makes 2 2/3 cups batter.)

Pour batter into the 2 well greased baking pans to form very thin layers of batter.

Bake at 180°C/350°F until golden brown (about 12 minutes). (Cakes are 1 cm or 1/2 inch thick.)***

Cut cakes into squares (about 5 cm or 2 inches). (Each cake makes 16 squares.)

Arrange squares of polenta cake, well separated, on baking trays. Cover surface of each square generously with sliced goat cheese (6 mm or 1/4 inch thick).

Just before serving, place in oven 15 cm or 6 inches below a pre-heated broiler until the cheese melts and bubbles (about 2 to 3 minutes).

To serve, arrange warm squares of Broiled Goat Cheese on Polenta Cake on a platter or on individual plates in an overlapping manner; sprinkle with walnuts; garnish with fresh basil leaves and tomato wedges.

Offer Garlic Dressing at table to bathe polenta cake and tomato according to personal taste. (It is not recommended to heat platter or plates, as the basil leaves may discolour rapidly from the heat.)

Serve immediately.

*Option Cheddar cheese may be used for a milder and more casual version.

**Add more or less cheese, according to taste. (Very soft goat cheese cuts more easily when chilled in the freezer for 1 to 2 hours to become firmer.)

***At this point, the polenta cake may be wrapped securely in plastic wrap, placed in a well sealed plastic bag, and frozen until required. The cake will retain its quality for weeks if frozen properly.

SOUPS

Soups can be wonderfully delicious. A truly excellent soup is memorable. Unfortunately, far too frequently soups do not create great excitement. Unlike most other courses, soups are usually presented in a bowl which restricts their artistic and culinary potential.

Soups can be very attractive when creatively presented, and enhanced through flavour, colour, and texture. I prefer chilled fruit soups to look graceful, vegetable soups to look impressive, but all soups to capture the attention of guests. When it comes to soups, my imagination goes into high gear, conjuring up edible containers, complementary decorations, or simply deciding on what else can be done to make soups a memorable experience.

Mango Soup with Kiwi (page 119)

Almond Strawberry Soup

I like to present Almond Strawberry Soup in small ramekin dishes placed in baskets made of Novelty Craft Dough. The dishes are fitted into the baskets, and then the soup is spooned into the dishes. Immediately before serving, the soup is garnished, and the dough handles are secured in position on the basket with chilled White Chocolate Cream.

Ingredients

250 g or ¹/₂ lb fresh strawberries, well ripened
3 tablespoons strawberry yoghurt
2 tablespoons strawberry jam
2 tablespoons evaporated milk
2 tablespoons whipping cream
2 tablespoons orange flavoured liqueur
1 teaspoon liquid honey
1¹/₂ teaspoons almonds, blanched and ground
a drop of almond extract
a pinch of ginger powder

*Garnish**
3 tablespoons whipped cream, sweetened
a few fresh parsley leaves

(Makes 1¹/₂ cups, or 4 small servings of ¹/₃ cup size)

To prepare strawberry soup, remove stems from strawberries. Carefully rinse berries under gently running cold water; drain well. Set aside 3 attractive small berries.

Place remaining berries and all other soup ingredients in a blender; blend to form a smooth mixture. Adjust flavours according to taste.

Refrigerate soup for at least 3 hours to allow enhancement of flavours.

To serve, pour soup into small bowls or glass dishes. If desired, garnish soup with a little whipped cream and top with a very thin vertical slice of strawberry. Add a single parsley leaf to resemble stem end of strawberry slice.

**Optional

Mango Soup with Kiwi

(illustrated on page 114)

The availability of mangos in many parts of the world has inspired me to create this recipe. It is astonishingly easy to make. The slightly tart flavour of the kiwi garnish complements that of the rich mellow mango. Mango Soup with Kiwi may also be served for dessert.

Ingredients

1¼ cups ripe mango flesh (fresh or frozen)
½ cup whole milk
½ cup whipping cream
2 tablespoons orange flavoured liqueur

Garnish*
2 fresh kiwi fruit, peeled
orange flavoured liqueur or water as required

(Makes 2¼ cups, or 6 to 8 small servings)

To make Mango Soup, place mango flesh and milk in a blender; blend until smooth. Add cream and liqueur; blend well.

Refrigerate Mango Soup for several hours or overnight to allow for the enhancement of flavours.

Mash peeled kiwi with a fork, adding only sufficient liqueur or water to enable the mashed kiwi to flow in a heavy thread when poured from a spoon.

To serve, pour mango soup (¼ to ⅓ cup) into individual chilled flat bowls.

Place a spoonful of kiwi purée in centre, on surface of soup. Using a heavy toothpick flip out kiwi purée to create 5 or more points, in a modified star formation, radiating from middle of soup.

*Option For another simple but successful garnish, sprinkle a touch of ground nutmeg (or cinnamon or cloves) on the surface of the soup. Enhance the presentation with a light spray of fresh basil leaves and flowers.

Strawberry and Peach Soup Eclipse

Guests are struck by the artistry of this soup and its beautifully delicate and compatible fruit flavours.

Ingredients

1½ cups Almond Strawberry Soup (page 117)
1½ cups Champagne Peach Soup (page 120)

Garnish
8 fresh whole strawberries

(Makes 8 or 9 small servings of ⅓ cup size)

Just before serving, place the peach soup and the strawberry soup in separate pouring jugs; hold them over opposite sides, and close to edge of a chilled flat bowl. Simultaneously pour both soups (3 tablespoons of each) into the bowl, allowing soups to flow evenly. Continue pouring carefully until bottom of bowl is covered, and soups meet in middle. Repeat process with remaining bowls.

Garnish with fresh strawberries.

Strawberry and Peach Soup Eclipse

Champagne Peach Soup

This soup is amazingly simple to prepare, and looks attractive served in flat champagne glasses which have been frosted with lime flavoured gelatin dessert powder.

Ingredients

1^1/$_2$ cups canned peaches, drained and sliced
1 cup evaporated milk
^{1}/$_2$ cup whole milk
^{1}/$_2$ cup sour cream
^{1}/$_2$ cup champagne (or dry white sparkling wine)
^{1}/$_4$ teaspoon lemon juice
^{1}/$_4$ teaspoon ginger powder
^{1}/$_8$ teaspoon almond extract
orange flavoured liqueur to taste
1 to 2 tablespoons peach (or apricot) jam

Garnish*

very thin peach slices as required
Minted Coconut (page 227) or sprigs of fresh mint as required

(Makes 4 cups, or 12 servings of ^{1}/$_3$ cup size)

Place peaches, evaporated milk, whole milk, sour cream, champagne, lemon juice, ginger, and extract in a blender; blend to form a smooth mixture. Add liqueur to taste (2 tablespoons), and jam as required. Blend well.

Chill soup overnight, to allow enhancement of flavours.

Stir before serving. If necessary, add a little extra champagne or milk to make a thinner soup. Adjust flavours if desired. To serve, pour soup into sherbet or flat champagne glasses.*

Garnish surface of each serving of soup with a peach slice and Minted Coconut or a sprig of fresh mint.*

*Optional

Coriander Zucchini Soup

(illustrated on page 26)

Coriander Zucchini Soup is a very light soup. A spicier version may be prepared by adding more crushed black peppercorns. I serve Coriander Zucchini Soup in glasses frosted with chopped coriander. (If parfait glasses are used, parfait spoons should be provided; however, the soup should eventually be drunk from the glasses.) This soup is not suitable for freezing. It may be served hot or chilled.

Ingredients

2$\frac{1}{2}$ cups hot water

2 tablespoons medium flavoured chicken bouillon cubes, very well crushed

500 g or 1 lb zucchini, washed and grated

1 teaspoon fresh garlic, finely chopped

$\frac{1}{4}$ to $\frac{1}{2}$ teaspoon* fresh ginger root, finely chopped

$\frac{1}{8}$ teaspoon black peppercorns, crushed

2 tablespoons* fresh coriander leaves, coarsely chopped

salt to taste

$\frac{1}{4}$ to $\frac{1}{2}$ teaspoon** sugar

$\frac{1}{3}$ cup whipping cream

(Makes 4 cups, or 12 servings in parfait glasses, or 8 servings of $\frac{1}{2}$ cup size)

Place hot water in a medium saucepan; add bouillon cubes, and stir to dissolve. Place saucepan with bouillon mixture over medium heat; add zucchini, garlic, ginger*, and pepper; bring to a boil.

Reduce heat, and cover; simmer zucchini mixture until zucchini is very soft (about 30 minutes). Remove from heat. Allow to cool for a few minutes. Pour cooked zucchini mixture into a blender. Add coriander*; blend to form a smooth mixture. Adjust seasoning, adding a pinch of sugar if desired.**

If soup is to be served hot, reheat soup before serving. (If soup is to be served chilled, refrigerate overnight or for at least 3 hours.)

To serve, pour soup into individual glasses*** (parfait, juice, or drink type) or into small soup cups. Decorate surface of soup with cream ($\frac{1}{2}$ teaspoon per serving). (Cream should be stirred into soup before soup is consumed.)

*Option Add ingredients according to taste.

**If desired, add a little sugar (less than $\frac{1}{2}$ teaspoon) to enhance the flavour of the soup.

***When pouring hot soup into glasses, first place a metal spoon into each glass to prevent the glass from cracking. Remove spoons before serving. (For convenience, pour the soup into parfait glasses through a small funnel.)

Escargot Soup

(illustrated on page 45)

When a very special menu is desired, Escargot Soup deserves serious consideration. The recipe can be prepared in minutes. If the soup is served in Turtle Bread Bowls*, the turtle breads can be made in advance.

To add another unique touch, partially fill escargot shells with medium dry sherry (¹/₂ teaspoon). They may then be arranged in the small concave circles of special escargot plates to restrict the movement of the shells and the spilling of the sherry. At the table, invite guests to take a shell and pour a few drops of sherry into their soup.

Ingredients

Sautéed Escargots
2 tablespoons butter or margarine
1 to 1¹/₂ teaspoons fresh garlic, finely chopped
1 to 1¹/₂ teaspoons fresh ginger root, finely chopped
2 cans escargots, drained (can size: 115 g or 4 oz drained weight)
¹/₄ teaspoon ground nutmeg
¹/₄ teaspoon ground cinnamon
pinch of ground cloves
salt to taste

Basic Soup
2 tablespoons butter or margarine
1 to 1¹/₂ teaspoons fresh garlic, finely chopped
¹/₂ to 1 teaspoon fresh ginger root, finely chopped
2 tablespoons onion, finely chopped
1 tablespoon dark beef bouillon cubes, crushed
2¹/₄ cups hot water
3 tablespoons flour
¹/₄ cup cold water
¹/₈ to ¹/₄ teaspoon ground nutmeg

pinch of black peppercorns, crushed
pinch of ground cloves
1 to 2 tablespoons medium dry sherry
1 tablespoon parsley, chopped

(Makes 3 cups, or 9 servings of ¹/₃ cup size)

To prepare escargots, melt butter in a skillet over medium heat; add garlic and ginger; sauté for 2 minutes. Stir in escargots, nutmeg, cinnamon, cloves, and salt; sauté gently over medium low heat for 5 minutes. Cover; reduce heat to warm.

To prepare soup, melt butter in a saucepan over medium heat; add garlic, ginger, and onion; sauté for 2 minutes.

Dissolve crushed bouillon cubes in hot water; add to saucepan.

Whisk flour into cold water; blend well. Add to bouillon mixture in saucepan, stirring constantly until sauce bubbles and thickens.

Stir sautéed escargots into sauce; add nutmeg, pepper, and cloves according to taste. Stirring constantly, bring soup back to a boil.

Stir in sherry and parsley. Immediately reduce heat to very low. Keep soup over gentle heat for 10 minutes. Remove from heat.**

Before serving, reheat soup over medium heat until very hot, adding a little extra water to ensure that the total volume of soup is 3 cups. If necessary, adjust seasoning.

*Optional To prepare Turtle Bread Bowls use the Deluxe Brown Bread recipe (page 224) to make the bread dough. Divide the dough into 8 portions (each: 70 g or 2¹/₂ oz), and continue as outlined in recipe; keep lids together with corresponding boxes. (If more than 8 Turtle Bread Bowls are required for an occasion, increase the recipes accordingly.)

**To allow flavours to develop further, refrigerate soup overnight. (The soup becomes spicier.) Escargot Soup may also be frozen at this stage.

Dickenson's Fast-Track Borshch

(illustrated on page 34–35)

With my Ukrainian origins, Borshch was a frequent treat when I was growing up. Mother's recipe depended entirely on what was in the garden, besides beets. This recipe is my own quick version. I discovered the trick of using corned beef in Kuwait after the Gulf War when we had cases of corned beef to help us through the times when fresh meat was not available.

Ingredients

2 cans sliced beets, plus juice (can size: 340 g or 12 oz)

$2/3$ cup cold water

1 tablespoon dark beef bouillon cubes, crushed

2 cups hot water

$1^1/_2$ cans corned beef (can size: 340 g or 12 oz)

2 teaspoons fresh garlic, crushed

$2/3$ teaspoon black peppercorns, crushed

$2/3$ teaspoon ground nutmeg

1 to 2 tablespoons fresh dill, chopped

2 teaspoons white vinegar

Garnish

$1/2$ cup sour cream

sprigs of fresh dill* as required

Makes 7 cups, or 12 small servings**,
or 4 to 6 main course servings)

Drain juice from beets into a large saucepan; set juice aside. Cut two-thirds of drained beets into matchstick pieces; set aside.

Place remaining beets in food processor; add $2/3$ cup cold water; process to form a smooth purée. Sieve purée into saucepan with beet juice.

To make the soup, dissolve bouillon cubes in hot water. Add bouillon mixture, corned beef, garlic, pepper, nutmeg, and dill to beet juice mixture in saucepan. Bring contents of saucepan to a boil over medium heat; cover and reduce heat immediately to very low. Allow soup to barely simmer for about 10 minutes. Add vinegar. If desired, adjust flavours according to taste, adding a little more spice, vinegar, and/or water.***

Just before serving, heat cut beets in a saucepan or microwave oven.

To serve, arrange hot beets in bottom of heated bowls; add only enough hot soup to just cover the beet sticks.

Top each serving with sour cream (1 teaspoon to 1 tablespoon) and a sprig of fresh dill.

*Optional

**This is a very hearty soup. For those occasions when the menu consists of several courses, a $1/2$ cup serving of soup is advisable.

***Soup may be frozen at this stage.

Mushroom Cappuccino

Guests are amazed when Mushroom Cappuccino arrives at the table: "Coffee time already? Are your dinners always this brief?"

Ingredients

250 g or 1/2 lb fresh mushrooms, chopped
1 teaspoon lemon juice
2 tablespoons butter
1/8 teaspoon fresh garlic, finely chopped
1/4 teaspoon fresh ginger root, finely chopped
2 teaspoons onion, finely chopped
2 teaspoons medium flavoured chicken bouillon cubes, crushed
2 1/4 cups boiling water
1/8 teaspoon black peppercorns, crushed
1 1/2 teaspoons cornstarch
1 tablespoon medium dry sherry

Garnish

1/4 cup whipped cream, unsweetened
pinch of ground cinnamon

(Makes 2 1/2 cups, or 8 servings in demi-tasse cups)

Toss mushrooms with lemon juice; let stand for 30 minutes.

Melt butter in a large heavy skillet over medium heat; sauté garlic, ginger, and onion. Add mushrooms; continue cooking, stirring frequently, until all liquid evaporates.

Dissolve crushed bouillon cubes in boiling water. Add bouillon and pepper to skillet; bring to a boil over medium heat.

Blend cornstarch with sherry; add to skillet, stirring constantly until soup bubbles and thickens. Remove from heat; allow to cool for a few minutes.

Transfer soup to a food processor; purée. Reheat puréed soup in a saucepan before serving. Adjust seasoning and add salt if necessary.

To serve, pour soup (almost 1/3 cup per serving) into heated demi-tasse cups*. Top each with 2 teaspoons whipped cream; sprinkle with ground cinnamon. Place filled cups on saucers. Serve immediately. (The soup should eventually be drunk from the cups.)

*__Option__ Regular coffee or soup cups may be used. If so, increase size of individual portions (which will decrease the number of servings).

Hearty Carrot and Wild Rice Soup

This is a hearty, non-traditional soup. Vegetarians will appreciate a generous serving of Hearty Carrot and Wild Rice Soup as a main course dish for a casual lunch. The coarsely shredded vegetables and the wild rice offer a unique and delicious touch. They should be tender but firm when the soup is served.

Ingredients

1 cup boiling water

3 tablespoons wild rice, uncooked

2 tablespoons butter

3 cups carrots, peeled and coarsely grated

$2/3$ cup potato, peeled and coarsely grated

$2/3$ cup onion, peeled and coarsely grated

1 teaspoon medium flavoured chicken bouillon cube, crushed

$2^1/_2$ cups water

1 cup whole milk

$1/3$ to $1/2$ teaspoon* ground nutmeg

$1/3$ teaspoon ginger powder

1 to $1^1/_2$ teaspoons* seasoned salt, commercial

$1/2$ teaspoon salt

$1/4$ cup** evaporated milk

2 tablespoons** whipping cream

1 tablespoon parsley, finely chopped

(Makes 5 cups, or 10 servings of $1/2$ cup size)

Place water in a small saucepan over medium heat; add wild rice. Bring contents of saucepan to a boil; reduce heat to simmer. Parboil wild rice only slightly (about 5 minutes). Drain; discard liquid; set parboiled wild rice aside.

Melt butter in a large heavy saucepan over low heat. Add grated carrots, potato, and onion; sauté gently for 5 minutes, not allowing vegetables to brown.

Dissolve bouillon cube in hot water. Add bouillon mixture, milk, parboiled wild rice, nutmeg, ginger, seasoned salt, and salt to sautéed vegetables in saucepan. Bring mixture to a boil over medium heat.

Reduce heat immediately to very low. Cover saucepan; allow soup to barely simmer until vegetables are just tender (about 8 to 10 minutes). Immediately add evaporated milk**, cream**, and parsley; remove from heat within 1 to 2 minutes. (Take care not to overcook soup.) If desired, adjust seasoning according to taste.

Set soup aside for at least 1 hour before serving to allow flavours to develop.*** Before serving, reheat soup carefully over medium heat. If desired, add a little extra milk, prepared bouillon, or cream; adjust seasoning.

*Add according to taste.

****Option** For a creamier soup, add less evaporated milk and more whipping cream.

***For best results, refrigerate soup overnight.

SALADS

Salads for daily menus do not require recipes as it is often simply a matter of buying and putting together a variety of fresh salad items. To create something tempting or unusual, however, a conscious effort must be made to arrange salads in different ways even if ingredients are similar. A variety of serving bowls, dishes, and techniques should be considered.

Some occasions call for salads which offer a touch of the exquisite. This may be achieved quickly through clever additions of fruit, nuts, cheese, fresh herbs, or grilled vegetables, as well as the perfect sauce or dressing. The excitement of presenting unexpected combinations has also inspired me to develop sherbet or sorbet salads.

Thoughtful presentation can do much for a salad. Salads become more enticing when arranged on novelty plates, in baskets, in edible containers, or in stemmed sherbet glasses or bowl type champagne glasses.

Strawberry Asparagus Salad (page 130)

Strawberry Asparagus Salad

(illustrated on page 128*)*

The sauces make this recipe outstanding. For occasions such as buffets or barbecues, I simply serve large platters of chilled cooked asparagus, bathed in Citrus Peel Dressing and garnished with fresh strawberries. Guests add the Honey Mustard Mayonnaise according to taste.

If white asparagus is used, it must be peeled after it is cooked. The peeled asparagus is particularly tasty and colourful when bathed in Citrus Peel Dressing and allowed to marinate for at least 3 hours before serving.

Ingredients

2 young leek leaves* (length: 30 cm or 12 inches)
8 fresh strawberries, well ripened
2 teaspoons orange flavoured liqueur*
a few stems of fresh parsley*
$^1/_2$ kg or 1 lb fresh green asparagus
salt to taste
$^1/_2$ cup Citrus Peel Dressing (page 230)
$^1/_2$ cup Honey Mustard Mayonnaise (page 229)

Garnish
cracked black peppercorns

(Makes 4 servings)

Cut each leek leaf lengthwise into 2 long ribbons, about 6 mm or $^1/_4$ inch wide. Blanch leek ribbons in boiling water for about 30 seconds until suitably flexible for tying; chill immediately in cold water; drain well; set aside.

Cut off tough ends of asparagus. (If desired, set ends aside to make soup.) Cook asparagus** until tender crisp. Transfer immediately to a large glass baking dish containing a generous quantity of ice and cold water. Allow cooking process to stop and asparagus to chill thoroughly; drain well over wire racks.

Pat asparagus dry with paper towels; divide asparagus into 4 equal servings. Tie* each serving into a bundle at centre with a leek ribbon; trim base evenly if necessary. Refrigerate.***

Rinse strawberries under running cold water; drain well. Remove stems. Carefully cut 4 berries into a fan formation, keeping berries intact at the stem end. Using a thin metal skewer, make a little hole in each strawberry at stem end; insert a parsley leaf (with stem attached) to resemble original stem of strawberry. Cut remaining 4 strawberries in half lengthwise to produce 8 half strawberries. Refrigerate. (If desired, strawberries may be prepared up to this stage 2 hours before serving.)

Just before serving the salad, sprinkle berries with orange flavoured liqueur. Arrange asparagus bundles on 4 individual plates. Bathe length of the asparagus bundles with Citrus Peel Dressing. If desired, add salt according to taste. Cover base of each bundle generously with Honey Mustard Mayonnaise (2 tablespoons).

Garnish each bundle with a fanned strawberry, and 2 strawberry halves, appropriately accessorizing the latter with small parsley leaves, if desired. For accent, lightly sprinkle the serving plates with coarsely cracked black peppercorns. (Asparagus cuts more easily with serrated dinner knives.)

*Optional

**The asparagus may be cooked several hours in advance of the event. It can be cooked in an electric fry pan or a large skillet. Take a wooden spoon of appropriate length to fit into the fry pan or skillet; lay the wooden spoon in fry pan or skillet, about $^1/_3$ distance from top edge of pan. Add water to a depth of about 1$^1/_2$ cm or $^1/_2$ inch; bring to a boil. Arrange asparagus in a single row along, and perpendicular to, the wooden spoon and its handle so that the tops of the asparagus are raised above the water. Sprinkle asparagus with salt. Rotate asparagus frequently until lower stem areas are just barely tender crisp (about 1$^1/_2$ minutes or more depending on the size and type of asparagus). Usually, it is necessary to cook the asparagus in several batches.

***This may be done 2 hours before serving.

Pineapple Carrot Salad

(in Pineapple Bird of Paradise)

(illustrated on pages 54–55)

Pineapple Carrot Salad arouses great excitement when presented in a Pineapple Bird of Paradise. The extra salad is placed in an accompanying bowl. The hostess/host may want to personally serve the salad at the table to the guests. For the salad course, I usually place 1/3 cup salad into individual Frosted Sherbet (or flat champagne) Glasses. Before the filled glasses are passed on to guests, each is topped with 1 or 2 teaspoons of Ginger Sour Cream, a cluster of 3 Frosted Grapes, and a few parsley leaves. The sherbet glasses of salad look elegant set in Tulip Napkins.

Pineapple Carrot Salad is also delicious served in choux pastry cups. Place a little Ginger Sour Cream in bottom of each cup; fill cups very generously with salad tossed with a little Ginger Sour Cream. Present cups on a bed of lettuce; garnish with more Ginger Sour Cream, Toasted Almonds, and cherries.

Ingredients

250 g or 1/2 lb carrots, peeled and grated
1 cup pineapple, slivered
1 cup fresh coconut, shredded
(or 1/2 cup dry shredded, commercial type)
2 tablespoons icing sugar
1 cup Ginger Sour Cream (page 235)
or Ginger Mayonnaise (page 231)*

Garnish
parsley leaves

(Makes 4 cups, or 12 servings of 1/3 cup size)

Lightly toss together carrot, pineapple, coconut, and sugar.** Refrigerate at least 2 hours before serving.

To serve, garnish with fresh parsley leaves if desired.

At the table, top with Ginger Sour Cream or Ginger Mayonnaise according to individual tastes.

*Option Other dressings or sauces of choice (e.g. Coriander Mayonnaise: page 231) may be used.

**If desired a little extra sugar and/or a touch of orange flavoured liqueur (about 1 teaspoon) may be added to enhance flavours. Also, a particularly exquisite taste can be created by adding only 1 drop of each of the following extracts: coconut, pineapple, lemon, and banana.

Mushroom Salad Intrigue

I serve Mushroom Salad Intrigue in Tomato Lotus Flowers which are surprisingly quick to make. Another option, especially for buffet occasions, is to arrange the mushrooms over a bed of sliced tomatoes. The Red Bell Pepper Mayonnaise is not a must, although it does make the salad a memorable dining experience.

Ingredients

125 g or 4 oz fresh mushrooms
$1^{1}/_{2}$ teaspoons lemon juice
$^{1}/_{8}$ to $^{1}/_{4}$ teaspoon* black peppercorns, cracked
4 medium size ripe tomatoes
$^{3}/_{4}$ cup Red Bell Pepper Mayonnaise (pages 230–231)
fresh basil leaves (long and narrow) as required

(Makes 4 generous servings)

Clean and rinse mushrooms; drain very well; slice thinly. Gently toss sliced mushrooms with lemon juice and pepper.

Slice tomatoes**; arrange in an overlapping manner on serving plates or platter; season with additional pepper according to taste.

Arrange mushrooms on top of tomato, leaving a border of tomato exposed around the salad.

Top mushrooms generously with Red Bell Pepper Mayonnaise (e.g. about $^{1}/_{3}$ cup).

Decorate the salad with basil leaves.

Offer extra Red Bell Pepper Mayonnaise at the table.

*Add according to taste.

****Option** Cut each tomato into a Tomato Lotus Flower (page 208) with rather thin petals. Remove the central ball of soft pulp, keeping the petals intact. Open the petals as desired. Just before serving, season with salt and pepper according to taste. Pile mushrooms high in centre of Tomato Lotus.

Coeur de Palmier, Avocado, and Watercress Salad

(illustrated on pages 52–53)

The ingredients in this salad complement the coeur de palmier in colour, shape, flavour, and texture.

Ingredients

1 can coeur de palmier (can size: 400 g or 14 oz)

2 avocados

5 cups fresh young watercress sprigs

1 can mandarin orange sections, drained
(can size: 312 g or 11 oz)

²/₃ to 1 cup Herb Vinaigrette (page 229)

Garnish

¹/₃ cup whole black olives, drained

(Makes 8 to 10 servings)

Drain the coeur de palmier; cut crosswise into slices (6 mm or ¹/₄ inch), discarding any woody sections. Bathe with Herb Vinaigrette (¹/₄ cup); refrigerate to chill.*

About 10 or 15 minutes before serving, peel avocado; cut into thin slices. Arrange slices in a single layer in a large flat glass baking dish; bathe generously with Herb Vinaigrette (¹/₄ cup). Refrigerate.

To assemble salad, scatter watercress sprigs on flat plates or trays, in a shallow bed arrangement. Add avocado slices, slices of coeur de palmier, and orange sections. Garnish with black olives.

Drizzle salad with Herb Vinaigrette according to taste.

*If desired, this may be done 1 day in advance.

Pesto Pasta Salad

Pesto Pasta Salad is a convenient precaution for buffets when the number of guests is uncertain.

Ingredients

375 g or 13 oz spiral tri-flavoured vegetable* pasta

1 tablespoon salt

3 litres or 2¹/₂ quarts boiling water

3 to 4 tablespoons Pesto** (page 226)

3 tablespoons black olives, pitted and sliced

2 tablespoons sun dried tomatoes seasoned in oil,
drained and cut into small pieces

²/₃ cup artichoke hearts, drained and cut into wedges

³/₄ cup sliced mushrooms, sautéed and seasoned

¹/₃ teaspoon black peppercorns, crushed

75 g or 3 oz fresh Parmesan cheese***, finely diced

salt to taste

**(Makes 8 cups, or 18 to 25 buffet servings,
or 8 to 12 regular servings)**

Cook pasta uncovered in boiling salted water until *al dente* (tender but firm). Drain well. Immediately add Pesto, tossing carefully to coat pasta evenly. Add olives, sun dried tomatoes, artichoke, mushrooms, and pepper; toss well. If desired, add Parmesan cheese according to taste. Adjust seasoning (including Pesto, salt, pepper, and cheese) according to taste. Serve Pesto Pasta Salad warm or chilled.

***Option** Other types of pasta or other varieties of spiral pasta may be used; however, the resulting product will be different.

**If commercial pesto is used, experiment to produce the desired balance of flavours.

*****Optional**

Avocado Sherbet Salad

In this recipe, salad is added to Avocado Sherbet to enhance its refreshing temperature, flavour, and texture. Avocado Sherbet Salad is particularly attractive arranged in individual Frosted Sherbet (or flat champagne) Glasses. Each filled glass may then be set in a Tulip Napkin for its presentation at the table.

Ingredients
1¹/₂ ripe avocados
³/₄ to 1 cup red cabbage, very finely shredded
²/₃ to ³/₄ cup Herb Vinaigrette (page 229)
2 tablespoons walnuts, chopped
³/₄ cup Avocado Sherbet (page 227–228)
carrot pieces* as required

Garnish
parsley leaves

(**Makes 6 servings**)

Several hours before serving, scoop 6 mini balls (1¹/₂ tablespoons each) of slightly softened sherbet; arrange on a chilled tray; freeze.

About 15 minutes before serving**, peel avocados; remove stones; cut lengthwise into thin slices. Arrange slices in shallow glass baking dish; bathe generously with Herb Vinaigrette.

Arrange 6 individual salads by loosely scattering shredded cabbage (2 tablespoons) in centre of small serving glasses or bowls; drizzle with vinaigrette.

Arrange 3 bathed avocado slices in the top left area of each salad. Place a ball of sherbet in centre; drizzle with a little more dressing, and sprinkle with walnuts. Garnish front right corner of each salad, with a few carrot pieces* and a tuft of parsley. Serve immediately.

*__Options__ Cut raw or tender crisp cooked carrots into mini Carrot Flowers (page 214), fine short sticks, or other suitable small shapes.

**If the avocados are of a variety that does not discolour too rapidly, they may be prepared up to 30 minutes before serving.

Warm Sesame Tofu Salad

Warm Sesame Tofu Salad is delicious with Garlic Cheese Mayonnaise.

Ingredients

300 g or 10 oz tofu, firm and cut into 2$^1/_2$ cm or 1 inch cubes
$^1/_3$ teaspoon ground cinnamon
$^1/_8$ teaspoon ground cloves
$^1/_3$ teaspoon ground fennel
$^1/_4$ teaspoon ground star anise
pinch of cayenne pepper
3 tablespoons sesame seeds, roasted brown
$^1/_4$ cup dry breadcrumbs
3 tablespoons flour
1 egg, beaten
2 cups oil for deep-frying
2 cups fresh watercress (or coriander) sprigs
$^1/_3$ to $^2/_3$ cup Garlic Cheese Mayonnaise* (page 230)

(Makes 18 cubes, or 4 to 6 servings)

Drain tofu cubes well; set aside.

Combine spices and sesame seeds with breadcrumbs in a flat bowl.

Arrange flour and beaten egg separately, in 2 other flat bowls.

Dust individual tofu cubes with flour; dip in beaten egg; then press firmly into breadcrumb mixture.

Heat oil for frying in a wok over medium high heat. Deep-fry coated tofu cubes in two batches, turning cubes regularly until golden brown (about 3 minutes). Drain on paper towels.

Immediately arrange crusty tofu cubes on a light bed of fresh watercress.

Garnish with Garlic Cheese Mayonnaise (allowing about 1 teaspoon per cube).

Serve promptly. (Sesame Tofu Salad is best served hot or warm.)

*Option A commercial garlic cheese mayonnaise may also be used.

MAIN COURSES

The main course is the most substantial part of a meal and it can be a challenge to offer a dish with the appropriate culinary and artistic qualities which measure up to this role. My recipes for main course include those tastes which I adore. This reflects my philosophy: "Give people something which you yourself would appreciate receiving." The list includes very tender and tasty meat and poultry recipes, creative fish dishes, combinations with seafood, phyllo or regular pastry wrappings, rolls and packages in any form, a wide variety of fillings and stuffings, barbecue tastes, sweet and sour gingered flavours, and deliciously unique sauces.

In our home, main course is served in several ways. If there are fewer than 10 guests, I may decide to arrange everything on serving platters which are placed in front of me at the table. Guests' plates are then prepared personally by myself. Or, at any size of sit-down dinner, individual plates may be partially or completely arranged in the kitchen, and then placed in front of each person at the table. This formula offers better control over the artistry of the guest's plate. When partially prepared plates are served, guests then choose the other items from trays which are served or passed immediately, or from trays/bowls placed directly on the table. When appropriate, a sauce flambé is also served at the table to add an extra bit of magic to the main course.

Pesto Beef Steak (page 142)

Marinated Beef Fillet Supreme

Marinated Beef Fillet Supreme was developed during our time in Moscow. It is advisable not to arrange all the beef with the crab topping, allowing an option for those who may be allergic to crab. To give height to the serving plate, the slices of beef may be arranged "pouring out" of Fried Spaghetti (or Potato) Straw Baskets.

Ingredients

1 kg or 2¼ lb beef fillet(s), marinated* (page 225)
2½ cups Whisky Parsley Sauce (page 235)
250 g or 8 oz crab meat, cooked and flaked**
chilli powder (or fresh hot red chilli pepper, finely chopped) as required
1 cup fresh parsley, coarsely chopped
1 cup tomato (seeds and soft pulp removed), chopped
seasoned salt (or salt) to taste

(Makes 8 to 10 servings)

Drain marinated beef well. Place on a baking tray.

Bake at 140⁰C/275⁰F to preferred point of doneness (e.g. 20 to 25 minutes for medium rare fillet of diameter 7 cm or 2½ inches, regardless of weight of fillet).

Cut roasted fillet into 7 mm to 1 cm or ¼ inch to ⅓ inch thick slices. If desired, sprinkle with seasoned salt.

Carefully heat Whisky Parsley Sauce in a small heavy saucepan (covered) over low heat, stirring occasionally.

To serve, arrange slices of beef in an overlapping manner; drizzle with Whisky Parsley Sauce. Top sauce with warm flaked crab meat and a pinch of chilli powder. Add garnish of chopped parsley and (slightly warmed) diced tomato; season according to taste.

Offer extra sauce at the table.

*Immediately before marinating the beef, sprinkle ½ teaspoon ground nutmeg and ½ teaspoon ground cinnamon over beef; rub the spices into the flesh.

**Canned crab meat may be used successfully. Drain well; carefully remove any pieces of shell before using crab meat.

Pesto Beef Steaks

(illustrated on page 138)

The filling gives an enhanced flavour to the steaks without being identifiable as Pesto. This is a rather quick recipe, if Pesto is on hand. The steaks are excellent bathed in Red Wine Mustard Sauce and drizzled with Cognac Cream. To add colour and character to the final presentation, I perch Mini Tomato Lotus Flowers (one per steak) on top of the Cognac Cream, and prop a few snow peas up against each steak. Rims of plates or platters may be decorated with a few more Mini Tomato Lotus Flowers to create a graceful balance.

Ingredients

1¹/₂ kg or 3¹/₃ lb beef fillet(s)*, marinated** (page 225)

¹/₂ cup Pesto (page 226)

1 tablespoon Dijon mustard

2 teaspoons fresh garlic, crushed

1 teaspoon dried tarragon

2 tablespoons butter

salt as required

crushed black peppercorns as required

2 cups fresh mushrooms, quartered or thickly sliced

2 to 3 tablespoons Garlic Butter (page 223)

2¹/₂ cups Red Wine Mustard Sauce** (page 234)

*Cognac Cream**

1 cup sour cream

2 tablespoons cognac

¹/₂ teaspoon ground nutmeg

1¹/₂ teaspoons soya sauce (not sweet)

(Makes 8 to 10 servings)

Prepare Cognac Cream** in a bowl by combining sour cream, cognac, nutmeg, and soya sauce; blend well until smooth and creamy; refrigerate. (This may be prepared hours or days in advance.)

Cut fillet into 3 cm or 1¹/₄ inch thick steaks.

Make a small horizontal incision in each steak at the middle of one side. Insert point of a small sharp knife into incision; carefully cut a large horizontal interior pocket, cutting fairly close to outside walls of steak.

Fill each pocket with 1 to 2 teaspoons of Pesto. Close pocket with a metal skewer.

Rub steaks with Dijon mustard and garlic. Sprinkle with tarragon.

Just before serving, carefully grill prepared steaks over medium heat to almost desired degree of doneness in a lightly buttered skillet (or on a barbecue). Season with salt and pepper. (If necessary, transfer cooked steaks to a heated tray and place in a warm oven for a few minutes until served.)

In a separate skillet, sauté mushrooms with Garlic Butter; season with salt and crushed peppercorns to taste.

Carefully heat Red Wine Mustard Sauce in a small heavy saucepan (covered) over low heat, stirring occasionally; add sautéed mushrooms.

Remove skewers from steaks. Serve grilled steaks bathed in mushroom and Red Wine Mustard Sauce**. Top with Cognac Cream** according to taste. (Do not heat Cognac Cream.)

*Option Other types of tender beef steaks may be used.
**Optional

Roast Chicken with Wild Rice Dressing

(illustrated on page 28)

The Barbecue Glaze and the Wild Rice Dressing in this recipe bring out the wonderful flavour of the chicken.

Ingredients

1 whole chicken (about 1 kg or 2$^{1}/_{4}$ lb)
1 teaspoon salt
1 teaspoon fresh ginger root, finely chopped
$^{1}/_{2}$ teaspoon black peppercorns, crushed
1$^{1}/_{2}$ cups Curry Sauce (page 232)
$^{3}/_{4}$ cup Orange Cranberry Sauce* (page 235)

Wild Rice Dressing

1$^{1}/_{4}$ cups basmati or long grain rice, cooked
$^{1}/_{4}$ cup Doubly Dark Wild Rice (page 223)
$^{1}/_{2}$ cup Toasted Coconut (page 227)
$^{1}/_{4}$ cup walnuts, chopped
2 teaspoons orange marmalade
1 teaspoon orange peel, grated
$^{1}/_{2}$ teaspoon ginger powder
$^{1}/_{2}$ teaspoon garlic powder
$^{1}/_{4}$ teaspoon ground nutmeg

Barbecue Glaze

$^{1}/_{4}$ cup tomato sauce
1 teaspoon chilli sauce
2 teaspoons smoked barbecue sauce

(Makes 4 servings)

Wash and dry chicken thoroughly, removing extra interior fat. Rub interior thoroughly with salt, fresh ginger, and pepper.

To prepare dressing, toss all Wild Rice Dressing ingredients together. Stuff cavity of chicken well; close with metal skewers.

To prepare Barbecue Glaze, mix together tomato, chilli, and barbecue sauces. Paint exterior of chicken completely and evenly with Barbecue Glaze.

Fold ends of wings under body of chicken; tie drumsticks loosely together to allow for more even browning.

Place chicken on a wire rack arranged on a baking tray. Roast at 160^{0}C/325^{0}F until tender (about 2 hours). If skin is browning too rapidly, cover chicken loosely with aluminium foil (shiny side out).

Remove from oven. Remove skewers, and untie legs.

Carefully heat Curry Sauce in a small heavy saucepan (covered) over medium heat, stirring occasionally.

Transfer chicken to serving tray. If desired, wrap ends of drumstick bones in paper "hats".

Serve with Curry and Orange Cranberry Sauces.

*Optional

Apricot Garlic Chicken
(with Peppercorn Prawns*)

Apricot Garlic Chicken is one of my early creations from Moscow days where chicken, garlic, and apricot jam were always available. Whole chicken is best for casual occasions; breasts or thighs work better for more elegant events. It is advisable to keep the skin attached, but to remove any excess fat. If skinless breasts are used, the chicken must be cooked slowly and carefully.

Ingredients
1 whole chicken (1 kg or 2¼ lb), cut into parts
½ cup Seasoned Flour (page 226)
1 to 2 tablespoons** vegetable oil
1 to 2 teaspoons** fresh garlic, minced
3 tablespoons apricot jam

(Makes 4 to 6 servings)

Dust chicken pieces with Seasoned Flour.

Heat oil in a large heavy skillet over medium heat. Add chicken (skin side down). Cook one side until golden brown. Gradually turn pieces to ensure chicken is evenly browned. (Do not cover skillet.) As final browning is taking place, promptly rub top side of chicken with minced garlic, and spread with apricot jam. (Ensure that garlic or jam does not fall on skillet. These ingredients tend to burn easily.)

If necessary, add a few drops of water (only enough to provide a little vapour); cover skillet tightly; reduce heat to barely simmer.

Cook chicken until tender. Check flavours. (It may be necessary to add a pinch of salt.)

If desired, serve Apricot Garlic Chicken topped with Peppercorn Prawns*.

*Peppercorn Prawns

(for 6 chicken breasts)
350 g or 12 oz or 12 medium size prawns (fresh or frozen), unpeeled
1½ tablespoons Garlic Butter (page 223)
salt to taste
coarsely crushed black peppercorns to taste

Peel prawns, leaving tails attached; remove veins; rinse and drain well.

In a heavy skillet, sauté prawns in Garlic Butter over medium heat until cooked (about 4 minutes). Season to taste with salt and pepper. Be generous with the crushed black peppercorns.

*Optional
**As required or desired.

Escargot Stuffed Chicken Breasts

(in Phyllo Parcels*)

The phyllo parcel in this dish keeps the chicken moister.

Ingredients

6 chicken breasts (each: 85 g or 3 oz)
1 recipe Chicken Marinade (page 225)
1 can escargots, well drained and cleaned
(can size: 115 g or 4 oz drained weight)
1/4 cup margarine
1 teaspoon fines herbes
salt to taste
crushed black peppercorns to taste
1/4 cup fresh coriander leaves, very finely chopped
(or blanched spinach leaves, as desired)
40 g or 1 1/2 oz mozzarella cheese, cut into 6 bars
1/3 cup Seasoned Flour (page 226)
1 1/2 cups Red Bell Pepper Sauce (pages 233–234)**

(Makes 6 servings)

Rub chicken with marinade; refrigerate for at least 24 hours, turning occasionally.

Sauté escargots gently in 1 tablespoon of margarine, over medium heat, for about 3 minutes. Season with fines herbes, salt and pepper; cover; keep over very low heat for another 7 minutes to enhance flavours.

Remove breasts from marinade; drain. Open breasts; pound carefully to flatten; season with salt and pepper. Spread 2 teaspoons chopped coriander leaves over central area of each flattened breast; place 3 to 5 escargots in centre of flattened breast; add a bar of cheese (2 teaspoons). Close breasts over filling; secure with fine metal skewers.

Roll filled chicken breasts in Seasoned Flour. Melt remaining margarine in a skillet over medium heat. Add stuffed chicken breasts; fry carefully, uncovered, until golden brown on all sides. Reduce heat to low; cover; cook carefully until tender (about 15 minutes); remove from heat; remove skewers. (If the sautéed stuffed chicken breasts are to be wrapped in phyllo parcels*, allow chicken breasts to cool first.)

Carefully heat Red Bell Pepper Sauce in a small heavy saucepan (covered) over medium low heat, stirring occasionally.

Serve Escargot Stuffed Chicken Breasts, accompanied by Red Pepper Sauce or a sauce of choice**.

Phyllo Parcels*

(for 6 chicken breasts)

12 sheets phyllo pastry (28 cm x 45 cm or
11 inches x 18 inches)
1/3 cup melted butter
1 teaspoon sesame seeds

To make individual Phyllo Parcels, lay out one sheet of phyllo pastry and paint with melted butter; put a second sheet of phyllo on top of first, and brush with melted butter; fold double thickness of pastry in half to make a thickness of 4 layers. (Use 1 1/2 sheets of phyllo to make a finer pastry wrapping with a thickness of 3 layers.)

Place one cooked chicken breast in middle of folded pastry; bring ends of pastry over chicken; roll up to form a parcel. Repeat process to make more Phyllo Parcels.

Arrange Phyllo Parcels, well separated, on a baking sheet; refrigerate. Just before serving, brush parcels with melted butter; sprinkle with sesame seeds. Bake at 180°C/ 350°F until golden brown (about 20 minutes). (During baking, cover edges of phyllo parcels with aluminium foil, shiny side out, to prevent excess and uneven browning.)

*Optional The phyllo wrapping allows the chicken to be prepared a day in advance, and baked immediately before serving.

**Options Other sauces may be used (e.g. Brandy Cream Sauce: page 234), depending on other elements in the final menu.

Indonesian Sweet Blackened Chicken with Kiwi

(illustrated on pages 54–55)

This Dickenson version of a wonderful Indonesian dish brings a tasty change to traditional barbecues or to more casual events. The chicken can also be grilled in an oven, with equal success. The fresh kiwi cuts the sweetness while adding contrasts of colour and texture. Pineapple Carrot Salad is a delicious accompanying dish. Served hot or cold, Indonesian Sweet Blackened Chicken is always very flavourful. Specific chicken pieces (e.g. legs, thighs, breasts) may also be used in this recipe.

Ingredients

1 whole chicken (about 1 kg or 2¼ lb)

¼ cup hoisin sauce

3 tablespoons soya sauce

1 tablespoon brown sugar

1½ tablespoons soft butter

⅓ teaspoon anise seed

3 fresh kiwi fruit, peeled

Marinade

2 teaspoons fresh garlic, minced

½ teaspoon salt

½ teaspoon black peppercorns, crushed

3 tablespoons lemon juice

1 tablespoon water

(Makes 4 servings)

To prepare marinade, mix together garlic, salt, pepper, lemon juice, and water.

Remove backbone from chicken; cut chicken into 6 pieces. Rub chicken pieces thoroughly with marinade; set aside for at least 1 hour.

Mix together hoisin sauce, soya sauce, brown sugar, butter and anise seed in a large baking dish. Set aside.

Gently grill chicken over hot charcoal*, turning regularly, until skin is dark and crispy (about 20 minutes). Remove grilled chicken from heat.

Transfer grilled chicken to dish with soya sauce mixture. Bathe (to coat) grilled chicken with soya sauce mixture. Immediately return soya sauce bathed chicken to medium hot charcoal until done (about another 30 minutes), turning and brushing chicken with soya sauce mixture frequently. Remove chicken from charcoal.

To serve, arrange chicken on plates or platter; garnish generously with fresh kiwi. Offer any extra sauce or Honey Mustard Mayonnaise at table. (Serve with white rice.)

*__Option__ With some modifications to the recipe, the chicken may be grilled in the oven under a pre-heated broiler. First, moderately paint chicken pieces with sweet soya sauce mixture. Next, arrange painted chicken on a wire rack set on a baking tray, and place 15 cm or 6 inches below broiler. Turn pieces every 5 minutes, painting chicken with more soya sauce mixture as required. Grill until surfaces are brown, and skin is crispy (about 15 minutes). Lower grilled browned chicken to 20 cm or 8 inches below broiler. Continue to turn and brush chicken with soya sauce mixture until chicken is tender and cooked.

Triple Fettuccine Experience with Sun Dried Tomatoes and Chicken*

(illustrated on page 38)

To keep this recipe quick and simple, one or two varieties of fettuccine may be used instead of three. But for an ultimate pasta experience, 3 varieties of pasta (preferably, if possible, some home-made) are recommended. An exciting combination is Garlic Spinach, Tomato Chilli, and Black Peppercorn (or Double Sesame).

Ingredients

350 g or 12 oz chicken breasts*, marinated (page 225)
1/4 cup Seasoned Flour (page 226)
3 tablespoons butter
350 g** or 12 oz fettuccine (preferably a combination of 3 varieties**)
3 tablespoons Garlic Butter (page 223)
1/4 cup olive oil
1/2 to 1 teaspoon fresh hot red chilli pepper, finely chopped
1 tablespoon fresh garlic, crushed
1 tablespoon fresh ginger root, finely chopped
3 tablespoons fresh basil, chopped
1/2 cup sun dried tomatoes in oil, drained and sliced
2 cups fresh shallots, cut into thin diagonal slices
1 can tomatoes, drained and cut into wedges
(can size: 410 g or 14 oz)
freshly cracked black peppercorns to taste
1 tablespoon Parmesan cheese, grated
1 teaspoon toasted sesame seeds***

Garnish

fresh shallots, cut into thin diagonal slices***
Red Bell Pepper Mayonnaise (pages 230–231) as desired

(Makes 4 servings)

Cut chicken breasts* into diagonal strips 7 mm or 1/4 inch wide. Dust with Seasoned Flour. Melt butter in a very large skillet over medium heat. Carefully fry chicken strips until golden brown and tender, turning pieces once and cooking each side for about 1 minute. Cover; set over low heat for another 2 minutes. Set aside.

Cook fettuccine uncovered in a generous amount of salted boiling water until *al dente* (tender but firm). (If more than one variety is used, cook each variety separately because cooking time may be different.) Drain well. Carefully toss all fettuccine together with Garlic Butter; set aside.

Heat oil in a large wok over medium heat. Add chilli pepper (according to taste), garlic, ginger, basil, sun dried tomatoes, and shallots. Cook, stirring constantly, for 1 minute.

Add canned tomatoes; stir-fry for about another minute. Transfer fried chicken strips from skillet to wok; combine ingredients together.

If necessary, reheat cooked pasta. Add hot pasta to chicken mixture in wok. Carefully combine ingredients; heat thoroughly. Season pasta mixture to taste with cracked black peppercorns. Add Parmesan cheese.

If desired, serve Triple Fettuccine Experience sprinkled with toasted sesame seeds, more cut shallots, and a touch of Red Bell Pepper Mayonnaise.

***Options** Seafood may also be used instead of chicken; or to produce a vegetarian version, omit the chicken; however, the quantity of pasta used should be increased by 60 g or 2 oz.

**If commercial varieties are chosen, quantities may need to be adjusted. The varieties of fettucine should be chosen to create a colourful and tasty combination.

***Optional

Tarragon Veal with Roasted Bell Peppers

The tarragon in this dish adds a subtle touch of flavour to enhance the veal while the roasted bell peppers offer a graceful contrast, without being overpowering.

Ingredients

500 g or 1 lb veal loin
2 fresh red bell peppers
1 tablespoon olive oil
pinch of salt
pinch of crushed black peppercorns
1^1/$_2$ cups Caper Cream Sauce (page 233)
^{1}/$_4$ cup Seasoned Flour (page 226)
2 tablespoons margarine
1 teaspoon dried tarragon

Garnish
fresh tarragon (or celery) leaves*

(Makes 4 servings)

Cut veal loin into 4 steaks. (If necessary, tie circumference of each steak with string to ensure a round shape.) Set steaks aside.

Cut bell peppers in half; remove and discard stem, seeds, and ribs. Brush pepper halves generously with olive oil; season with salt and pepper. Grill over hot charcoal or under a pre-heated broiler, turning occasionally, until skin is evenly blackened. Peel off and discard blackened skin. Cut into desired shapes.

Carefully heat Caper Cream Sauce in a small heavy saucepan (covered) over medium low heat, stirring occasionally.

Dust veal with Seasoned Flour.

Heat margarine in a large skillet over low medium heat; add veal, sprinkling top side with tarragon. Carefully cook veal (sprinkling second side with tarragon as well) until lightly browned on both sides (about 3 to 4 minutes per side).

If necessary transfer to a platter, and place in a warm oven for a few minutes, until ready to serve.

Serve veal with roasted bell peppers and Caper Wine Sauce. If desired, garnish with fresh tarragon or celery leaves.

*Optional

Herb Pork Farci
(with Vine Leaf Wrapping*)

This recipe often leaves guests convinced that they have dined on veal. I marinate several small pork fillets and keep them on hand for unexpected occasions. The fillet is easier to cut if the vine leaf wrapping is omitted. However, the vine leaf wrapping does offer a unique experience for most palates. Both versions are equally delicious.

In general, pork fillet is very lean. Serving Herb Pork Farci with a light coulis of Saffron Sauce further enhances the combination of flavours. Pasta is an excellent choice as an accompanying dish. Herb Pork Farci is also delicious served cold with Apricot Curry or Ginger Mayonnaise.

Ingredients

2 pork fillets**, preferably marinated (page 225)
(each fillet: 300 g or 10 oz)
3 tablespoons Dijon mustard
1 1/2 tablespoons ginger marmalade
1/2 teaspoon fresh garlic, crushed
1 teaspoon fresh ginger root, finely chopped
1/2 teaspoon salt
1/4 teaspoon black peppercorns, freshly crushed
3 tablespoons red maraschino cherries, sliced
4 dried prunes, slivered
4 dried apricots, slivered
3 tablespoons pine nuts
1/4 cup vegetable oil
1/2 cup Pesto (page 226)
Preserved Vine Leaves* (page 226) as required
1 1/2 cups Saffron Sauce* (page 232–233)
1/3 cup Orange Cranberry Sauce* (page 235)

(Makes 4 to 5 servings)

Cut a deep pocket along length of pork fillets. Carefully open out pockets to produce flat fillets. (This will make adding the filling easier.)

Combine half the mustard (i.e. 1 1/2 tablespoons) with the marmalade, garlic, ginger, salt, and pepper. Rub flattened surfaces of fillets with the mustard mixture.

Distribute cherries, prunes, apricots, and nuts evenly along middle of fillets. Close fillets by restoring them to their original shape; secure with fine metal skewers. Paint exterior of fillets with remaining mustard.

Heat oil in a large heavy skillet over medium heat. Add fillets; cook carefully until all sides are evenly browned (about 10 to 15 minutes). Remove from skillet. Remove metal skewers from meat.

When fillets are cool enough to handle, paint exterior of sautéed fillets with Pesto. (If desired, arrange vine leaves in an overlapping fashion to form 2 sheets, each of a suitable size to wrap one fillet. Wrap each Pesto bathed fillet in a vine leaf sheet, folding in ends of sheet. Paint surface of vine leaf wrapping with more Pesto.)*

Place pesto painted fillets on baking trays.*** Bake at 160°C/325°F, painting fillets occasionally with additional Pesto. Bake until done (about 15 minutes for unwrapped fillets/20 to 25 minutes for vine leaf wrapped pork). Allow baked fillets to rest for a few minutes before slicing.

To serve, carefully cut into 7 mm or 1/4 inch thick slices. Serve with a light coulis of Saffron Sauce if desired; garnish with Orange Cranberry Sauce.

*Optional

**Option With appropriate modifications to the recipe, pork roasts or chops may also be used successfully. (Definitely omit the vine leaf wrapping if chops are used.)

***Pesto bathed fillets (with or without the vine leaf wrapping) may be prepared to this stage in advance, and baked just prior to serving.

Grilled Oriental Lamb Chops

I serve Oriental Lamb Chops on a very light bed of fresh herb and salad leaves. Cracked Black Peppercorn Pasta is delicious with the lamb chops.

Ingredients

1 kg or 2$^{1}/_{4}$ lb young lamb ribs
(thickness: 1$^{1}/_{2}$ cm or $^{2}/_{3}$ inch)
1 recipe Oriental Marinade (page 225)
fresh herb and salad leaves as desired

(Makes 4 servings)

Brush lamb chops with about half the Oriental Marinade (i.e. $^{1}/_{2}$ cup), saving remaining half to be used later as a dressing for fresh leaves and grilled chops. Refrigerate, allowing chops to marinate for at least 6 hours; turn chops every hour in marinade.

Just before serving, remove chops from marinade. Grill chops carefully on a barbecue (or under a pre-heated broiler), bathing with drained marinade if desired. Cook chops until exterior surfaces are well browned but interior flesh is still pink (just a few minutes).

Arrange grilled chops on a very light bed of herb and salad leaves. Serve immediately, accompanied by remaining Oriental Marinade.

Poached Fish Fillets with Crab Meat Mousse

Poached Fish Fillets with Crab Meat Mousse can be prepared in ramekin dishes or by using a rolled fillet technique. The Ramekin Dish technique is quicker and quite simple; however, we serve slices of rolled fillets on individually prepared plates. A thin coulis of heated sauce is spread on very hot plates. The slices of fish fillet are then laid on the sauce. Rims of the plates are decorated with alternating small touches of Doubly Dark Wild Rice, and mini clusters of cooked zucchini and carrot sticks bathed in a little honey and soya sauce. Squid Ink Pasta makes the final presentation superb.

Ingredients

3 fish fillets (white flesh variety suitable for rolling),
(each fillet: 125 g or 4 oz; length: 23 cm or 9 inches)
1 egg white
1 cup fresh watercress leaves, lightly packed
2 cups Tomato Brandy Cream Sauce (page 234)
1 recipe Fish Poaching Bath* (page 226)

Crab Meat Mousse

135 g or 4$^{1}/_{2}$ oz crab meat, cooked
2 egg whites (small eggs)
$^{1}/_{4}$ cup whipping cream
salt to taste
pepper to taste
$^{1}/_{2}$ teaspoon fresh dill, finely chopped
$^{1}/_{2}$ teaspoon dried tarragon leaves
$^{1}/_{8}$ teaspoon ginger powder
$^{1}/_{8}$ teaspoon ground nutmeg

(Makes 4 servings)

To prepare mousse, place half frozen crab meat in food processor; turn processor on and off. At the lowest speed, add egg whites, one at a time; blend to form a smooth paste. Continue at slow speed, and gradually add cream; blend in seasoning (salt, pepper, dill, tarragon, ginger and nutmeg). Refrigerate.

For the Ramekin Dish technique, flatten fillets to a thickness of $^{1}/_{2}$ cm or $^{1}/_{4}$ inch (by partially slicing thick areas of flesh to allow fillet to be opened out, and/or by gently pounding fillet). Cut fillets into suitable pieces in order to line sides and bottom of 4 buttered ramekin dishes ($^{1}/_{2}$ cup size), reserving a portion of fish fillet to cover tops. (Line dishes with prepared fillets so that lighter coloured flesh is arranged against inside surface of dishes.)

Brush exposed surface of fish in dishes with egg white; cover all exposed surfaces evenly with watercress leaves. Add prepared crab meat mousse to fill dishes; cover surface of mousse with remaining pieces of fish fillet.

Place prepared dishes in a metal baking pan of hot water so that dishes are half submerged in the water bath. Cover baking pan with aluminium foil (shiny side facing inward); bake at 200°C/400°F until done (about 15 to 20 minutes**).

Remove dishes from oven and pan; drain dishes of any liquid; discard liquid. Leave parcels in dishes for at least 15 minutes, allowing mousse to set.

Carefully heat Tomato Brandy Cream Sauce in a small heavy saucepan (covered) over low medium heat, stirring occasionally. Invert dishes to remove poached fish parcels.

Serve parcels in inverted position; bathe with Tomato Brandy Cream Sauce. Offer remaining sauce at the table.

Poached Fish Fillets with Crab Meat Mousse (Rolled Fish Fillet option)

Rolled Fish Fillet

(Makes 6 servings)

Prepare a double recipe of Crab Meat Mousse. Place in an airtight container; refrigerate for at least 1 to 1¹/₂ hours, allowing mousse to set. (The chilled set mousse is easier to handle and offers best results.) Also prepare twice the amount of watercress leaves (i.e. 2 cups).

Flatten fish fillets to a thickness of ¹/₂ cm or ¹/₄ inch. (Each fillet should be about 23 cm or 9 inches long. The width is not important.) Cut a strip of aluminium foil (25 cm or 10 inches long) for each fillet. (The strips should be wider than the width of fillets.) For convenience in handling fillets, place each foil strip on a separate baking tray. Butter surface of foil strips.

Arrange each fillet, darker flesh up, on a strip of aluminium foil. Cover fillets with plastic wrap; refrigerate.

Prepare a strip of cheese cloth for each fillet; cut strips about the same length as, but 10 cm or 4 inches wider than, each fillet; set cheese cloth strips aside.

Prepare Fish Poaching Bath in a large deep skillet or electric frying pan; bring to a boil; simmer for 5 minutes.

About 1¹/₂ to 2 hours before guests arrive, remove trays of fillets from refrigerator. Discard plastic wrap. Season fillets with salt and pepper; brush with egg white. Top each fillet completely with a fine layer of watercress leaves, except for 3 cm or 1¹/₄ inches at wide end of fillet. Arrange spoonfuls of crab meat mousse on top of watercress layer; spread mousse carefully over watercress (using tip of a fork) to form an even layer of mousse (¹/₂ cm or ¹/₅ inch thick).

Starting at narrow end of fillet, roll up fillet tightly. Transfer rolled fillet to a strip of cheese cloth, discarding foil strip. Wrap rolled fillet securely in cheese cloth, tucking in ends. Repeat process for remaining fillets.

Poach rolled fillets immediately, by bringing Poaching Bath back to a boil and adding filled rolls, seam side down. Cover tightly, and reduce heat to low. Simmer very gently for about 25 minutes. Turn rolls over in poaching bath;

Poached Fish Fillets with Crab Meat Mousse (Ramekin Dish option)

simmer for about another 25 minutes. (Total poaching time is about 50 minutes.)

Remove poached rolls from bath; place on wire racks to drain. Allow rolls to rest and set at room temperature for about 15 minutes before removing cheese cloth. Cut each roll into slices (7 mm to 1 cm or ¹/₄ inch to ¹/₃ inch wide), exposing inside spiral arrangement of fillet and mousse.***

To serve, arrange slices to display spiral design. Serve with Tomato Brandy Cream Sauce.

*This is only necessary when using the Rolled Fish Fillet technique.

**If ramekin dishes of fish are prepared in advance and refrigerated, the poaching time may be 5 to 7 minutes longer.

***If not served immediately, reassemble sliced fillets into rolls. Wrap rolls in aluminium foil (shiny side inside); place in a warm oven until ready to be arranged on serving plates or platter.

Chinese Sweet and Sour Fish

(illustrated on pages 26–27)

Whole fish or fillets may be used with equal success; however, the effect is different. For family dining and more casual occasions, whole fish gives a touch of character to the menu. To arouse the expectation of guests, I serve Chinese Sweet and Sour Fish flambéed at the table. White rice should accompany this dish.

Ingredients

1 kg or 2 lb whole* fish (with head and tail),
(white flesh variety such as red snapper), cleaned
1 teaspoon coriander paste (leaves crushed into a paste)
1 teaspoon fresh ginger root, grated
$^1/_2$ teaspoon salt
$^1/_4$ teaspoon black peppercorns, crushed
$^1/_4$ cup cornstarch
1 cup oil for frying

Chinese Sweet and Sour Sauce
1 tablespoon vegetable oil
2 teaspoons fresh garlic, finely chopped
1 to 1$^1/_2$ tablespoons fresh ginger root, finely chopped
2 teaspoons fresh ginger root, slivered
$^1/_4$ teaspoon fresh hot red chilli pepper, finely chopped
2 tablespoons brown sugar
2 teaspoons white sugar
$^1/_3$ cup cherry jam
3 tablespoons tomato sauce
3 to 4 tablespoons** wine vinegar
2 tablespoons cornstarch
1 cup dry white wine
$^1/_2$ cup water
1$^1/_2$ tablespoons Calvados (or medium dry sherry)

(Makes 3* servings)**

First prepare the Chinese Sweet and Sour Sauce, by heating 1 tablespoon of oil in a skillet over medium heat; add garlic, ginger, and chilli pepper; fry carefully for 2 minutes.

Stir in brown sugar, white sugar, jam, tomato sauce, and vinegar.

Whisk cornstarch with wine and water; add to skillet, stirring constantly until sauce thickens and bubbles. Remove sauce from heat; add Calvados. Set Chinese Sweet and Sour Sauce aside. (Makes 2 cups sauce.)

Wash fish*; dry thoroughly; make 3 diagonal slashes on each side.

Mix together coriander paste, grated ginger, salt, and pepper; rub interior cavity of fish with mixture. Dust exterior of fish with cornstarch.

In a large electric fry pan, heat the oil for frying over medium high heat; add dusted fish. Fry fish, turning it occasionally to ensure even browning; cook until flesh flakes when tested with a fork (about 30 to 35 minutes). Remove; drain on paper towels.

To serve, heat Chinese Sweet and Sour Sauce; spread $^1/_2$ cup sauce on a serving platter. Place the fried fish on top of sauce; bathe fish generously with remaining sweet and sour sauce.

Option** Fish fillets ($^1/_2$ kg or 1 lb) may also be used. (Do not slash the fillets.) Lightly rub all surfaces of the fillets with the mixture made from combining coriander paste, grated ginger, salt, and pepper. (Quantities of these ingredients do not need to be adjusted.) Continue as outlined in recipe. (Fillets take less time to cook.) Makes 3 servings.

**Add according to taste.

***It may be necessary to use several whole fish and/or to multiply this recipe in order to make the number of servings required. If whole fish is being used, avoid choosing individual fish larger than 1$^1/_2$ kg or 3 lb.

Grilled Marinated Salmon

This recipe was developed to subtly bring out the delicate flavour of the fish while adding a discreet bouquet of other interesting flavours. The salmon may be grilled, with equal success, on a barbecue or under a pre-heated broiler.

Ingredients

8 salmon steaks (about 2 kg or 4$\frac{1}{2}$ lb)
1 recipe Oriental Marinade (page 225)
2$\frac{1}{2}$ cups Horseradish Mayonnaise (page 232)
$\frac{3}{4}$ cup capers*

(Makes 8 servings)

Arrange salmon steaks in a single layer, in glass baking dishes. Bathe with Oriental Marinade; set aside for about 6 hours, turning regularly in marinade.

Just before serving, remove salmon from marinade. Grill carefully on a barbecue (or under a pre-heated broiler). Turn regularly and baste with marinade, until exterior surfaces are well browned, and interior flesh is cooked. (Flesh flakes easily with a fork.)

Serve immediately, accompanied by Horseradish Mayonnaise and capers if desired.

*Optional Regular or Fried Capers (page 214) may be used.

160

Fish en Papillote

(à la Belge)

In Belgium, we used to go to a fabulous restaurant off the Grande Place, where long sheets of white paper were torn from a huge roll to make a fresh tablecloth for newly seated guests, where white sawdust was tossed on floors to prevent slips, and where we feasted on enormous servings of delectable Fish en Papillote. Having been denied the papillote experience for almost 20 years, I have created my own version of that treat. The only difficult part in this recipe may be obtaining parchment paper. It is usually available in large supermarkets. Oregano seasoned saffron rice may be attractively arranged with the papillote packages as an accompanying dish.

Ingredients

6 fish fillet portions (white flesh variety),
(each portion: 150 g or 5 oz)

2 cups fresh spinach (small leaves)

salt to taste

pepper to taste

nutmeg to taste

ginger to taste

garlic powder to taste

1 recipe Fish Poaching Bath (page 226)

vegetable oil as required

3 cups Newburg Sauce (page 235)

1/2 cup red bell pepper, cut into strips

1/4 cup Toasted Almonds, sliced (page 226)

1 1/2 m or 5 feet parchment paper*

(Makes 6 servings)

Place spinach in a large glass baking dish; cover with boiling water; drain immediately. Continue to drain leaves, in a single layer, on paper towels. Season well drained spinach leaves to taste with salt, pepper, ground nutmeg, ginger, and garlic powder.

In a large deep skillet or electric frying pan, prepare Fish Poaching Bath; bring mixture to a boil; simmer for 5 minutes.

Carefully arrange fillets in poaching bath; bring to a boil; cover skillet tightly; reduce heat to allow fish to simmer very gently until flesh begins to flake with a fork. Remove fish from skillet; drain well on wire cooling racks. Adjust seasoning if necessary.

Cut 6 pieces of parchment paper (each 25 cm or 10 inches square in size). Fold each square into a triangle; and then open parchment paper out into a flat square again. (The diagonal fold line divides the square into 2 triangles.)

Brush top surface of each parchment square with oil. Arrange 1/6 of spinach within one of the triangles of each square (in area where fish is to be placed); add one portion of fish.

Continue to prepare each parchment parcel by topping each portion of fish with Newburg Sauce (about 1/4 to 1/3 cup); decorate with red bell pepper and almonds. Fold the other triangle of the parchment square over garnished fillet to make a triangular package.

At the two open sides of triangle package, take top and bottom parchment layers together and make a 1 cm or 1/3 inch deep double fold towards the centre, sealing package closed.

Place filled parchment packages on baking sheets.** Bake at 210°C/425°F for about 12 minutes until contents of packages are well heated.

Serve fish in parchment triangles garnished according to taste. Offer extra Newburg Sauce at table.

*Option Aluminium foil (dull side out) may be used; however, care must be taken when removing the fish from the foil. The fish should be removed from the foil papillotes and transferred to dinner plates. (This may be done in the kitchen, or rather dramatically at the table.)

**Fish en Papillote can be prepared to this stage a day in advance, and immediately refrigerated. Transfer to oven for baking.

Pasta Duet with Mushroom Herb Cream Sauce

(and Scallops*)

Mushroom Herb Cream Sauce is usually on hand in our freezer, ready to be added to pasta. Vegetarian and non-vegetarian versions of the recipe may be prepared. A delicious non-vegetarian dish can be prepared by adding sautéed scallops or pepperoni. Smoked salmon is another excellent choice. Home-made Garlic Spinach fettuccine coupled with Orange fettuccine is delicious in this recipe.

Ingredients

170 g or 6 oz Orange Pasta (page 222)**, fettuccine style
170 g or 6 oz Garlic Spinach Pasta (page 222)**, fettuccine style
$^1/_4$ cup Garlic Butter (page 223)
salt to taste
freshly crushed black peppercorns to taste

Mushroom Herb Cream Sauce

$^1/_{16}$ teaspoon saffron threads, very finely chopped
2 tablespoons hot water
1 tablespoon butter
$1^1/_2$ teaspoons fresh garlic, finely chopped
$1^1/_2$ teaspoons fresh ginger root, finely chopped
$^1/_2$ cup onion, sliced
$^2/_3$ cup mushrooms, sliced
$^1/_2$ cup green bell pepper, cut into strips
$^1/_3$ cup tomato, sliced
2 cups whole milk
$^1/_2$ cup evaporated milk
$^1/_2$ teaspoon dried basil
$^1/_4$ teaspoon dried oregano
$1^1/_4$ teaspoons salt
$^1/_4$ to $^1/_2$ teaspoon black peppercorns, cracked
$^1/_4$ cup whipping cream
Parmesan Cheese (optional) as required

(Makes 4 servings)

To make Mushroom Herb Cream Sauce, soak saffron in hot water for about 30 minutes. (If the saffron is not strong in flavour, increase the quantity used. The final Mushroom Herb Cream Sauce should be a definite pale yellow in colour.)

In a large deep skillet, melt butter over medium heat. Add garlic, ginger, onion, mushrooms, green pepper, and tomato. Cook about 3 minutes, stirring frequently. Add saffron mixture, whole milk, evaporated milk, basil, oregano, salt, and pepper. Bring to a boil; reduce heat, and allow mixture to simmer for 3 minutes. Remove from heat; stir in whipping cream to produce Mushroom Herb Cream Sauce. Set aside*** until pasta is cooked. (Makes $2^2/_3$ cups of liquid cream sauce.)

Using 2 separate pots, cook Orange and Garlic Spinach Pasta separately and uncovered, in generous amounts of salted boiling water until *al dente* (tender but firm). Drain well.

Carefully toss the two types of pasta together with Garlic Butter; season with salt and pepper according to taste.

Place skillet with Mushroom Herb Cream Sauce, over medium heat. When sauce is hot, add pasta.* Heat Pasta Duet, turning carefully and frequently, until hot. (If necessary, add more evaporated milk or whipping cream to make a moister combination.) If desired, add grated Parmesan cheese according to taste, and adjust flavours.

Serve immediately in oversized bowls or on large plates.

*Optional For a non-vegetarian version, add one of the following options:

sautéed and seasoned scallops (raw weight: $^2/_3$ kg or $1^1/_4$ lb)
strips (8 mm or $^1/_3$ inch wide) of smoked salmon (250 g or 8 oz)
sautéed pepperoni slices, uncooked (60 g or 2 oz)
strips of ham (275 g or 9 oz)

**Commercial varieties of choice may be used; however, quantities may need to be adjusted. A twin colour (e.g. white and green) pasta combination is attractive.

***Mushroom Herb Cream Sauce may be prepared in advance, placed in an airtight container, and stored in the refrigerator or freezer until required.

Vegetarian Omelettes in Crêpe Bowls

This is an interesting vegetarian alternative to traditional main course dishes. To make a non-vegetarian version, substitute ham or salmon for the asparagus or broccoli.

Ingredients

butter as required
6 Basic Crêpes (page 221),
(diameter: 15 cm or 6 inches)
2 tablespoons margarine
1/2 cup mushrooms, sliced
2 tablespoons green bell peppers, thinly sliced
2 tablespoons red bell peppers, thinly sliced
1 tablespoon onion, finely chopped
1/4 teaspoon fresh ginger root, finely chopped
3/4 cup asparagus or broccoli pieces, blanched
6 eggs
1 tablespoon French mustard
2 tablespoons cheddar cheese, grated
1/4 cup evaporated milk
3/4 teaspoon salt
1/4 teaspoon black peppercorns, crushed
1/4 teaspoon ground nutmeg
3/4 cup Hollandaise Mayonnaise (page 231)*

(Makes 6 servings)

Butter interiors of 6 ramekin dishes (1/2 cup size); set aside.

Prepare thin crêpes using approximately 2 tablespoons of batter for each crêpe, and cooking only on one side. Remove from pan.

Gently fit each crêpe, with cooked side down, into a well buttered ramekin dish, arranging edges to resemble a ruffle. Set aside.

Melt margarine in a skillet over medium heat; add mushrooms, bell peppers, onion, and ginger; sauté for 2 minutes. Remove from heat; add cooked asparagus or broccoli. Set asparagus (broccoli) mixture aside.

In a bowl, combine eggs, mustard, cheese, evaporated milk, salt, pepper, and nutmeg.

Place 2 1/2 tablespoons of asparagus (broccoli) mixture into each crêpe lined ramekin dish. Almost fill dishes with egg mixture. Arrange ramekin dishes on baking trays for convenience in handling.

Bake at 190°C/375°F. (If crêpe fringe browns too quickly, arrange a strip of aluminium foil, shiny side out, around the outside surface of dishes to cover crêpe fringe.) Bake until a knife inserted in centre of omelette bowl comes out clean (about 25 to 30 minutes); remove omelettes from oven.

Allow ramekin dishes to stand for a few minutes. Remove crêpe omelette bowls from ramekin dishes; transfer directly to individual plates or a serving platter.

Serve the omelette bowls in a coulis of Hollandaise Mayonnaise.** (Do not heat Hollandaise Mayonnaise.) Garnish as desired.

*Optional

**Note: For convenience, spread the plates with a coulis of Hollandaise Mayonnaise while the omelette bowls are baking.

167

DESSERTS

Desserts are usually the highlight of a meal. They are meant to be irresistible, tempting even the "already too well-nourished" guest. Much of the secret of a dessert lies in its presentation. Delicious ingredients can be arranged together in delectable layers and combinations and served in intriguing edible containers.

If desserts are to be easy and magical, it is advisable to learn the basic skills of making pastry, crêpes, mousse, and ice cream, as well as hard and soft meringue. The degree to which all these skills are mastered is really not critical. Such treats can be served in wonderful compositions where perfect quality becomes irrelevant.

Frequently at sit-down events of up to 18, I serve the dessert personally, from large trays placed in front of me. For these occasions, the dessert plates are piled on a tea wagon (or small portable table) located at my left elbow. Often, to add an extra touch of drama, some element on the plate is flambéed, or individual plates are personalized with the guests' initials inscribed with melted chocolate.

Probably everyone has been served a dessert which is uncomfortable to manage, resulting in awkward moments for the host/hostess and the guests. Frozen desserts or chocolate cups may be too hard, pastries too crisp or tough, and meringues too brittle. To minimize such risks, potentially mobile desserts can be fixed in position on plates with White Chocolate Cream, chocolate hazelnut spread, or with some type of coulis. Served with a fork and spoon, the dessert can be secured in place with the fork (usually held in the left hand) and cut with the spoon (located in the right hand).

Delectable Chocolate Mousse (page 191)

Chocolate Lattice Fruit Baskets

Chocolate Lattice Fruit Baskets is my version of strawberries and cream. Creating the Pastry Lattice Baskets is the only real work required in preparing the recipe. The baskets may be prepared and painted weeks in advance of being used, and refrigerated. The rest is simple. This recipe is a favourite in our home for those occasions when preparation time is at a premium on the day of the event. (Note: Painting the baskets is not necessary; but the final effect may be compromised.)

Ingredients
175 g or 6 oz semi-sweet chocolate*, coarsely chopped
6 Pastry Lattice Baskets with Handles (page 212), prepared
400 g or 14 oz fresh strawberries**, stems removed
2 teaspoons orange flavoured liqueur (optional)
1 cup whipped cream, sweetened

Garnish
mint or parsley leaves (small and delicate)

Cinnamon Strawberry Sauce
$2/3$ cup strawberry jam
2 teaspoons brandy
$2/3$ teaspoon lemon or lime zest
$1/5$ teaspoon ground cinnamon

(Makes 6 servings)

Partially melt chocolate over hot water; remove from heat; stir vigorously until chocolate is melted and smooth.

Using a small spoon***, paint exterior of prepared Pastry Lattice Baskets with a very thin coating of melted chocolate, leaving lattice work exposed. (A heavy toothpick is useful for this task.) Arrange painted baskets in an inverted position on wax paper lined baking trays, with chocolate side up. Refrigerate for about 10 minutes until chocolate is set. Then paint all remaining surfaces of baskets. Paint handles in a similar manner, returning them to baking tray, with freshly painted sides up. Refrigerate to set. Finally, attach handles to baskets with melted chocolate. Refrigerate to set completed basket. Keep baskets refrigerated until about $1/2$ hour before being served. (The baskets are easier to break apart if they are not cold and brittle.)

To make Cinnamon Strawberry Sauce, mix together strawberry jam, brandy, lemon zest, and cinnamon until smooth. Refrigerate. (This may be prepared days in advance.)

Just before serving, sprinkle strawberries with liqueur if desired.

To assemble dessert, place a generous portion of whipped cream ($2^{1}/_2$ tablespoons) in each basket, drawing the cream up around sides to create a soft nest. Generously fill with strawberries. If desired, garnish with delicate mint or parsley leaves (or "refit" a few of the surface strawberries with parsley stems).

Serve Chocolate Lattice Fruit Baskets on a coulis of Cinnamon Strawberry Sauce ($1^{1}/_2$ tablespoons per serving).

(When consuming this dessert, hold basket securely at centre with a fork and break it apart with a spoon.)

*Option For a tastier option, use 25 g or 1 oz chocolate mint morsels and 150 g or 5 oz semi-sweet chocolate.

**If strawberries are large, it may be necessary to slice them. (Other berries or fruit pieces may be used in this recipe.)

***If a softer chocolate is used, the lattice baskets and handles may be dipped. The chocolate coating must be thin, allowing the basket to be broken easily with a fork and spoon.

Sour Cream Blueberry Brûlée

I only make Sour Cream Blueberry Brûlée in very small ramekin dishes (¼ cup size). Care must be taken to seal the surface of the filling well with heavy sour cream, and to broil this dessert only for about 2½ to 3 minutes, or until the sugar bubbles. Sour Cream Blueberry Brûlée is best served immediately.

Ingredients

Topping

½ cup brown sugar
1½ teaspoons ground cinnamon

Filling

2 teaspoons orange flavoured liqueur*
1¼ cups blueberry pie filling, commercial
¾ cup thick sour cream

Garnish

½ cup whipped cream, sweetened

(Makes 6 servings of ¼ cup size)

To make sugar topping, combine brown sugar and cinnamon; set aside.

If desired, blend liqueur into blueberry pie filling. Fill small individual ramekin dishes (¼ cup size), not quite two-thirds full with pie filling.

Carefully top with a deep layer of thick sour cream to almost fill the dishes, and to form a seal over the fruit filling. Arrange dishes, well separated, on a baking tray.** (If the brûlées are not to be served immediately, refrigerate until about 15 minutes before serving.)

When guests are ready for dessert, sprinkle surface of sour cream evenly and to edges of dishes with a generous amount of cinnamon sugar topping (2 teaspoons per dish); place tray of ramekin dish desserts 15 cm or 6 inches below a pre-heated broiler. Grill until most of the sugar bubbles and melts (about 2 to 3 minutes); avoid over baking. (Some crystals may remain unmelted in the centre.)

Serve immediately before cream sets. If desired, offer whipped cream at the table, after guests have started their desserts.

*Optional

**The dessert may be prepared to this stage, up to 2 days in advance of being served.

Peaches and Cream Meringue Combo

I usually crown the combo with fresh mint or basil leaves. A fork and spoon are essential for this dessert.

Ingredients

3¹/₂ cups fresh* or canned peach slices, drained

Garnish
fresh herb leaves** (e.g. basil, parsley, mint)

Crisp Walnut Meringue
1 cup castor sugar
3 egg whites, room temperature
¹/₄ teaspoon cream of tartar
¹/₂ teaspoon vanilla extract
¹/₃ cup walnuts, coarsely chopped

Coffee Sour Cream Sauce
³/₄ cup sour cream
1 tablespoon castor (super fine) sugar
2 to 3 teaspoons instant coffee crystals

Coffee Liqueur Cream Topping
1³/₄ cups whipping cream, chilled
3 tablespoons castor (super fine) sugar
2 to 4 tablespoons coffee flavoured cream liqueur

Strawberry Sauce
¹/₂ cup strawberry jam
1¹/₂ teaspoons orange flavoured liqueur (or water)

(Makes 12 servings)

Line baking trays with parchment paper. Draw 12 circles (diameter: 8 cm or 3 inches) on paper. Turn paper over with pencil drawings face down against tray (to avoid possible transfer of pencil lead to meringues). Set aside.

To make meringue mixture, sift castor sugar. Beat egg whites with cream of tartar and vanilla extract until soft peaks form. Gradually add 3 tablespoons of sugar, beating constantly until stiff peaks form. Remove beaters.

Pour all remaining sugar into beaten egg white mixture, and fold carefully together. (Makes 2¹/₄ cups meringue mixture.)

Promptly, while meringue mixture is stable, pipe or drop about 3 tablespoons of soft meringue into each circle outlined on parchment paper. Using the back of a spoon, evenly spread meringue within limits of circles. Sprinkle unbaked meringue discs with chopped walnuts. Using the tip of a fork, carefully blend nuts into soft meringues.

Bake at 140⁰C/275⁰F until meringues are crisp (about 40 to 50 minutes); turn off oven. When meringues are completely dry, remove from oven. When meringues are cool, peel away parchment paper.***

To prepare Coffee Sour Cream Sauce, mix together sour cream, coffee crystals, and castor sugar until well blended. Refrigerate. (Coffee Sour Cream Sauce may be prepared days in advance.)

Shortly before serving, make Coffee Liqueur Cream Topping by beating chilled cream until soft peaks form; gradually add sugar, beating constantly until peaks become firm. Gradually beat in liqueur, a small quantity at a time, being careful not to significantly reduce the thickness of the whipped cream.

Immediately before serving, arrange each walnut meringue disc on a little Coffee Sour Cream Sauce (1 tablespoon); generously top meringue with Coffee Liqueur Cream (2¹/₂ tablespoons), and then peaches (¹/₄ cup). Garnish with Strawberry Sauce (1 teaspoon), and fresh herb leaves if desired.

*If fresh peaches are used, they should be appropriately sweetened (e.g. sprinkled with sugar and orange liqueur if desired).

**Optional

***Baked meringues retain their quality for weeks, if arranged in an unsealed box and stored in a cool dry place.

Strawberry Peppercorn Duet

(illustrated on page 28)

In this recipe, the berries are tastier when cut in halves, allowing the whisky and sugar to bring out the flavour of the strawberries more effectively. Usually, I place the berries in a crystal bowl, with pre-scooped Whisky Peppercorn Ice Cream arranged separately in a second chilled bowl, or in chilled individual glasses (e.g. large cognac glasses or sherbet). We add the whisky, sugar, and crushed peppercorns to the strawberries at the table, asking guests to sample and to check if the additions are according to taste. Depending on the occasion, a noisy pepper grinder – even a battery operated one – can also contribute to the theatrics and humour at the table! The strawberry concoction is then spooned over the ice cream.

Ingredients

1/2 kg or 1 lb fresh strawberries
1/3 to 1/2 cup* whisky
1/4 to 1/3 cup* sugar
1/2 teaspoon or more* black peppercorns, freshly crushed
3/4 litre or 11/4 pints Whisky Peppercorn Ice Cream (page 184)**

(Makes 6 servings)

Toss berries lightly with whisky, sugar, and pepper. Adjust flavours if necessary. Serve flavoured and seasoned berries over Whisky Peppercorn Ice Cream**.

*Add quantities according to taste.

****Option** Vanilla ice cream may also be used.

Fresh Fruit and Whipped Chocolate Medley

This recipe is another quick way to serve just fruit for dessert, but with a gourmet flair.

Ingredients

3 fresh ripe kiwi fruit, peeled
3 cups fresh raspberries or blackberries
orange flavoured liqueur* as required
2 recipes White Chocolate Cream (page 228)

(Makes 6 servings)

Cut fresh kiwi fruit as desired (e.g. in halves, wedges, slices); sprinkle with liqueur.* Arrange kiwi and berries together on a serving platter or on individual dessert plates. Serve fresh fruit with White Chocolate Cream. Garnish appropriately (e.g. fresh mint leaves, crushed praline, or small edible flowers).

*Optional

Fruit Pastry Blossoms

I prepare the Pastry Blossoms and outline the petals in piped dark chocolate, a week or longer prior to an event. The morning of the event, I pipe chocolate stems and leaves on individual plates. The chocolate painted plates are then transferred to tablecloth covered beds and/or card tables in a cool room. Hours before the guests arrive, the Pastry Blossoms are lined with White Chocolate Cream, filled with fruit, and returned to the refrigerator on trays. At dessert time, the blossoms are removed from the refrigerator, and arranged directly on the plates, fixed into position on a drop of White Chocolate Cream located at the top of the painted chocolate stems.

For an extra special presentation and heartier appetites, one large and one small blossom may be arranged together on a plate for each individual serving.

Strawberry Fruit Pastry Blossoms

Ingredients

25 g or 1 oz semi-sweet chocolate*, coarsely chopped

6 Large Pastry Blossoms (pages 210–211), prepared
(base diameter: 5 cm or 2 inches)

2 cups fresh fruit (e.g. mango or peaches, cut into pieces)
or berries**

2 to 3 teaspoons orange flavoured liqueur*

3/4 to 1 cup White Chocolate Cream (page 228)

(Makes 6 servings of 1 large blossom per serving)

If Pastry Blossoms trimmed with chocolate* are desired, partially melt semi-sweet chocolate over hot water; remove from heat; stir vigorously until chocolate is melted and smooth. Place melted chocolate in a piping bag with a small nozzle. Pipe melted chocolate around top of Pastry Blossoms to outline petals. Refrigerate to set, and until ready to use. (This may be done 1 week or more in advance.)

Sprinkle fruit with liqueur according to taste.

To assemble blossoms, line interior of each Pastry Blossom with White Chocolate Cream (1½ tablespoons). Fill blossoms with fruit; top with an extra drop of White Chocolate Cream. Refrigerate until ready to serve.

To serve, secure the blossoms in position on plates with a little White Chocolate Cream (or chocolate hazelnut spread). This assists in holding blossoms in place while guests break the pastry. Garnish filled blossoms as desired (e.g. with piped chocolate stems and leaves***, or with fresh mint leaves).

(To consume, hold blossom securely at centre with a fork, and break apart with a spoon.)

*Optional

Option Peach pie filling (not heated) or a fruit mousse may also be used.

***About an additional 50 g or 2 oz of semi-sweet chocolate (melted), are required to make the piped stems and leaves.

177

Decadent Butterscotch Banana Noodle Soup

Noodle soup makes an entirely new and elegant debut with this recipe. The Butterscotch Sauce and Fried Rice Noodles can be prepared 1 week or more in advance. Once the cream is whipped and the bananas are cut, arranging the final composition takes only a few minutes. I avoid being too generous with the Butterscotch Sauce Supreme because it is decadently rich!

Ingredients

2 cups ripe bananas, sliced
2 tablespoons orange flavoured liqueur*
1 cup Butterscotch Sauce Supreme (page 236)
1 cup whipped cream, sweetened

Fried Rice Noodles
15 g or 1/2 oz rice vermicelli noodles, uncooked
2 cups oil for deep-frying

(Makes 4 to 6 servings)

To prepare Fried Rice Noodles, drop uncooked rice noodles (small quantities at a time) into hot oil. Cook until crispy (about 10 seconds or more). Drain on paper towels. Set aside.**

Just before serving, slice bananas, and sprinkle with liqueur.

To serve, carefully heat Butterscotch Sauce Supreme in a small heavy saucepan over medium low heat. Arrange bananas in the bottom of flat soup bowls.

Add hot Butterscotch Sauce Supreme to just barely cover bananas (1 1/2 to 2 tablespoons per serving). Garnish with whipped cream; top delicately with Fried Rice Noodles. If desired, add a few leaves of fresh mint or basil.

*Optional

**Fried Rice Noodles may be prepared 1 week or longer in advance. Arrange noodles carefully in an unsealed box lined with paper towels. Store in a cool dry place.

Irresistible Triple Chocolate Cheesecake

In general, cheesecakes tend to be filling, and final bites are not always savoured with the pleasure they deserve. When serving Irresistible Triple Chocolate Cheesecake, it is advisable to first offer guests thin wedges which may be presented on plates dusted with cocoa powder, if desired. Additions of fresh pineapple (cut into matchstick size pieces) and Butterscotch Sauce Supreme enhance both the flavour and presentation of the cheesecake.

Ingredients

Crust
1¼ cups graham cracker crumbs, finely crushed
¼ cup sugar
¼ cup cocoa powder
1 teaspoon ginger powder
⅓ cup butter, melted

Cheesecake Mixture
175 g or 6 oz semi-sweet chocolate, coarsely chopped
1¼ cups sugar
1 kg or 2¼ lb cream cheese
½ cup sour cream
2 teaspoons vanilla extract
4 eggs
2 teaspoons lime (or lemon) zest

Topping
½ cup sour cream
125 g or 4 oz cream cheese
1 tablespoon icing sugar
60 g or 2 oz semi-sweet chocolate
½ teaspoon butter
1 tablespoon (approximate) water

(Makes 24 servings)

To make the crust, combine graham cracker crumbs, sugar, cocoa, ginger, and butter; press into bottom of a well buttered springform pan (diameter: 25 cm or 10 inches); chill.

To make the cheesecake mixture, heat chocolate with ½ cup sugar over hot water until chocolate melts; set aside.

Beat together cream cheese, sour cream, ¾ cup sugar, and extract. Add eggs, one at a time, beating well after each addition. Divide cream cheese mixture into 2 equal portions.

Add melted chocolate mixture and lime zest to one portion of cream cheese mixture (i.e. half of the cream cheese mixture); combine well; spread over crust in springform pan.

Add remaining portion (or half) of cream cheese mixture to springform pan (on top of chocolate cheese layer), to make a second layer.

Bake at 170⁰C/340⁰F until cheesecake is set (centre springs back to the touch), and cake has come well away from edge of pan (at least 1¼ hours).

Allow cake to cool. Chill overnight in refrigerator. Trim off any raised outer rim; smooth cut area with a dampened metal spatula.

To make topping, mix together cream cheese, sour cream, and icing sugar; spread over top of cheesecake, allowing it to drip over sides (as desired).

Melt chocolate over hot water. Stir in butter; blend well. Very gradually add only enough water to make chocolate just sufficiently fluid to run in a slow stream when poured from a spoon. Decorate cheesecake by drizzling thick heavy lines of melted chocolate over cream cheese topping. Refrigerate to chill.*

Cut cake into thin (2 cm or barely 1 inch) wedges.

*The cheesecake may be frozen very successfully for several weeks. Allow the cheesecake to thaw in refrigerator before serving. For best results, add the topping after the cheesecake thaws.

Almond Tiramisu Cups

A very subtle touch of almond in the cream mixture makes this Tiramisu recipe different. The combination of instant coffee crystals and cocoa powder dusted on the surface of the Tiramisu is an unexpected surprise for many palates.

Ingredients

250 g or 8 oz cream cheese
1 teaspoon almond extract
3 eggs, separated
pinch of salt
6 tablespoons castor sugar
1/4 cup whipping cream, chilled
12 (approximate) Lady Finger Biscuits (page 227*), or commercial
1 1/2 tablespoons Toasted Almonds (page 226), slivered

Coffee Mixture for Dipping**
3 to 4 tablespoons instant coffee crystals
1/3 cup hot water
2 to 3 tablespoons coffee flavoured liqueur***

Garnish
instant coffee crystals
cocoa powder
20 almonds***, whole and unblanched

(Makes 10 to 12 servings in demi-tasse cups)

First, beat together cream cheese, extract, and egg yolks until well blended.

Beat egg whites with salt until soft peaks form; gradually add 3 tablespoons sugar, beating constantly until peaks become firm; set aside.

Beat chilled cream until soft peaks form; gradually add 1 tablespoon sugar, beating until peaks become firm.

Then with a wire whisk, carefully fold beaten egg whites into cream cheese mixture. Finally, fold in whipped cream to produce a Tiramisu cream. (Makes 3 cups.)

To prepare Coffee Mixture for Dipping**, dissolve instant coffee crystals and remaining 2 tablespoons sugar in hot water; stir in 1 tablespoon liqueur.

With a sharp knife*, cut Lady Finger Biscuits horizontally into very thin (1/2 cm or 1/5 inch) slices. (Biscuits may crack and break. This is not serious. The biscuits may still be used.)

Carefully and quickly dip biscuit pieces into Coffee Mixture, only to moisten pieces; arrange on a flat platter. (Also dampen any crumbs.) Very lightly sprinkle dampened pieces and crumbs with a little more liqueur. Arrange pieces of dampened biscuits in a single layer in bottom of demi-tasse cups (1/3 cup size), filling any spaces with dampened crumbs. Into each cup, spoon only enough cream cheese mixture (2 1/2 tablespoons) to fill half the cup. Drop 3 Toasted Almond slivers into centre of cream filling.

Add another layer of moistened biscuits; add cream cheese mixture, filling cup to a regular full cup of coffee level (i.e. about three-quarters full).

Cover cups individually with plastic wrap. Refrigerate overnight. (Note: Tiramisu may be kept frozen for several weeks. A few hours before serving, transfer Tiramisu Cups to refrigerator.)

Just before serving, use a fine small sieve to dust creamy surface of cups with both instant coffee crystals and cocoa powder. (Remove any dust from exterior of cups and handles.) To serve, arrange Almond Tiramisu Cups on saucers. If desired, present Tiramisu accompanied by whole unblanched almonds.

*If making Lady Fingers, prepare thin biscuits of a suitable size and shape to fit exactly into serving cups or container. (When arranging the Tiramisu, only a slight trimming of these biscuits may be required.) Coffee flavoured Lady Fingers add extra flavour to the dessert.

**It may be necessary to prepare additional quantities of this Coffee Mixture. The final quantity required depends on thickness and dryness of biscuits, as well as on type of container used.

***Optional

Ice Cream and Frozen Mousse

I have no special equipment for making ice cream. Anyone can make successful home-made ice cream and frozen mousse with these recipes. They are not difficult. The basic technique is the same. It is also important to know that water and ice crystals can affect quality. In general, the less water and the finer the crystals, the smoother the product. A very cold freezer is crucial.

Home-made ice cream and frozen mousse are so delicious that they can be happily consumed on their own. It is therefore more practical for me to keep those basic recipes separate from other recipes which I have developed to emphasize presentation and/or interesting combinations. Of course, for the latter group of recipes, commercial ice cream may be substituted for the home-made varieties of ice cream and frozen mousse.

Whisky* Peppercorn Ice Cream

Crushed black peppercorns add a bit of spark to traditional vanilla ice cream; so does the whisky. I use Whisky Peppercorn Ice Cream as one might normally use vanilla ice cream.

Ingredients
2 cups whipping cream
2 egg yolks
1/3 cup sugar
1/4 cup whisky*
1/3 teaspoon black peppercorns, crushed

(Makes almost 1 litre or 1½ pints, or 4 cups)

In a large bowl, whisk together cream, egg yolks, sugar, and whisky until sugar dissolves.

Cover bowl with plastic wrap. Place bowl with contents in freezer until crystals begin to form around edge.

Remove from freezer. Place bowl with cream mixture into a shallow ice water bath. Whip mixture until firm peaks begin to form (several minutes). Fold in crushed peppercorns.

Pour mixture into a chilled airtight container, covering surface of ice cream closely with plastic wrap to prevent ice crystals from forming. Freeze and store in a very cold freezer.

*Option For a non-alcoholic and quicker version of this recipe, simply add about 1/3 teaspoon of crushed black peppercorns to 1 litre or 1½ pints vanilla ice cream. The resulting product is Black Peppercorn Ice Cream.

Lemon Ice Cream

The grated peel in this recipe adds a subtle touch of tartness and texture.

Ingredients

2 cups whipping cream
2 egg yolks
1/4 cup sugar
1 packet lemon* flavoured gelatin dessert powder
(packet size: 85 g or 3 oz)
1/4 cup boiling water
2 teaspoons lemon* extract
1/2 to 3/4 teaspoon yellow food colouring**
2 tablespoons lime (or lemon) peel, grated

(Makes more than 1 litre or 1 quart, or 5 cups)

In a large bowl, whisk together cream, egg yolks, and sugar until sugar dissolves.

Cover bowl with plastic wrap. Place bowl with cream mixture in freezer until crystals begin to form around edge. Immediately, dissolve gelatin powder completely in boiling water. Allow gelatin mixture to cool briefly at room temperature, stirring occasionally, until mixture begins to thicken (not gel).

Remove bowl with cream mixture from freezer. Place bowl into a shallow ice water bath. Whip mixture until firm peaks begin to form. Add thickening gelatin mixture in a quick steady stream, beating constantly at high speed. Beat in extract (and food colouring if desired); fold in peel.

Pour Lemon Ice Cream into a chilled airtight container, and cover with plastic wrap to prevent ice crystals from forming. Freeze and store in a very cold freezer.

*Option To make Pineapple Ice Cream, use pineapple gelatin dessert powder and pineapple extract.

**Optional

Chocolate Mint Frozen Mousse

Ingredients

1 cup whipping cream
1 egg yolk
3 tablespoons sugar
1/4 cup Crème de Menthe liqueur
pinch to 1/2 teaspoon* peppermint extract
1/2 teaspoon green food colouring**
1/2 cup semi-sweet chocolate, chopped (not too finely)

(Makes 1/2 litre or almost 1 pint, or 2 1/3 cups)

In a medium bowl, whisk together cream, egg yolks, and sugar until sugar dissolves. Cover bowl with plastic wrap. Place bowl with contents in freezer until crystals begin to form around edge.

Remove from freezer. Place bowl with cream mixture into a shallow ice water bath. Whip mixture until firm peaks begin to form; beat in liqueur, and extract (as well as food colouring if desired). Fold in chocolate.

Pour mixture into chilled airtight container; cover surface of mousse closely with plastic wrap. Freeze and store in a very cold freezer.

*Option The extract is optional, or add according to taste.

**Optional The food colouring produces a much more attractive product. Add as desired. The colour tends to become darker after a day.

Frosted Lemons

(illustrated on pages 26–27)

Frosted Lemons are perfect for lunches or those occasions which call for a light but interesting dessert.

To serve Frosted Lemons, I plant a small decorative paper umbrella (opened) in the lid of each lemon. (To facilitate adding the umbrella, pierce a small hole in the lids with a skewer, after removing the flesh from the lemon, and before freezing.) Frosted Lemons look particularly attractive arranged on doily lined dessert plates, and garnished with clusters of Frosted Grapes.

Ingredients

6 whole lemons (good shape and colour)
2 to 3 teaspoons blackberry or blueberry jam
$^3/_4$ litre or $1^1/_4$ pints Lemon Ice Cream (page 185)

(Makes 6 servings)

Stand lemons with stem end up. If necessary, trim bottoms of lemons so that they stand securely.

Cut off upper part of lemons with a neat horizontal cut, about one-third of the way down from top. Set lemons aside, keeping corresponding lids and bottoms together.

Using a sharp pointed spoon, remove interior flesh from lids and bottom portions of lemons. Scrape away any membranes, taking care not to pierce or break the peel of the lemon shells.

Arrange hollowed shells, with their lids, in a standing position in an airtight plastic box. Freeze until stiff.

Place about $^1/_2$ teaspoon jam in bottom of each frozen lemon shell. Fill body of lemon shells and lids with lemon ice cream. Reassemble lemons to original form; return to freezer until firm and ready to serve.*

(If ice cream filled lemons are frozen very firmly, transfer them to refrigerator about 10 minutes before serving, allowing ice cream to soften slightly.)

*Frosted Lemons may be prepared several days in advance. Keep frozen in an airtight container.

Ice Cream Cherry Crêpes

(illustrated on page 55)

I serve these ice cream filled crêpes to guests myself at the table. Just before serving, the ice cream filled crêpes are prepared in the kitchen. They are then arranged, side by side, on a long chilled serving platter. Finally, cherry sauce is poured down the centre of the row of crêpes (1 tablespoon per crêpe). Usually, a small heated bowl of flaming rum accompanies the platter of crêpes to the table. As guests watch, the crêpes are transferred to individual dessert plates, more cherry sauce is added, and the crêpe is bathed with a "coffee" spoonful of flaming rum. A little Ginger Sour Cream crowns the crêpe, before it is passed to a guest.

Ingredients

1/2 litre or about 1 pint Pineapple* Ice Cream
(see Lemon Ice Cream: page 185)
1 1/2 cups cherry pie filling, commercial
pinch of almond extract
1 tablespoon orange flavoured liqueur**
12 Basic Crêpes (page 221), prepared and chilled
(diameter: 15 cm or 6 inches)

(extra) orange flavoured liqueur**
(for sprinkling on crêpes) as required
1/2 cup Ginger Sour Cream (page 235)

(Makes 6 large servings of 2 crêpes per serving, or 12 servings of 1 crêpe)

Cut ice cream into bars (2 1/2 cm x 8 cm or 1 inch x 3 1/2 inches), each 2 tablespoons in volume; arrange bars on a chilled tray; return to freezer, allowing ice cream to set firmly before serving.

Combine cherry pie filling, extract, and 1 tablespoon liqueur to make a cherry sauce; refrigerate.

At serving time, quickly separate and arrange chilled crêpes (with first side-cooked down), on a flat surface. If desired, sprinkle with liqueur.

Place an ice cream bar at one edge of each crêpe; roll up crêpe rather tightly around ice cream.

Serve crêpes topped with cherry and Ginger Sour Cream sauces.

***Option** Lemon Ice Cream is equally delicious.
**Optional

Caged Frozen Mint Mousse

Under a Pastry Cage, Chocolate Mint Frozen Mousse is truly presented in all its glory. The dessert is particularly charming crowned with chocolate pieces.

Ingredients

¹/₂ litre or ³/₄ pint Chocolate Mint Frozen Mousse (page 185)
3 tablespoons mango or pineapple jam
¹/₂ teaspoon orange flavoured liqueur*
pinch of water
¹/₃ cup chocolate hazelnut spread
6 Pastry Cages (page 211)**, ¹/₃ cup size

(Makes 6 servings)

Using a ¹/₄ cup size measuring cup, scoop and mould 6 individual portions of Chocolate Mint Frozen Mousse; arrange the moulded portions on a wax paper lined chilled baking tray. Cover frozen mousse closely with plastic wrap. Place in freezer; allow to freeze thoroughly.

Blend together jam, liqueur, and a pinch of water to form a barely fluid fruit sauce.

To assemble dessert, spread a circular coulis (diameter: 10 cm or 4 inches) of chocolate hazelnut spread (less than 1 tablespoon) on 6 individual dessert plates. (This may be done hours before serving.)

Immediately before serving, add a portion of Chocolate Mint Frozen Mousse to centre of each coulis; drizzle mousse with fruit sauce (¹/₂ teaspoon); cover with a Pastry Cage. Add a little extra fruit sauce to each plate, just outside the cage. Garnish plate and top of cage as desired (e.g. mint leaves, chocolate curls, praline). Serve immediately.

*Optional

**Option If desired, the exterior of each cage may be partially painted in advance with lines of melted chocolate; refrigerate to set.

Favourite Dessert Mousses

(Not Frozen)

Dessert mousses of the non-frozen type deserve a section of their own. Some hosts and hostesses may like the simplicity of serving mousses in individual sherbet glasses or in a large crystal bowl. Mousse recipes are very flexible; presentation is limited only by one's imagination, time available, and the degree of elegance desired.

Dark Chocolate Mousse

Ingredients

280 g or 10 oz semi-sweet chocolate, coarsely chopped
2 eggs
2 tablespoons dark rum
1 tablespoon vanilla extract
1⅓ cups whipping cream, chilled

(Makes about 3 cups, or 8 servings)

Melt chocolate over hot water.

Beat eggs in top of double boiler over hot water, until thick and creamy. Remove from heat; transfer to a bowl.

Immediately add melted chocolate, rum, and extract to warm beaten eggs; allow to cool at room temperature.

Whip cream until firm peaks form; fold whipped cream into chocolate mixture.

Pour mousse into suitable containers such as dessert glasses, crystal bowl, or edible containers, lined ramekin dishes, or moulds. Refrigerate to set (overnight, or for at least several hours, depending on size of container).

If desired, serve mousse garnished with whipped cream or white chocolate curls.

Maple Syrup Mousse

Being Canadian, we are always eager to serve this recipe – made with Canadian maple syrup of course!

Ingredients

1 tablespoon unflavoured gelatin
3 tablespoons cold water
1 to 3 teaspoons maple extract (to taste)
1¼ cups maple syrup
3 eggs
1½ cups whipping cream, chilled

(Makes 5 cups, or about 12 servings)

Sprinkle gelatin over water, and let stand until softened.

Heat maple syrup in heavy saucepan; add softened gelatin; stir until gelatin dissolves; remove from heat; stir in maple extract. Let stand at room temperature until warm.

Separate eggs. With electric beater, beat egg yolks until light.

By hand, very gradually stir warm gelatin syrup mixture into beaten yolks; refrigerate mixture until it is quite thick.

Beat egg whites until firm peaks form; set aside.

Whip cream until firm peaks form. Using a wire whisk, carefully fold whipped cream into thickening gelatin mixture; then fold in beaten egg whites.

Pour mousse into suitable container(s). Refrigerate until set (overnight, or for several hours, depending on size of container).

Strawberry Mousse

Some strawberries are not as sweet as others. I have introduced strawberry jam into this recipe to produce a more "standard product".

Ingredients

1 tablespoon gelatin
1¹/₂ tablespoons cold water
2 tablespoons orange flavoured liqueur
250 g or 9 oz fresh strawberries
¹/₂ cup strawberry jam
1 cup whipping cream, chilled*
¹/₄ to ¹/₂ teaspoon strawberry extract
¹/₄ to ¹/₂ teaspoon red food colouring**

(Makes 3¹/₂ to 4 cups, or 6 to 8 servings)

Sprinkle gelatin over water; set aside for 2 minutes, allowing gelatin to soften. Place gelatin mixture over hot water, and stir until dissolved. Add liqueur; set aside to cool to room temperature.

Remove stems from strawberries. Wash berries under gently running cold water; drain well.

Place berries and strawberry jam in a food processor; purée until smooth. Transfer to a bowl.

Stir cooled gelatin mixture into strawberry mixture.

Whip chilled cream until soft peaks form; fold whipped cream into strawberry gelatin mixture. If desired, add extract and food colouring.

Pour mousse into suitable container(s). Refrigerate until set (overnight, or for several hours, depending on size of container).

*The final product is a delicate soft mousse. Use less cream for a firmer but heavier mousse.

**Optional

Delectable Chocolate Mousse

(*illustrated on page* 168)

Delectable Chocolate Mousse is so delicious that I opt for a simple presentation, serving it over a touch of cherry liqueur arranged in sherry glasses. Other flavoured liqueurs may be possible, but they definitely do not charm the palate in the same way as cherry liqueur. To top off this dessert with more taste and character, add Marzipan Cherries, as an alternative to fresh or maraschino cherries.

Ingredients

1 recipe Dark Chocolate Mousse (page 190)
¹/₄ to ¹/₂ cup cherry flavoured liqueur
1¹/₃ cups whipped cream, sweetened
10 fresh, maraschino, or marzipan cherries (with stems)

(Makes 10 sherry glass size servings)

Prepare Dark Chocolate Mousse.

Pour 1 to 2 teaspoons of liqueur into individual small glasses (e.g. sherry glasses) or demi-tasse cups (about ¹/₃ cup size).

Carefully spoon mousse (¹/₄ cup) into each glass. Cover glasses individually with plastic wrap, fitting the wrap almost to the surface of mousse.* Refrigerate for at least several hours until mousse sets.

To serve, remove plastic wrap, pipe generous amounts of whipped cream (1¹/₂ to 2 tablespoons per serving) on surface of mousse; crown with a cherry.

*This dessert may be prepared 2 days in advance, and refrigerated.

Fenced Maple Syrup Mousse

I usually prepare individual servings of Fenced Maple Syrup Mousse. However, with a few logical modifications to the recipe, one large Fenced Maple Syrup Mousse Torte may also be assembled and presented in a similar manner. For a single large mousse torte, use a springform pan instead of individual ramekin dishes. The Coffee Sour Cream Sauce harmonizes beautifully with the Maple Syrup Mousse, offering an agreeable balance of sweet and tart flavours.

For a touch of originality, a chocolate frame may be painted on individual dessert plates (or on a cake plate*) to surround the dessert. Coffee Sour Cream Sauce may be spooned inside the chocolate frame before arranging the Fenced Maple Syrup Mousse inside the chocolate frame. Another novel addition might be a sugar frosted bow (egg white "paint", dusted with flavoured gelatin dessert powder crystals), strategically located below the chocolate frame.

Ingredients
30 (approximate) Lady Finger biscuits**, (page 227) or commercial
$^1/_2$ recipe Maple Syrup Mousse (page 190)

Coffee Sour Cream Sauce
1 tablespoon instant coffee crystals
$1^1/_2$ teaspoons hot water
1 recipe Ginger Sour Cream (page 235)
evaporated milk as required

Garnish
1 cup whipped cream, sweetened and flavoured with vanilla extract
$^1/_4$ cup chocolate curls

(Makes 8 servings)

Line 8 ramekin dishes ($^1/_2$ cup size)* with plastic wrap; set aside.

Trim curved ends off lady finger biscuits; discard trimmings. Cut trimmed biscuits into short pieces, about 3 cm or $1^1/_4$ inches long; set pieces aside.

Make Maple Syrup Mousse as outlined in recipe.

To assemble mousse* in a lady finger fence, arrange trimmed lady finger pieces (5 or 6) around inside edge of each plastic wrap lined ramekin dish. Using 5 tablespoons mousse per dish, fill the inner space with the soft Maple Syrup Mousse to the top of the lady finger fence; allow the mousse to flow through any spaces between lady finger pieces. Refrigerate until set (overnight, or for at least 4 hours).***

To prepare Coffee Sour Cream Sauce, dissolve instant coffee crystals in hot water. Stir coffee into Ginger Sour Cream until well blended. Refrigerate. (This may be done days in advance.) If a thinner sauce is required, add evaporated milk, 1 teaspoon at a time, to create desired consistency.

To serve dessert, turn or lift moulded mousse out of ramekin dishes; peel away and discard plastic wrap. Arrange mousse on serving plate(s); garnish with whipped cream (about $1^1/_2$ tablespoons per serving) and chocolate curls. Serve with Coffee Sour Cream Sauce.

***Option** One large Fenced Maple Syrup Mousse Torte may be made in a springform pan (diameter: 25 cm or 10 inches). Line pan completely in plastic wrap. Trim one end of lady finger biscuits (about 30) so that the length of the biscuits is just shorter than the depth of the pan. Place trimmed lady finger biscuits side by side, in a standing position around inside edge of pan. (Arrange biscuits with cut end down, and with length and top surface of biscuits against plastic wrap.) Prepare 2 recipes of Maple Syrup Mousse (i.e. 10 cups); pour mousse into pan and within fence formed by lady finger biscuits. Refrigerate to set. To serve, remove mousse torte from pan; peel away plastic wrap and discard. Garnish and present the torte as outlined. Cut torte into thin wedges. Serve with Coffee Sour Cream Sauce and whipped cream. (Prepare twice the quantities as outlined, of Coffee Sour Cream Sauce, whipped cream, and chocolate curls.) Makes about 16 to 24 servings.

**Coffee flavoured Lady Fingers are preferable.

***Fenced Maple Syrup Mousse may be made 2 or 3 days in advance; cover with plastic wrap; refrigerate.

FINISHING TOUCHES

The importance which I bestow upon hors d'oeuvres in my menus is only equalled by that given to the finishing touches offered with coffee or tea after a meal. These two elements are often ignored or omitted in menu planing. This may be the reason why their addition to a menu is valued and appreciated by guests. Nothing could be more appropriate after a lovely dining experience than to be offered a final tasty treat. On this last culinary note, a host/hostess once again conveys the subtle message that he/she has made a very personal effort to please guests. In menu planning, I always include this last touch – even for cocktail receptions or for drink, coffee, and tea parties.

I always keep a few home-made chocolates, marzipan mini fruit, and a jar of ginned dates on hand in our refrigerator. If more than the supply on hand is required for unexpected entertaining, some simpler recipes can be prepared in minutes. Home-made chocolates have their own special appearance and taste; they are often recognized because they tend to be more appealing than the shiny and moulded commercial varieties. If time is limited, and no home-made post-coffee sweets are on hand, Frosted Grapes take less than 5 minutes to prepare. They can be charmingly presented on their own or on a tray with purchased chocolates.

Finishing touches lend themselves to being served rather artistically in or pouring out of baskets, boxes, and unusual containers. The sweets should be accompanied by a supply of small paper napkins. If a host/hostess feels that post-coffee treats are not on the menu, the coffee or tea tray can be personalized with a few home decorated sugar cubes, as a final salute to guests. On some occasions, the serving of chocolates or other petit sweets plays an important role in discreetly marking the conclusion of the event.

Chocolate Turtles (page 196), Marzipan Mini Fruit (pages 198–199), Pineapple Cream Chocolates (pages 196–197), Cream Cheese Strawberries (page 199), Chocolate Apricot Coins and Oysters (pages 197–198)

Chocolate Turtles

(and Nutty Chocolate Eggs)

Ingredients

10 large pecan halves
150 g or 5 oz semi-sweet chocolate, chopped
25 g or 1 oz mint chocolate chips

Coconut Coffee Paste
$^1/_4$ cup condensed milk
2 teaspoons instant coffee crystals
1 teaspoon hot water
$^2/_3$ cup desiccated coconut, unsweetened

(Makes 30)

Prepare Coconut Coffee Paste in a small heavy saucepan, by heating condensed milk over medium low heat until almost boiling. Turn off heat. Dissolve coffee crystals in hot water; blend into milk. Stir in coconut, and combine thoroughly. Allow to cool at room temperature.*

To make turtles, cut each pecan half crosswise into thirds, making 30 pieces. Cover and enclose each piece of pecan with $^3/_4$ teaspoon of Coconut Coffee Paste; shape into body of a turtle**. Arrange shaped bodies on wax paper lined baking trays; refrigerate to set and chill.***

Combine semi-sweet and mint chocolate; partially melt over hot water. Remove partially melted chocolate from heat; stir rapidly until chocolate is completely melted and well combined.

Using a small teaspoon, dip chilled turtle bodies, one at a time, into melted chocolate; bathe thoroughly. Allow excess chocolate to drip off bodies, before transferring to wax paper lined baking trays; make sure chocolate bodies are well separated.

To create 4 feet, a head, and a tail for each turtle, add (in the appropriate places) small amounts of melted chocolate to each chocolate coated body. (Use tip of a small sharp knife to add chocolate and to shape appendages.) Refrigerate to set.

Store Chocolate Turtles refrigerated, in an airtight container, to maintain freshness. (If it is necessary to enhance appearance of chocolate coating, dust Chocolate Turtles with cocoa powder before serving. The cocoa powder also keeps the exterior of the chocolates drier.)

*Coconut Coffee Paste may be prepared, refrigerated, and used over a period of time to make chocolates. Coconut Coffee Paste retains its quality for at least 3 weeks.

**To make Nutty Chocolate Eggs, form Coconut Coffee Paste into egg shapes, bathe in chocolate (as outlined for Chocolate Turtles), and arrange on wax paper lined baking trays.

***Shapes may be prepared in advance, stored in an airtight container, refrigerated or frozen, and dipped as required.

Pineapple Cream Chocolates

We were first introduced to handmade chocolates in Belgium. Hand dipped chocolates are usually more agreeable because they lack the strong and difficult to penetrate cases. I have developed Pineapple Cream Chocolates in order to offer a unique version of handmade and hand dipped Belgium Chocolates.

Ingredients

350 g or 12 oz semi-sweet chocolate, coarsely chopped

Pineapple Butter Cream
2 egg yolks
2 tablespoons water
$^1/_4$ cup sugar
pinch of cream of tartar
$^1/_4$ cup butter
1 teaspoon pineapple (or lemon) extract
$^1/_8$ teaspoon yellow food colouring
2 tablespoons pineapple jam

Coconut Coffee Paste
$^1/_2$ cup condensed milk
$1^1/_2$ tablespoons instant coffee crystals
2 teaspoons hot water
$1^1/_3$ cups desiccated coconut, unsweetened

(Makes 60)

To prepare Coconut Coffee Paste, heat condensed milk in a small heavy saucepan over medium low heat until almost boiling. Turn off heat. Dissolve coffee crystals in hot water; blend into milk. Stir in coconut, and combine thoroughly. Allow Coconut Coffee Paste to cool at room temperature.*

To make Pineapple Butter Cream, beat egg yolks until light and creamy. Mix water, sugar, and cream of tartar together in a very small heavy saucepan; bring to a boil over medium heat. (It may be necessary to tilt saucepan and contents to one side, if saucepan is not very small.) Boil vigorously (about 10 minutes) without stirring until syrup forms a soft ball. (i.e. When a small quantity of syrup is dropped into cold water it immediately forms a soft ball of toffee.) Remove from heat; pour hot syrup in a steady stream into beaten egg yolk, beating constantly with electric beater at medium high speed. Continue to beat mixture, at high speed, for another 5 minutes to produce an egg yolk cream. Refrigerate to cool (about 30 minutes).

In a medium size bowl, beat butter until creamy. Beat cooled egg yolk cream mixture into butter; beat at medium high speed (about 2 to 3 minutes) to form a smooth cream. Add extract, food colouring, and jam. Freeze Pineapple Butter Cream for ease in handling.** (Makes 2/3 cup Pineapple Butter Cream.)

To make Pineapple Cream Chocolates, shape small amounts of Coconut Coffee Paste (3/4 teaspoon) into small balls, and flatten into coins (3 mm or 1/8 inch thick). (Coconut Coffee Paste should be at room temperature to facilitate shaping.) Drop a small ball of freezer chilled Pineapple Butter Cream (1/3 teaspoon) on top of each coffee coconut coin; carefully close coffee coconut coin up and around pineapple cream; shape into a ball. Chill balls in refrigerator until ready for dipping.***

Partially melt semi-sweet chocolate over hot water; remove from heat; stir rapidly until melted.

Remove pineapple cream filled balls, a few at a time, from refrigerator. Pierce balls individually with a toothpick; dip into melted chocolate; bathe completely. Allow excess chocolate to drip off ball; transfer chocolate coated ball to a wax paper lined baking tray; remove toothpick. Immediately add finishing touches to chocolate ball by swirling chocolate on top of ball into a curl with toothpick, before dipping next ball.

Refrigerate to set.

Store Pineapple Cream Chocolates refrigerated, in an airtight container, to maintain freshness and firmness. Before serving, dust exterior of chocolates with cocoa powder if desired.

*Coconut Coffee Paste may be prepared, refrigerated, and used over a period of time to make chocolates. Coconut Coffee Paste retains its quality for at least 3 weeks.

**Pineapple Butter Cream may be frozen, and used over a period of time to make Pineapple Cream Chocolates.

***Pineapple cream filled balls may be prepared in advance, placed in an airtight container, stored in the refrigerator or freezer, and dipped as required. Allow frozen balls to thaw in refrigerator before dipping.

Chocolate Apricot Coins

Chocolate Apricot Coins are not sweet and rich like many traditional chocolates. It is important to use only "apricot halves" which make thinner and more delicious chocolates. The liqueur enhances the apricot flavour and balances the tartness of the fruit. Chocolate Apricot Oysters may be made in a similar manner, using whole dried apricots. Add a bit of marzipan and half a walnut to the interior of each apricot to make the Chocolate Apricot Oysters.

Ingredients
30 g or 1 oz or 12 dried apricots halves*, preferably small
1 1/2 tablespoons orange flavoured liqueur
85 g or 3 oz semi-sweet chocolate, chopped

(Makes 12)

Arrange apricots in a single layer, in a small heavy saucepan; sprinkle apricots with liqueur. Cover saucepan, and place over medium heat for about 3 minutes, turning once. Remove from heat; allow apricots to cool (and absorb liqueur) in covered saucepan (about 30 minutes).

Arrange flavoured apricot halves in a flat position on a wax paper lined baking tray; refrigerate to chill.

Partially melt chocolate over hot water; remove from heat; stir rapidly until chocolate is smooth and completely melted.

Using a toothpick, dip chilled apricot halves into melted chocolate; bathe completely. Allow excess chocolate to drip off apricot half. Transfer chocolate coated apricot halves to wax paper lined baking tray; make any necessary final touches to chocolate coating. Refrigerate to set.

Store Chocolate Apricot Coins in an airtight container, arranging coins in single layers separated by wax paper. Refrigerate until required.**

*Only 6 whole small apricots are required. Open whole apricots in a horizontal manner. (Remove and discard any stones.) Separate each whole apricot into 2 circular flat halves.

**If stored properly, Chocolate Apricot Coins retain their quality for several weeks.

Almond Praline

Almond Praline offers an interesting alternative to chocolates. It also makes an attractive and tasty decoration for desserts. Crushed Almond Praline may be added to ice cream or used as a decorative feature. Almond Praline is delicious dipped in melted chocolate.

Ingredients

1/3 cup almonds, whole and unblanched
1/3 cup sugar
1/4 teaspoon vegetable oil

(Makes 110 g or 4 oz)

Individually cut whole unblanched almonds lengthwise, and in a vertical manner, into four slivers.

Put sugar in a small heavy non-stick skillet; place over medium high heat. Carefully heat sugar without stirring, until sugar melts and begins to caramelize (about 5 minutes).

Add slivered nuts; stir with a fork until nuts are lightly browned and evenly coated with caramelized sugar (about 4 or 5 minutes).

Immediately turn out coated nuts onto a lightly oiled baking tray. Using 2 oiled forks, quickly separate nuts, and/or shape into clusters; cool to harden.*

Serve Almond Praline with coffee, or as tasty decoration detail, or as praline for ice cream, icing, and chocolates.

*Store Almond Praline in an airtight container, arranging praline in single layers separated by wax paper; refrigerate. If stored properly, Almond Praline retains its quality for months.

Mini Marzipan Carrots

Marzipan is another delightful alternative to chocolates. When prepared in fruit shapes, they add a charming touch of colour and originality to many presentations. Marzipan fruit may be served as a decoration, as a sweet, or both.

Ingredients

yellow food colouring as required
1/4 cup marzipan, commercial
long threads of Minted Coconut (page 227) as required

(Makes 12)

Knead food colouring into marzipan.

Take a small amount of marzipan (1 teaspoon); form into a carrot shape.

Pierce top centre of marzipan carrots with a thick toothpick; deeply insert a few long threads of Minted Coconut into each marzipan carrot to resemble carrot tops. Close marzipan in and around base of coconut threads to secure carrot tops in position.

Store Mini Marzipan Carrots in an airtight container, arranging them in layers separated by wax paper; cover marzipan closely with plastic wrap. Refrigerate until required.*

*If stored properly, Mini Marzipan Carrots retain their quality for at least 1 week.

Marzipan Cherries

Marzipan Cherries may look very real. The green Minted Coconut stems add a touch of character to the Marzipan Cherries. Marzipan fruit sweets are attractive and delicious. They may also be used as a garnish for dessert plates, a tea tray, or a cheese board.

Ingredients

1/3 teaspoon red food colouring
1/4 cup marzipan, commercial
long threads of Minted Coconut (page 227) as required

(Makes 16)

Knead red food colouring into marzipan. Take a small amount of marzipan (3/4 teaspoon); form into a cherry shape; arrange on a wax paper lined baking tray.

Pierce top centre of Marzipan Cherries with a thick toothpick; deeply insert one single long thread of Minted Coconut into each marzipan cherry to resemble a cherry stem. Close marzipan in and around base of coconut thread to secure stems in position.

Store Marzipan Cherries in an airtight container, arranging them in a single layer; cover marzipan closely with plastic wrap. Refrigerate until required.*

*If stored properly, Marzipan Cherries retain their quality for at least 1 week.

Cream Cheese Strawberries

Cream Cheese Strawberries make a colourful and delicious garnish for a tea or chocolate tray, cheese or fruit presentations, or desserts. Cream Cheese Strawberries may also be dipped in or coated with chocolate.

Ingredients

125 g or 4 oz cream cheese, softened
1/2 packet strawberry gelatin dessert powder
(packet size: 85 g or 3 oz)
1/4 teaspoon strawberry extract*
1 cup desiccated coconut, unsweetened
red food colouring* as required
1 egg white
2 1/2 tablespoons Minted Coconut (page 227)
36 whole cloves

(Makes 36)

On a large plate, use a fork to combine cream cheese, gelatin dessert powder, and extract; blend well to form a smooth and evenly coloured paste. Work in coconut; add a few drops of colouring if desired; blend well. Refrigerate mixture overnight. (It may be necessary to add more coconut if mixture is too soft, or more cream cheese if mixture is too dry for moulding.)

Take 1 teaspoon of mixture; form into a strawberry shape. (Strawberry cheese mixture should be at room temperature to facilitate shaping.)

Dip tip of stem end of cheese strawberry into egg white, and then into green Minted Coconut; shake off any excess coconut. Pierce stem end with a whole clove to form a pip.

Store Cheese Strawberries in an airtight container. Carefully arrange Cheese Strawberries in rows (and then layers), separating rows and layers with wax paper. (Make sure Minted Coconut is not transferred to bottom part of strawberries). Refrigerate or freeze until required.**

*Optional

**Cheese Strawberries may be frozen for 1 month or longer. Thaw in refrigerator before serving.

Ginned Dates

Ginned Dates served after coffee are indeed a special surprise. I serve unpitted dates as they retain their attractive shape; however, it is advisable to caution guests about the pits. On the same tray as the Ginned Dates, I arrange cocktail forks in a mini cognac glass, a small bowl for pits, and a supply of finger napkins.

Ingredients

500 g or 1 lb dates, whole and unpitted (excellent quality)

1/4 cup gin

1/4 cup vodka

(Makes about 50)

Rinse dates quickly and carefully under gently running cold water; drain well. Place dates in a plastic container with a securely fitting lid; add gin and vodka. Cover tightly; turn gently to bathe dates.

Refrigerate; turn occasionally. Allow flavours to develop over at least several days before serving dates.*

Serve Ginned Dates chilled or at room temperature.

*Ginned Dates keep for months; their flavour only improves! (If desired, add more alcohol over time.)

Dice Sugar Cubes

I have always loved the petit appearance of sugar cubes; however, they seemed to be in need of "something"; so I have created Dice Sugar Cubes. Only very small amounts of liquorice are used so that the beverage is not affected in any way.

Ingredients

1 small liquorice toffee

60* sugar cubes

(Makes 60)

Take very tiny amounts of liquorice toffee; roll into small balls about size of a pin head.

Press tiny liquorice balls, one by one, into top surface of a sugar cube to resemble one side of a dice. Repeat to produce more cubes, each representing a single side of a dice.

Arrange cubes, with decorated side up, in single layers (separated by wax paper) in an airtight container. Store in a cool dry place.**

Serve Dice Sugar Cubes, decorated side up, on a small dish or tray.

*This is about 225 g or 8 oz of regular size sugar cubes.

**If stored properly, Dice Sugar Cubes retain their quality for months. Avoid exposing Dice Sugar Cubes to moist conditions (such as a humid outdoor environment); the liquorice may run a small dark stain on the sugar cubes.

Painted Sugar Cubes

The icing in Painted Sugar Cubes does leave a residue in the beverage. Therefore, I only add a few floral Painted Sugar Cubes to a dish of Dice Sugar Cubes, as a garnish.

Ingredients

4 teaspoons Royal Icing (page 228)

1 or 2 drops green food colouring

1 or 2 drops red (or yellow) food colouring

1 or 2 drops flavourings*

35 sugar cubes

(Makes 35)

Divide icing equally into 2 portions (i.e. 2 teaspoons each); arrange portions in 2 separate small dishes. Blend green food colouring into icing arranged in one dish, and red (or yellow) colouring into other. If desired, blend in appropriate flavourings according to colour of icing (e.g. mint, strawberry, and lemon extracts for green, red, and yellow coloured icings respectively).

Use a toothpick or piping bag with a tiny opening to add small amounts of coloured icing to surface of sugar

cubes; paint creative images (such as flowers and tied parcels). Allow icing to dry.

Arrange Painted Sugar Cubes, with decorated side up, in a single layer in an airtight container. Store in a cool dry place.**

It is best to serve only a few Painted Sugar Cubes, principally as a garnish, along with regular sugar cubes or Dice Sugar Cubes.

*Optional

(e.g. mint, strawberry, and lemon or pineapple)

**If stored properly, Painted Sugar Cubes retain their quality for months.

DECORATION

Decoration is a crucial element in my cuisine, regardless of the occasion. In our home, paper doilies are taped in advance onto plates of different sizes, ready to carry individual bowls of cereal, soup, fruit, salad, and dessert to the table. Regular family meals are not an exception. Decoration has that wonderful capacity of adding a positive element to all occasions. When a menu is relatively simple, it does not need to appear unimaginative. Well decorated food makes menus more exciting, enhances guests' appreciation not only of the food, but also of the occasion, and the personal efforts of the host/hostess.

Decoration used in combination with food must be edible. There are only a few rare exceptions such as frilly "hats" on the ends of exposed bones. My repertoire of edible decorations include a variety of flora and fauna shapes, nests, bowls, and containers made of different ingredients. These choices are very appealing. Also glasses, bowls, plates, and fruit may be frosted to make colourful, textured, even tasty, decorations. Another agreeable decorating technique, suitable for food or plates, is painting with chocolate and icing, or dusting with cracked black peppercorns, cocoa powder, icing sugar, instant coffee, and coloured sugar crystals.

Skilfully folded napkins always succeed in offering a decorative touch. Tulip napkins sitting on flat plates cradle stemmed glasses gracefully. If the glass is also frosted, the entire effect is enough to render any creation particularly elegant and more tempting. Bird napkins strategically perched on a dinner or side plate delight guests.

Many decorative recipes may be prepared in advance, and appropriately stored until required. Often decorative ideas are versatile and may be used in different parts of a menu, in a variety of ways and combinations. Frequently, decorative elements bring additional shapes, textures, and flavours to a culinary experience.

Anti-clockwise (from bottom left): Pineapple Bird of Paradise (page 205)

Apple Swan

For Each Apple Swan
3 toothpicks (fine)
1 Red Delicious apple
2 dark raisins, small
¹/₄ cup orange juice

Break toothpicks in halves; set 5 halves aside; discard 1 half.

Break stem off apple; cut apple vertically in half.

Take one half of apple; place it, with cut-side down, on a flat surface. Working only at one long side of the half apple, and using a fine sharp knife, place blade of knife on top of apple but near (e.g. 5 mm or ¹/₅ inch from) outer edge. Make a shallow cut (e.g. 8 mm or ¹/₃ inch) perpendicularly towards base. Then, starting at outer edge but at a position corresponding to the end of the first cut, make another shallow cut, parallel to base of apple (or

perpendicular to first cut), so that the second cut just meets the first at the bottom of the first cut. Release and remove the slim V-shaped wedge.

Still working on same side of half apple, make a second pair of cuts slightly beyond and below first pair of cuts, to free another (and slightly larger) V-shaped wedge. Carefully repeat process to obtain a third V-shaped wedge. (Note: The wedges are of increasing size. The final wedge should be cut about half the distance towards centre, and slightly above the base of the half apple.)

Restore wedges to their original positions on one side of apple half. Push each wedge, individually about 6 mm or ¹/₄ inch, towards blossom end of apple to form a wing. Secure sections of wing to base of apple, by piercing through all 3 wedges with one half toothpick.

Repeat procedure on opposite side of apple half to create a second wing, securing wing section in place with another half toothpick.

Take other half of apple, and cut a complete slice (8 mm or ¹/₃ inch thick) off cut-side. Lay slice on a flat surface.

Clockwise (from bottom left): Making Apple Swan wings

Clockwise (from top left): Making Apple Swan head and neck

With a fine curved-bladed knife (if available), cut 8 mm or $1/3$ inch from edge, all around inside of peel edge from stem end to blossom end. Free 2 head and neck pieces; discard remaining central core section.

Using 2 half pieces of toothpick, vertically attach and secure one head and neck piece to swan's body above stem end of carved half of apple and between wings to represent head and neck of a swan. (Reserve other head and neck in case of breakage.)

With the one remaining half toothpick, attach 2 raisin eyes to sides of head in appropriate positions.

Bathe swan completely in orange juice to prevent discolouring; drain well. Place Apple Swan in an airtight container, protecting it with facial tissues; refrigerate.* (For safe storage, temporarily remove neck from body.)

When using Apple Swan, insert tufts of parsley leaves strategically around base.

*If bathed well in orange juice and stored properly, the Apple Swan retains its quality (and will not discolour) for 3 days or longer.

Pineapple Bird of Paradise

The Pineapple Bird of Paradise is very versatile, suitable for many occasions. Frequently after our Pineapple Bird of Paradise has done its salad duty, it is cleaned, wrapped in a tea towel, placed in a plastic bag, and refrigerated or frozen, ready for another occasion*. It might then make another grand entrance filled with Ginned Dates, fresh berries, fruit salad, Frosted Grapes, dessert sauces, or a variety of ice creams and sherbets.

For Each Pineapple Bird of Paradise
1 large fresh pineapple (attractive leaves,
good colour and shape)
1 maraschino cherry, cut in half from stem end to bottom
5 heavy toothpicks

Wash pineapple; drain and dry well. Place pineapple on its side allowing leaves to be displayed at their best, representing tail of the bird.

With pineapple in this horizontal position, cut off (from the top) a long horizontal slice, removing about $1/5$ of the pineapple in a single long oblong section.

Take freed oblong section; place on a cutting board with cut side down. Cut out an L-shaped piece to represent the head and neck of bird. To do so, begin cutting at top of one long side, about $2^{1}/_{2}$ cm or 1 inch from edge; continue cutting in a straight line, down length of side to within $2^{1}/_{2}$ cm or 1 inch of shorter side; make a right angle turn and continue cutting $2^{1}/_{2}$ cm or 1 inch above edge of short side. Remove the head and neck section. With half of a strong toothpick, pierce the head at an appropriate position for eyes. Add one half cherry to each side of head section, to resemble eyes. (Place cut side of cherry against pineapple.) Set head and neck piece aside. (Discard remaining half of toothpick.)

Use remainder of original oblong section (now with a right angle corner) to make 2 wings. To do this, cut section into 2 (fairly equal) triangular pieces, starting from newly produced right angle corner and cutting diagonally across section. Set wings aside.

Create a cavity in large part of pineapple (with top slice removed, but leaves still attached). Using a grapefruit knife and a strong metal soup spoon, remove pulp from interior, to within about 1 cm or $1/3$ inch of pineapple skin. (This represents the hollowed body of the bird.

To assemble Pineapple Bird of Paradise, place lower part of head and neck piece in a vertical position against inside wall of hollowed pineapple body, opposite tail end. Using 2 very heavy toothpicks, secure head and neck piece in position, with head pointing outwards and beyond body of pineapple.

Using 2 more toothpicks, attach wing pieces in a similar manner, at appropriate positions on exterior walls of hollowed pineapple, with skin side out and wing tips pointing toward tail.

Fill Pineapple Bird of Paradise with salad, fruit, or other items.

*The Pineapple Bird of Paradise freezes well for about 2 weeks. If the Bird of Paradise has been frozen, only use it in its frozen form (e.g. filled with ice cream or sherbets).

Black Olive Rabbits

I use Black Olive Rabbits as a decorative detail with hors d'oeuvres or savoury dishes.

For Each Black Olive Rabbit
1 black* olive, whole with pit

Cut a thin slice off length of olive (about 1/4 of olive).

To make a pair of rabbit ears, place removed slice (with flat side down) on a cutting board. Starting at base of slice, carefully cut out and remove a long inverted V-shaped piece from central area of slice, keeping slice intact at tip of V. Set resulting pair of ears aside. (Save the small V-shaped piece for adding to a salad.)

Place olive on a flat surface, cut side down. (Stem end of olive is considered as tail end of rabbit.) To position ears, cut a small deep slit across olive just above and diagonally towards nose end. Insert ears securely into slit, with cut-side of ears facing towards back of olive or tail end. Repeat procedure to make more Black Olive Rabbits.

Store Black Olive Rabbits in original olive brine.**

Clockwise (from top centre): Olive Rabbit

When required, remove Olive Rabbits from brine, reassembling bodies and ears if necessary. Drain on paper towels before transferring to serving plates or trays.

*Option Olives of other colours may be used.

**If stored properly, Olive Rabbits retain their quality for 2 to 3 weeks or longer.

Clockwise (from top centre): Kiwi Rabbit

Kiwi Rabbits

Kiwi Rabbits may be used to decorate drink, hors d'oeuvre, cheese trays or fruit platters.

For Each Kiwi Rabbit
1 fresh kiwi fruit, unpeeled
2 whole cloves

Use same technique as outlined for Black Olive Rabbits (see index). Trim flesh of lower back side of rabbit ears so that the ear piece may be inserted into the slit. Stem end of kiwi fruit becomes the tail, and blossom end becomes the nose. To make eyes, plant 2 whole cloves just above and on either side of nose.

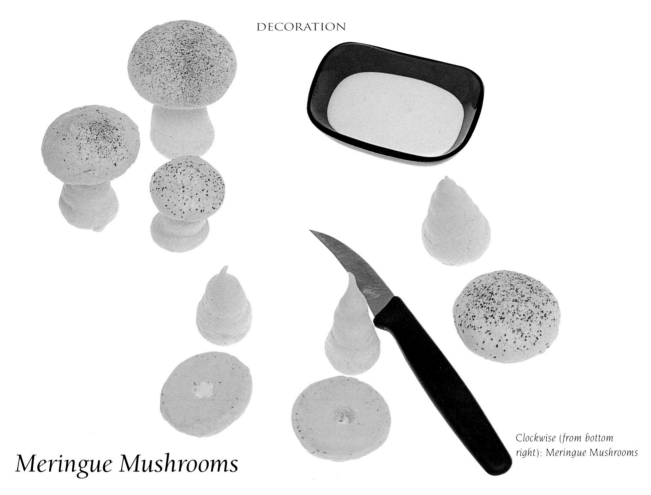

Clockwise (from bottom right): Meringue Mushrooms

Meringue Mushrooms

Meringue Mushrooms are particularly suitable for desserts or fruit trays.

For Meringue Mushrooms
1 cup castor (super fine) sugar
3 egg whites, room temperature
pinch of cream of tartar
paprika powder as required
instant coffee powder as required
marshmallow cream or Royal Icing (page 228) as required

(Makes 30)

Sift sugar. Beat egg whites with a pinch of cream of tartar until soft peaks form. Gradually add 3 tablespoons of sugar, beating constantly.

Remove beaters; pour in all remaining sugar, and fold carefully into beaten egg whites.

Line baking trays with parchment paper.

Put meringue mixture into a piping bag.

Prepare mushroom stems and caps separately on parchment paper. Pipe soft meringue into peaks of desired heights (e.g. 5 cm or 2 inches) to form mushroom stems. Then pipe soft meringue into round shapes of suitable size (e.g. diameter: 5 cm or 2 inches) to form mushroom caps. Dust caps with paprika or sifted instant coffee powder.

Bake at 140°C/275°F until meringues are crisp (about 40 minutes); turn off oven. When meringues are completely dry, remove from oven; allow to cool.

If not using immediately, arrange unattached stems and caps in an airtight container. Store in a cool dry place.*

To serve, attach caps to stems by making a little hole in middle of underside of caps with tip of a small sharp knife. Add a drop of marshmallow cream or Royal Icing, and secure caps to top of stems.

*If stored properly, Meringue Mushrooms retain their quality for months. Meringue Mushrooms may also be stored with stems and caps attached; however, more care must be taken.

207

Tomato Lotus Flower

Tomato Lotus Flowers are versatile. Use them as a garnish or as edible containers for salads, rice, or vegetables. All sizes of tomatoes may be used, from mini to large varieties. Hollowed mini Tomato Lotus Flowers become intriguing hors d'oeuvres when filled with crab meat, chopped and seasoned mushrooms, or flavoured cheese.

For Each Tomato Lotus Flower
1 tomato, round and evenly coloured

Arrange tomato with stem end down. Slit skin of tomato (with inner thick pulp attached) to divide outer firm area of tomato into quarters or 4 petals. To do this, make 2 right angled long cuts which pass through top centre and continue down and around sides of tomato to within about 1 cm or 1/3 inch of stem end (i.e. centre of base).

Carefully, release or detach each quarter section of skin from soft interior, to make a petal. Fold petals outwards and backwards to form a 4-petal lotus flower, and to expose a soft central core (ball). If desired, cut away exposed soft central ball of pulp to make a hollowed Tomato Lotus Flower. Garnish centre, or use the hollowed Tomato Lotus Flower as a container.

Potato Straw Baskets

Potato Straw Baskets are appropriate for serving individual portions of rice, small mushrooms, or vegetables. It is advisable to prepare Potato Straw Baskets 1 to 2 days before an event. (This task does require a certain amount of time, until one becomes familiar with the technique.)

For Potato Straw Baskets
1/2 kg or 1 lb potatoes, unpeeled
4 cups cooking oil

(Makes 12)

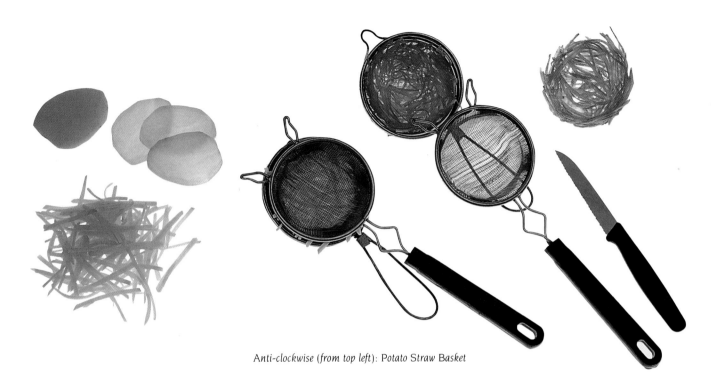

Anti-clockwise (from top left): Potato Straw Basket

Peel potatoes; shred or cut into sticks (size of fine match sticks)*. (Makes about 4 cups of cut sticks, shredded, or grated potato.)

Heat oil in a medium size saucepan or wok.

Take two small wire sieves** of slightly different sizes (diameter: 7¹/₂ cm and 8 cm or 3 inches and 3¹/₂ inches).

Dip larger sieve in hot oil, and remove. Carefully line sieve with a delicate layer of shredded potato. Use about ¹/₃ cup of potato for each basket.

Dip smaller sieve in hot oil, and remove. Fit into larger sieve, on top of potatoes, holding potatoes in place between the sieves. Press sieves gently together, keeping handles locked together.

Carefully and completely submerge sieves in hot oil; cook until potatoes are golden brown and crispy (about 3 minutes). (During cooking process, loosen grip on sieves.)

Remove sieves from hot oil. Release Potato Straw Basket from sieves, using point of a sharp thin-bladed knife if necessary. (If potato basket sticks to upper sieve only, place basket in palm of hand covered with a pot holder, and cautiously twist basket until it is freed.) Allow potato baskets to drain on paper towels.

Repeat procedure to make more Potato Straw Baskets. Cool.

Arrange Potato Straw Baskets in a covered cardboard box lined with paper towels. Store in a cool dry place until ready to use.***

*Potatoes may be shredded with a food processor, or coarsely grated (by hand). Baskets are light and delicate when prepared with potatoes shredded in a food processor, or cut by hand into matchsticks. Hand grated potatoes tend to produce a slightly heavier and denser basket.

**Sieves should be made entirely of wire if possible.

***If stored properly, Potato Straw Baskets retain their quality for more than 1 week. On the day the stored baskets are to be used, place them in an oven at 150⁰C/300⁰F for about 15 minutes to ensure crispness and fresh flavour.

Spaghetti Straw Baskets

Spaghetti Straw Baskets may be prepared for non-edible decorative purposes, or as edible containers. When making Spaghetti Straw Baskets, regardless of their final use, it is important to keep the spaghetti layer rather thin so that the basket is not too heavy. It is best to prepare Spaghetti Straw Baskets 1 to 2 days before an event, particularly if a fairly large number is required.

Arrange Fried Capers, pickles, radishes, or dates in Spaghetti Straw Baskets. Very fine Spaghetti Straw Baskets made with only a few strings of cooked spaghetti may be dipped in chocolate, to be used for desserts.

For Each Decorative (Non-edible)* Basket
15 pieces spaghetti, fine and uncooked
(length: 25 cm or 10 inches)
4 cups cooking oil

Cook spaghetti in a generous amount of boiling water until *al dente* (tender but firm). Drain; rinse with cold water; drain thoroughly.

Use exactly the same technique as outlined for Potato Straw Baskets (pages 208–209). Fry baskets for about 3 minutes.

To store, place Spaghetti Straw Baskets in a covered cardboard box lined with paper towels. Keep in a cool dry place until ready to use.**

***Option** A chewy, but edible Spaghetti Straw Basket may be prepared by using only 6 strings of cooked spaghetti. The technique is basically the same. The resulting "net type" basket can be broken apart easily with a fork and knife.

**If stored properly, decorative Spaghetti Straw Baskets retain their quality for weeks. The finer edible versions should be consumed within a few days, before they become too tough.

Pastry Blossoms

Pastry Blossoms make charming edible containers in a variety of sizes, from a mini version for hors d'oeuvres or tea party dainties to larger blossoms for desserts. Pastry Blossoms are even more delicious when lined with

Clockwise (from top left): Pastry Blossom

mayonnaise, whipped cream, or a variety of spreads. For special desserts, the exterior of the blossoms may also be painted with melted chocolate.

For Pastry Blossoms
1 recipe Basic Pastry (page 221)

(Makes 18 mini Pastry Blossoms of base diameter 3 cm or 1¼ inches, or 10 large Pastry Blossoms of base diameter 5 cm or 2 inches)

Prepare Basic Pastry according to recipe. Roll pastry out thinly (1½ mm or 1/16 inch thick) on lightly floured surface.

Measure diameter of bottom of cups of muffin (or tart) pans to be used.*

For each Pastry Blossom, cut out 6 circles of pastry slightly smaller in size than diameter of muffin cup bottom.**

Using ungreased muffin pans, line bottom of one cup with one circle of pastry. Line sides of cup with remaining 5 pastry circles in a slightly overlapping manner; dampen overlapping areas, and press lightly to seal layers of pastry together.

Repeat procedure to make more Pastry Blossoms.

Bake at 190ºC/375ºF until golden brown (about 10 minutes). Allow pastry blossoms to cool slightly in pan. Remove from pan. Allow to cool thoroughly.

Place Pastry Blossoms in a covered cardboard box; store in a cool dry place until required.***

*Any size of muffin tin may be used, from a mini (for hors d'oeuvres or petit sweets) to a jumbo size (for salads or main course).

**Option A Pastry Blossom may also be made with only 5 circles of pastry. Each circle must be the exact diameter of the bottom of the muffin cup. (Use one circle for the base, and 4 for the petals.)

***If stored properly, Pastry Blossoms may be prepared several weeks in advance of an event.

Pastry Cages

Pastry Cages greatly enhance culinary presentations. Frequently, I arrange a cage over something rather simple, such as a scoop of ice cream, a mousse, berries, fruit pieces, or mini vegetables, to give the dish a bit of pizzazz. Dessert Cages painted with touches of melted chocolate (dark or white) or frosted with flavoured dry gelatin dessert powder are irresistibly delicious as well as attractive.

For Pastry Cages
175 g or 6 oz puff pastry, commercial

(Makes 12 Pastry Cages* of base diameter 5 cm or 2 inches, and height 3 cm or 1¹/₄ inches)

Clockwise (from top left): Pastry Cage and Lattice Basket

Roll dough out into a thin (1¹/₂ mm or ¹/₁₆ inch thick) rectangle. Cut dough into long ribbons 6 mm or ¹/₄ inch wide.

Make cages around individual cups of inverted muffin pans. (Do not grease muffin pans. Muffin pans used must have cups similar in size to cages desired.)

For each cage, cut 4 equal strips* (length: diameter of base plus twice the height of the side of the muffin cup) from pastry ribbons. Carefully lay strips, one at a time, over middle and down sides of one inverted cup (ungreased) on back side of muffin pan, to resemble 8 evenly spaced spokes radiating from centre of muffin cup. (Dampen each strip as it overlaps previous strip at centre, using a fine artist's paint brush if necessary.) With the point of a small sharp knife, trim away any excess pastry ribbon which extends beyond cup.

Cut 3 more pastry strips of lengths* that would be sufficient to wrap around the circumference of cup at top, middle, and base of inverted muffin cup, allowing ends to overlap. (Strips are of slightly different lengths. It is advisable to keep a record of the measurements of the 4 different lengths of pastry ribbons required to make cage.*)

To form cage, wrap strips around exterior (of side) of inverted cup and over the 8 pastry spokes, at top, middle, and bottom of cup. Overlap ends of each strip; carefully moisten all overlapping areas of pastry; press to secure in position.

Repeat procedure to make more cages.

Bake at 190⁰C/375⁰F until golden brown (about 10 to 12 minutes). Remove from oven; allow to cool slightly before carefully loosening cages from bottom with a metal spatula and removing from muffin pan. Cool.

Carefully arrange Pastry Cages in a covered cardboard box lined with paper towels; store in a cool dry place until required.**

*For example: Muffin pans with individual cups with base diameter of 5 cm or 2 inches and depth of 3 cm or 1¹/₄ inches (and about a ¹/₄ cup capacity), may be chosen. To make Pastry Cages of a similar size, cut 4 strips 11 cm or 4¹/₂ inches long. Cut 3 more single strips: 24 cm or 9¹/₂ inches, 22 cm or 8¹/₂ inches, and 19 cm or 7¹/₂ inches each. (Note: These measurements may vary slightly even for muffin cups with an individual capacity of ¹/₄ cup.)

**If stored properly, Pastry Cages may be prepared several weeks in advance of an event.

Pastry Lattice Baskets

A Pastry Lattice Basket is actually a baked Pastry Cage arranged in its inverted position. If desired, a handle may be attached. I fill Pastry Lattice Baskets with mini vegetables, mushrooms, some light salads (e.g. Pineapple Carrot or herb leaf salads), shrimps, or hors d'oeuvres. Pastry Lattice Baskets completely painted with chocolate are exquisite for desserts, or when filled with sweets to be served with coffee.

For Pastry Lattice Baskets
Pastry Cages (page 211) as required
commercial puff pastry as required*

Prepare Pastry Cages as outlined in recipe; invert cages so that they resemble baskets.

To make handles* for baskets, roll out pastry to a thickness of 3 mm or ⅛ inch). Cut pastry into ribbons (5 mm or ⅕ inch wide). Cut lengths of pastry equal to circumference of top of muffin cup plus 1 cm or ½ inch. Wrap each strip loosely around an individual cup of an inverted muffin pan (at a position which is actually the top of the cup when the muffin pan is right side up.) Dampen overlapping areas and press together to form a ring. (One ring makes 2 handles.)

Repeat procedure to make half the number of rings as handles required. (Make extra rings in case of breakage.)

Bake at 190⁰C/375⁰F until golden brown (about 10 minutes). Remove from oven; carefully loosen rings and remove from pan as quickly as possible. When rings are cool, carefully cut each ring in half with a sharp knife to produce 2 semi-circle handles.

Store Pastry Lattice Baskets and handles separately, in a covered cardboard box. Keep in a cool dry place until required.**

It may be best to fit handles*** into or on baskets at serving time, when baskets are already filled.

*__Option__ Stems of fresh herbs may also be bent and arranged as handles for the Pastry Lattice Baskets.

**__Option__ Pastry Lattice Baskets used for desserts or for serving sweets may be partially or completely painted with melted chocolate or frosted with sugar. See Chocolate

Lattice Fruit Baskets (page 171) and Frosted Grapes (page 217) for basic techniques. When handles are also painted with melted chocolate, allow chocolate to set before securing the handles into position with additional melted chocolate. (Chocolate coated handles are usually fitted into position well in advance of baskets being used.)

***Herb handles are simply shaped, and then secured in position by poking them into the contents or the lattice work of the pastry baskets. If pastry handles are attached at time of serving (to either chocolate painted or plain Pastry Lattice Baskets), use chilled chocolate hazelnut spread or thick White Chocolate Cream to secure handles in position.

Bread Box

This is a trick I learned in Brussels. The top was cut off a loaf of bread, and the interior of the loaf was removed in one piece while keeping the outer crust intact. The interior portion was then carefully cut horizontally into thin large slices, and made into small sandwiches. Finally, the sandwiches were meticulously reassembled in layers in the bread crust container. I loved the idea, and quickly decided to adopt it, with some modifications.

For the Dickenson version, the top is sliced off the loaf to become a lid, and the interior is cut out in one piece. The resulting container resembles an empty box. However, I set the interior aside, and line the newly created Bread Box with a large oversized paper doily. A wide ribbon is then wrapped horizontally around the box and tied in an attractive bow at the front of the box. Shortly before serving, the Bread Box is filled with small sandwiches, in a loose but attractive arrangement. (The sandwiches are prepared using any type of bread.) The lid is restored to its original position on the box or propped up against the back of the box.

When I have finished using the Bread Box, the ribbon is removed (and put away for the next occasion); the paper doily liner is discarded; and the reserved interior section is returned to the Bread Box (to reinforce the box during storage). The Bread Box, covered with its lid, is placed in an airtight plastic bag, and stored in the freezer until required.

Round buns may be transformed into fascinating containers for individual servings of soups or salads. Often, I make breads of novel shapes. Turtle shapes are my favourite. Large Turtle Bread Boxes* carry hors d'oeuvres; small Turtle Bread Boxes are filled with soups and sauces.

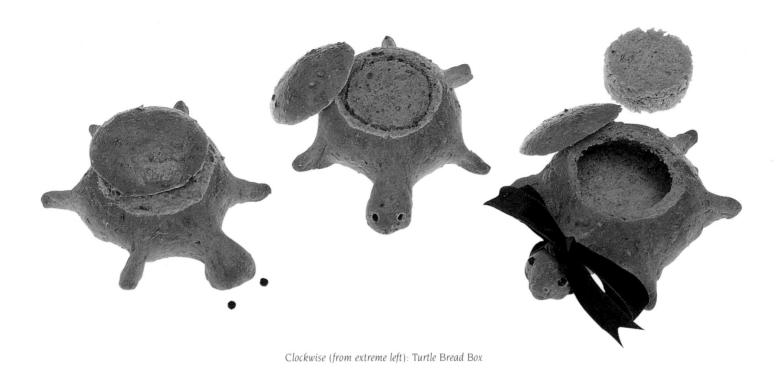

Clockwise (from extreme left): Turtle Bread Box

For Each Bread Box
1 loaf brown** bread (unsliced and with strong chewy crust)
(or see Deluxe Brown Bread: page 224)

Place loaf of bread in standing position. Cut off top of bread; set aside.

Make a deep cut all around inside edge of bread $1^{1}/_{2}$ cm or $^{2}/_{3}$ inch from crust, and to within $1^{1}/_{2}$ cm or $^{2}/_{3}$ inch of bottom.

Slip fingers in along cut, and loosen interior of loaf from bottom. Carefully remove interior, keeping it intact as one piece if possible; set aside.

To strengthen box, press soft inside bread walls and bottom towards crust; smooth inside surfaces. If not using boxes immediately, return reserved interior section and lid to Bread Box, before placing Bread Box in an airtight plastic bag until required.*** (Store Bread Box in freezer, if it is not being used.)

Use Bread Box as a container for hors d'oeuvres, salads, small buns, sandwiches, sauces, and thick soups.

*To make Turtle Bread Boxes, use the Deluxe Brown Bread recipe. After the dough has risen, divide it into portions of suitable size for the Turtle Bread Boxes desired. Shape each portion of dough into a ball, and then pull out the dough in appropriate positions to form appendages (head, tail, feet). Allow the turtle shaped dough to rest covered, for about 5 minutes. Pull out the appendages again to ensure that they retain their size and shape. (The appendages may be made slightly larger and longer than desired to allow for shrinkage during the last rising and baking.) To make Turtle Bread Boxes, cut the tops off the baked turtle shaped breads; remove their interiors as outlined in the recipe, keeping corresponding tops and bottoms together. Push whole black peppercorns into appropriate positions to form eyes. Use a skewer to make holes for nostrils.

****Option** Other types of bread may be used. However, slightly heavier brown bread varieties make the most versatile Bread Boxes.

***If the Bread Box is limited to serving dry items, and relined with a fresh paper doily for each occasion, it may be reused over an extended period of time. If kept frozen between use, Bread Boxes last for months. They may become rather dry, but that is not critical when the boxes are being used strictly as a serving container which is not to be eaten.

213

Rice Noodle Straw

Rich in texture but limited in flavour, Rice Noodle Straw is a useful filler for trays which might otherwise appear a little empty. Rice Noodle Straw is also an important component in Decadent Butterscotch Banana Noodle Soup.

For Rice Noodle Straw*
125 g or 4 oz rice vermicelli noodles, uncooked
2 cups cooking oil

(Makes 1¹/₂ litres or 1¹/₃ quarts, or 7 cups)

Drop uncooked noodles in hot oil, in very limited amounts. Cook until crispy (about 10 seconds or longer). Drain on paper towels.

Carefully arrange Rice Noodle Straw in a covered cardboard box lined with paper towels. Store in a cool dry place until required.**

Rice Noodle Straw may be used as a bed upon which to arrange hors d'oeuvres, or as a possible edible garnish for any course.

***Option** Linguine, in a cooked or uncooked form, may be fried in a similar manner to produce beautiful decorative material. Coloured varieties such as Squid Ink, Spinach, Saffron, and Tomato Chilli can be particularly exciting.

**If stored properly, Rice Noodle Straw retains its quality for weeks.

Fried Capers

Fried Capers offer a unique flavour and texture. Serve them with fish and veal dishes, or as a decorative detail.

For Fried Capers
very large bottled capers as required
1 cup cooking oil

Drain capers very well on paper towels. By hand, carefully open capers into flowers. Fry in hot oil over medium heat until crispy and golden brown (about 35 to 40 seconds). Drain Fried Capers on paper towels.

If not using immediately, gently place Fried Capers in a paper towel lined small plastic box; cover box loosely. Store in a cool dry place.*

*If stored properly, Fried Capers retain their quality for several weeks.

Carrot Flowers

Carrot* Flowers may be used as a decoration, or served as an attractive accompanying vegetable. To create contrasting centres for the Carrot Flowers, add a touch of black olive or a drop of mayonnaise. These combinations are also delicious. Raw or cooked carrots may be used to make Carrot Flowers.

For Carrot Flowers
whole and peeled fresh carrots* as required

If cooked Carrot Flowers are required**, cook whole peeled carrots until still very tender crisp. Drain; allow to cool slightly.

Cut out at least 5 (or more) long thin channels (about 4 mm or ¹/₆ inch wide) down length of whole carrot to sculpt petals; slice carrots crosswise (every 6 mm or ¹/₄ inch) to create flowers .***

***Option** Long white radish may be used to prepare cooked or uncooked White Radish Flowers. Use same techniques as outlined in recipe.

****Option** If raw Carrot Flowers are desired, do not cook the carrots. Directly cut channels in, or deeply score, peeled whole carrots; continue as outlined in the recipe.

*****Option** Flower shapes may also be made by cutting whole carrots horizontally into thin round slices (6 mm or ¹/₄ inch thick). Use a small flower shaped cookie cutter to cut out flowers.

Top and bottom (from left to right): Carrot Flowers

Chocolate Shapes

For Chocolate Shapes
coarsely chopped semi-sweet chocolate as required

Partially melt chocolate over hot water. Remove from heat; stir to melt chocolate completely.

Prepare Chocolate Shapes by:

Spooning melted chocolate evenly into shallow plastic moulds* of desired shapes; or by placing melted chocolate into a piping bag** fitted with a suitable nozzle, and piping desired shapes onto wax paper which has been arranged on baking trays. (Chocolate shapes and patterns may also be piped directly on to surface of cakes or plates.)

Allow Chocolate Shapes to set in refrigerator (e.g. about 20 minutes) before removing from moulds or peeling away wax paper.

Store Chocolate Shapes arranged in single layers separated by wax paper, in an airtight container. Refrigerate until required.***

*The moulds are available commercially.

****Option** A very small plastic bag may also be used. Cut off one bottom corner in a diagonal fashion to leave a very small hole. Pipe melted chocolate through the hole.

***If refrigerated, Chocolate Shapes retain their quality for weeks.

215

Butter Shapes

For Butter Shapes
butter as required

Prepare Butter Shapes in a number of different ways*:

Cut block of chilled butter into large slices (about 8 mm or 1/3 inch thick); arrange slices in a flat position on wax paper. Dip a petit cookie cutter of an appropriate motif in a small bowl of warm water and immediate cut out shape from large slice of butter. Arrange shape on a wax paper lined baking tray. Repeat process with warm cookie cutter to produce more shapes.

Or using soft butter, evenly fill shallow plastic moulds** of desired shapes; or place soft butter into a piping bag fitted with a suitable nozzle, and pipe desired shapes onto wax paper which has been arranged on baking trays.

Allow Butter Shapes to set in freezer (about 20 minutes) before removing from tray or moulds, or peeling away wax paper.

Store Butter Shapes arranged in single layers separated by wax paper, in an airtight container. Freeze until required.***

*Note: Also, use a small melon baller and fairly firm butter to form balls of butter. To add a special touch, roll newly formed balls in finely chopped fresh parsley, dill, edible flower petals, walnuts, or other suitable coatings. Arrange butter balls on a wax paper lined baking tray; refrigerate to set.

**The moulds are available commercially.

***If frozen, Butter Shapes retain their quality for weeks.

Frosted Glasses

The frosting technique is quick and effective. When we entertain virtually all juice glasses are frosted. Years ago, I came up with the idea of frosting glasses with flavoured dry gelatin dessert powder. The flavour of the commercial gelatin dessert powder chosen for frosting glasses should be co-ordinated with the colour and the flavour of the juice to be served. Juice appears refreshingly inviting. The sweet tangy flavour which greets the guest as the glass first

Frosted Glasses and Frosted Grapes

touches the lips is subtly sustained as the juice flows through the frost.

For Frosted Glasses
1/2 egg white
3 tablespoons sugar (salt or dry flavoured
gelatin dessert powder)
18 to 30 glasses*

(For 18 sherbet glasses, or 30 regular juice/parfait glasses)

Place egg white and sugar (salt or gelatin powder crystals) on 2 separate small plates.

Turn a glass upside down into egg white in order to coat rim (to a depth of 6 mm or 1/4 inch) with egg white. Remove glass, keeping it in an inverted position.

Immediately, transfer inverted glass to plate with sugar crystals; gently twist rim of glass into sugar, coating rim evenly with sugar crystals. Remove glass; set on its base.

Repeat process to frost remaining glasses.

Allow frosted glasses to dry. Store in a cool dry place until required.**

*Choose appropriate glasses for frosting. Frost juice glasses for special occasions. Use frosted sherbet glasses to serve sweet cold soups or some desserts. Frosted tall fluted champagne glasses are attractive for parfaits.

**Frosted glasses may be prepared 1 week or longer in advance if they are stored as outlined.

Frosted Grapes

Frosted Grapes have many versatile qualities. Guests are impressed by both the attractiveness of the grapes and the talents of the chef. Guests also enjoy touching the frosted grapes, biting into their sugar crust, and releasing the juice in an explosive crack. Dates may also be frosted in a similar manner.

For Frosted Grapes
250 g or 1/4 lb fresh grapes (preferably seedless*), stems well attached
1/2 egg white
1/2 cup sugar crystals (preferably castor*)

(Makes 300 g or 10 oz)

Wash grapes under gently running cold water; drain grapes and allow to dry thoroughly. If desired, use scissors to snip grapes into clusters of appropriate size.

Beat egg white with a fork until bubbles just begin to form.

Lightly bathe grapes with egg white, thoroughly and evenly coating each grape with egg white. (A pastry brush is useful for this task.) Remove any excess egg white.

Holding egg white coated grapes over a platter, sprinkle completely and evenly with sugar. Shake off excess sugar crystals.

Place Frosted Grapes on wax paper lined baking trays. Allow to dry, turning once or twice to ensure underside areas also dry completely. Cover Frosted Grapes loosely with wax paper; store in a cool dry place until ready to use.** Use Frosted Grapes to garnish drink or hors d'oeuvre trays, cheese or fruit presentations, salads (e.g. Pineapple Carrot Salad), or desserts.

*This is not essential.

**It is best to frost the grapes at least 1 day in advance of an event. If grapes are dried well after washing, and stored properly, Frosted Grapes maintain their quality for several days. Transfer Frosted Grapes to the refrigerator after 2 or 3 days, in order to keep them for an extended period of time.

Dough Napkin Rings

If Dough Napkin Rings are being used, guests may casually sit down at the table but once they reach for their napkin, conversation usually becomes more animated. Guests realize that what they have is not the average napkin ring, and that perhaps other exciting surprises await them during the meal which is about to begin.

For Dough Napkin Rings
1/4 recipe Basic Novelty Craft Dough* (pages 228–229)
1/4 teaspoon food colouring**
a little egg yolk**

(Makes 12*)

Prepare dough according to recipe.**

Roll dough, between the palms of both hands, into long strings (diameter: 6 mm or 1/4 inch). Cut into lengths of 15 cm or 6 inches. Braid 2 strings together; form rings, pinching ends together.

Dough Napkin Rings

Paint rings completely with egg yolk**. Place braided rings around top of individual cups (1 ring per cup) of an inverted mini muffin pan (diameter of base of mini cup: 3¼ cm or 1¼ inches).

Bake at 190⁰C/375⁰F until golden brown (about 20 minutes). Remove from oven. Allow to cool. Store Dough Napkin Rings in an airtight container; keep in a cool dry place.

To use napkin ring, roll napkins and insert them into rings.

*Novelty Dough Craft items, including napkin rings, are very hard; therefore, they are not edible. Objects made of Basic Novelty Craft Dough could possibly last for years.

**Optional If coloured napkin rings are desired, knead a small quantity of food colouring into the Basic Novelty Craft Dough. Before baking the coloured rings, paint rings with egg white instead of egg yolk. (To make colours darker, rub hot baked dough rings with a little oil, paint again with egg white, and bake for another 5 minutes.)

Tulip Napkin

Tulip Napkins are attractive in all sizes, from mini to jumbo versions.

For Each Tulip Napkin
1 square napkin, sturdy (not flimsy)
1 plate, large enough to hold Tulip Napkin

Using a hot iron, press napkin out flat.

Working on a clean flat table with right side of napkin up, fold all four corners of napkin to centre, producing a smaller square, containing 4 equal triangular shapes. By hand or with a hot iron, crease napkin along fold lines.

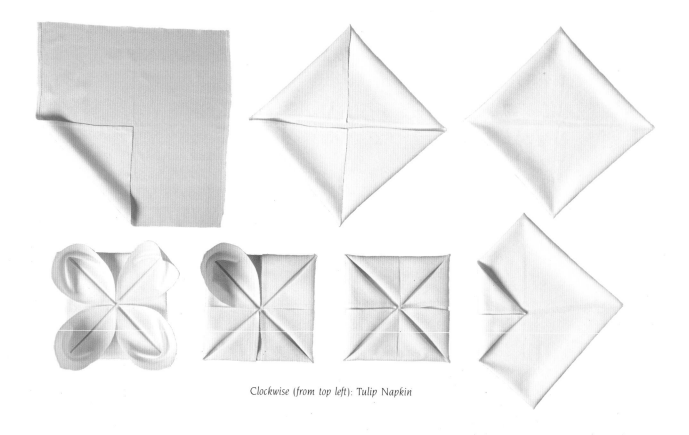

Clockwise (from top left): Tulip Napkin

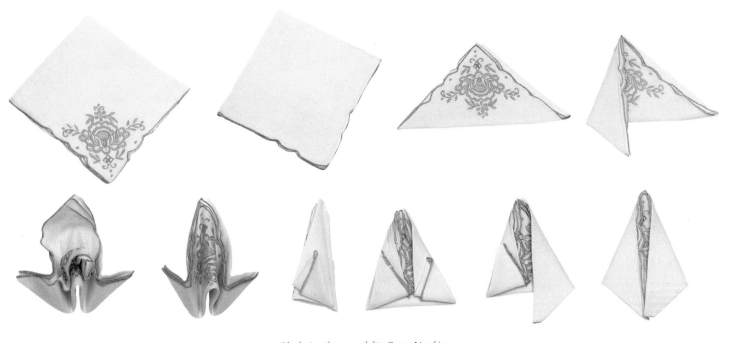

Clockwise (from top left): Swan Napkin

Place palm of one hand squarely over centre of folded napkin, pressing down securely to hold triangular shapes in position. Slip second hand under napkin to centre. Turn napkin upside down so that top of first hand is now against surface of table; slip hand out from under folded napkin.

Fold all four "new" corners to centre, producing another set of 4 equal triangular shapes. Crease or press napkin along fold lines.

Place one hand in centre of napkin, holding it firmly in position. Slip other hand under one corner; find open point of triangular piece at centre of underside of napkin. Carefully pull out loose corner (from the underside), and raise it to a standing position to form a petal of a tulip. Repeat procedure at three remaining corners to complete the Tulip Napkin.

With one hand securely in centre of Tulip Napkin, slip palm of other hand under Tulip Napkin. Carefully lift Tulip Napkin, transferring it to a flat plate ready to be fitted with a glass or dish of food for presentation at the table.

Swan Napkin

Learning the technique of how to make bird napkins was a wonderful discovery. Never having seen written instructions for these graceful birds, I would like to share one of my techniques with those who are eager to add bird napkins to their repertoire when entertaining. The instructions given are for the simplest variety of Swan Napkins. A hot iron is absolutely necessary to firmly press and secure the folds. Artistic licence may be used to create other types of bird napkins.

The colour of the birds may vary to suit the theme of the occasion. These napkins may be prepared in advance and kept on hand.

For Each Swan Napkin
1 square napkin, preferably lacy and sturdy (not flimsy)

Using a hot iron, press napkin out flat on an ironing board; fold into quarters, producing a small square; iron folds well.

Continuing to work on an ironing board, arrange folded square-shaped napkin, so that open corner of napkin (consisting of original corners), is pointing down to a 18:00 hour position. (Napkin now resembles a diamond shape.)* Fold napkin in half to produce a triangle by picking up all layers of open corner (at 18:00 hour position) and bringing them up to meet top of napkin (which is pointing upward at a 12:00 hour position). Using a hot iron, press base line firmly to crease napkin into a triangular shape. (Do not move triangular shaped napkin.)

With right hand, securely hold top of triangular napkin against ironing board (at 12:00 hour position). With left hand, fold left side of napkin to centre, placing left edge of napkin along central vertical axis of triangular napkin, with point protruding below base of triangle. Replace right hand with left; similarly, fold right side of original triangular napkin to centre. (Two edges of original triangular napkin meet along central vertical axis with points protruding below base of triangle.) Iron fold lines firmly to crease napkin in position.

Fold lower points (which protrude below base of original triangle), back up at base line, matching edges of napkin and creating a new triangular napkin shape. Iron fold lines firmly in position.

Fold new triangle in half, and backwards, along central vertical axis. Iron centre fold firmly. (Wing and body sections are visible on both sides of fold.)**

Pinch wing ends of napkin (broad end of new long triangle) together; stand napkin in a low lying horizontal position with free corner points (of original folded square napkin) on top, at narrow end of triangle. While continuing to hold wing sections together at front broad end of folded napkin, pull top corner point (at narrow end of triangle) vertically up and between wing sections. To transform raised section into a neck and head, fold section together vertically, roll tip under, and iron firmly to secure a final neck and head shape. One by one, pull remaining 3 corner points up to different heights to form tail feathers of a swan. (Never use pins or such devices to hold shaped napkin in position.)

Repeat procedure to make more Swan Napkins.

*When using an embroidered or decorated napkin, it may be necessary to turn napkin over at this stage so that a decorated corner is facing downward against surface of ironing board.

**Swan Napkins may be folded in advance of an event, and stored at this stage in their tightly folded positions. When required, stand napkins in appropriate position and arrange as outlined.

BASIC RECIPES

Basic recipes are used with great versatility as part of many different recipes and for a variety of occasions. They may appear in various forms and sizes, and for different purposes. Used independently, these basic recipes play an essential role in my daily cuisine as well as when entertaining.

Basic recipes are valuable familiar tools in the personal repertoire of every host/hostess. This section has been created for quick and efficient access.

GENERAL

Basic Crêpes

Ingredients

1 egg

1 egg yolk

1¹/₂ teaspoons sugar

¹/₂ cup flour

³/₄ cup milk

2 tablespoons butter or margarine, melted

vegetable oil as required

(Makes 32 crêpes of diameter 7¹/₂ cm or 3 inches,
or 21 crêpes of diameter 12 cm or 4¹/₂ inches,
or 10 crêpes of diameter 15 cm or 6 inches)

To make crêpe batter, beat together egg, egg yolk, sugar, flour, and ¹/₄ cup of the milk with an electric mixer at medium speed, until mixture is well blended. Beat in melted butter and remaining milk to form a smooth batter. Refrigerate for at least 30 minutes before using.* (Makes about 1¹/₃ cups of crêpe batter.)

To make larger crêpes, place a very lightly oiled crêpe pan (of appropriate diameter) over medium high heat. Pour only enough batter** into pan to form a thin even layer by tilting and rotating pan. (To make small crêpes, drop spoonfuls of batter on a lightly oiled skillet, and quickly spread batter from centre in a circular fashion, using underside of a spoon.) Cook until bottom side of crêpes are golden brown. Carefully free sides of crêpes; turn over; lightly brown second side. Remove crêpes from pan, stacking crêpes on a plate.

Place plate of crêpes in a sealed plastic bag. Refrigerate crêpes if they are to be used later. (Usually, Basic Crêpes are best used immediately or within a few hours of being cooked.)

*Product may be frozen at this stage.

**Adjust the amount of batter used according to the size of the crêpe desired: Use about 2 teaspoons batter to make 1 small appetizer crêpe of diameter 7¹/₂ cm or 3 inches. Recipe makes about 32 crêpes.

Use about 1 tablespoon batter to make 1 small hors d'oeuvre crêpe, suitable for a crêpe sachet of diameter 12 cm or 4¹/₂ inches. Recipe makes about 21 crêpes.

Use about 2 tablespoons batter to make 1 crêpe of diameter 15 cm or 6 inches. Recipe makes about 10 crêpes which may be used for dessert or Vegetarian Omelettes in Crêpe Bowls.

Basic Pastry

Ingredients

1 cup flour

pinch of salt

¹/₃ cup shortening

2¹/₂ to 3 tablespoons ice water

(Makes 1 pie crust of diameter 20 to 23 cm
or 8 to 9 inches)

In a medium bowl, mix together flour and salt. Add in shortening using a pastry blender or wire whisk, until consistency resembles that of crumbs.

Add ice water, 1 tablespoon at a time, tossing mixture lightly with a fork. Gently press pastry into a ball.*

Flatten ball, and carefully roll out on a lightly floured surface, always placing rolling pin in centre of dough and rolling out towards edges with light, quick, brisk movements. Roll pastry to desired thickness (usually about 3 mm or ¹/₈ inch).

Cut and arrange dough as required for recipe.*

*Dough may be refrigerated or frozen at this stage.

Basic Pasta Dough

Ingredients

1¹/₂ cups flour

2 eggs

¹/₄ teaspoon salt

1¹/₂ tablespoons olive oil

extra flour for kneading as required

(Makes about 350 g or 12 oz,
or 6 large servings with a main course,
or 4 main course servings)

Place 1¹/₂ cups flour in large bowl*; make well in centre.

Beat egg, salt, and oil together**. Pour egg mixture into the well. Gradually pull flour into egg mixture, a little at a time.

When dough forms ball, turn out on a clean floured surface. Knead until smooth (about 5 minutes).

Cover dough with plastic wrap; refrigerate for at least 30 minutes, allowing dough to rest.

Roll dough out into paper thin sheets, with either a pasta dough roller or by hand.

Cut sheets of dough into strands of desired width. Hang strands over a clothes drying or towel rack, at room temperature. Allow pasta to dry (about 20 minutes).***

Just before serving pasta, add 1 teaspoon oil to a generous amount of salted boiling water in a large pot. Drop pasta into boiling water; bring water back to a gentle boil. Cook pasta to *al dente* or until tender but firm (about 1 to 3 minutes, depending on the width of the pasta).

Remove pot with pasta from heat. (If not serving pasta immediately, add 1 cup or more of very cold water to stop cooking. Allow pasta to remain in the warm water for a few minutes, until ready to serve.)

Drain pasta well; toss with butter or Garlic Butter to taste. Add additional salt if desired.

*Food processor option: Combine flour and salt in a food processor. In a separate bowl, mix together eggs and oil (and other ingredients required for specialty pastas). With food processor operating, add egg mixture to flour and salt. Process until dough begins to form a ball (about 2 minutes). Remove dough; turn out on a clean floured surface; knead dough, and proceed as outlined.

**At this stage, it may be necessary to add other ingredients required for specialty pastas.

***Dried pasta strands may be wrapped as a bundle in wax paper, placed in large airtight shallow boxes, and frozen until required.

Pasta Choices

To prepare pasta of different flavours*, use the Basic Pasta Dough recipe, making appropriate additions as outlined in the recipes.

Cracked Black Peppercorn Pasta

(Makes about 350 g or 12 oz, or 6 large servings with a main course)

Replace half of the olive oil in the Basic Pasta Dough recipe with sesame oil (i.e. about 2 teaspoons). Add $1^1/_2$ to 3 teaspoons (according to taste) freshly cracked black peppercorns to the flour mixture.

Lime Thyme Pasta

(Makes about 350 g or 12 oz, or 6 large servings with a main course)

Using the Basic Pasta Dough recipe, add $^2/_3$ to 1 teaspoon dried thyme and 2 to 3 tablespoons grated lime peel to the flour mixture.

Garlic Spinach Pasta

(Makes 300 g or 10 oz, or 5 large servings with a main course)

Make a spinach paste by cooking about 50 g or 2 oz fresh spinach leaves. Drain well in a sieve, pressing firmly to remove all possible water and juice; discard liquid. Blend pressed leaves in a blender to form a smooth spinach paste. (Makes $^1/_4$ cup.)

Using half of the Basic Pasta Dough recipe, add 1 teaspoon garlic powder to the flour, and then add $^1/_4$ cup prepared spinach paste and 1 to $1^1/_2$ tablespoons crushed fresh garlic to the egg mixture. Draw in about $^1/_4$ cup extra flour during kneading process.

Tomato Chilli Pasta

(Makes 225 g or 8 oz, or 4 large servings with a main course)

Using half of the Basic Pasta Dough recipe, add 1 to $1^1/_2$ tablespoons tomato paste and $1^1/_2$ to 2 tablespoons chilli sauce to the egg mixture. Draw in about 3 tablespoons extra flour during kneading process.

Violet Caviar Pasta

(Makes about 200 g or 7 oz, or 10 small portions)**

Use half of the Basic Pasta Dough recipe, omitting the salt. Add 3 tablespoons lumpfish caviar (with ink) to the egg mixture.

Squid Ink Pasta

(Makes about 175 g or 6 oz, or 8 small portions)**

Using half of the Basic Pasta Dough recipe, add $2^1/_2$ to 3 teaspoons squid ink to the egg mixture.

Double Sesame Pasta

(Makes about 375 g or 13 oz, or 6 large servings with a main course dish)

Replace half of the olive oil in the Basic Pasta Dough recipe with sesame oil (i.e. about 2 teaspoons). Add $^1/_4$ cup dark roasted sesame seeds to the egg mixture.

Orange Pasta

(Makes about 350 g or 12 oz, or 6 large servings with a main course)

Using the Basic Pasta Dough recipe, add $^1/_3$ cup coarsely grated orange peel to the flour mixture; add 1 tablespoon lemon extract and 2 tablespoons orange juice to the egg mixture.

Saffron Pasta

(Makes about 350 g or 12 oz, or 6 large servings with a main course)

Soak $^1/_4$ teaspoon*** very finely chopped saffron threads in 2 tablespoons hot water for 30 minutes. Add saffron mixture to Basic Pasta Dough recipe along with the egg mixture. If desired, also replace half of the olive oil in the Basic Pasta Dough recipe with sesame oil.

*Many of these pastas may be served in combinations of 2 or 3 different varieties. They may be served with commercial varieties as well.

**These pastas are best served in small portions, or in combination with other pastas, because of their distinctive flavour and colour.

***If saffron is not strong in flavour, an increased quantity may be required.

Pirozhki (Ravioli, Wanton) Dough

Pirozhki dough may also be used to make ravioli or wanton dough. For best results, a pasta roller machine should be used to roll the ravioli and wanton dough out very thinly.

Ingredients
2/3 cup flour

pinch of salt

2 teaspoons sugar

3 to 4 tablespoons potato water*

1 teaspoon vegetable oil

(Makes sufficient dough for 70 mini pirozhki dough circles of diameter 3¹/₂ cm or 1¹/₂ inches, or 18 ravioli dough circles of diameter 8 cm or 3 inches, or 12 to 14 wanton squares 10 cm or 4 inches square)

To prepare dough, put flour, salt, sugar, potato water, and oil together in a small bowl; combine thoroughly with a fork. Turn dough out on a clean surface; knead dough until soft and elastic (about 10 minutes).**

Roll dough out very thinly*** on a lightly floured surface, or with a pasta roller machine. Cut dough as desired. (Always keep cut dough closely covered with plastic wrap to prevent drying.)

*Use water in which potatoes have been cooked.

**Dough may be frozen at this stage.

***For pirozhki and ravioli, dough should be just thicker than "paper thin" (1¹/₂ mm or ¹/₁₆ inch). For wanton squares, roll out dough as thinly as possible.

Chelo Rice

This recipe has been developed from an Iranian technique where the rice is half cooked and then steamed with butter. I serve a combination of Chelo Rice and Doubly Dark Wild Rice, prepared separately, and then folded together. Other gourmet rice dishes are also possible.*

Ingredients
2¹/₂ cups long grain rice (e.g. Basmati)

cold water as required

8 cups hot water

2 tablespoons salt

¹/₄ cup** melted butter or Garlic Butter

(Makes 7¹/₂ cups)

Wash rice several times in cold water. Cover rice generously with cold water. (Rice should be 2¹/₂ cm or 1 inch below surface of water.) Soak rice for 45 minutes. Drain rice; discard water.

Pour hot water into a large saucepan; add salt; bring to a boil. Pour rice in a steady stream into boiling water. Allow to boil, uncovered, for about 6 minutes, stirring occasionally. Drain rice very well.

Place 2 tablespoons melted butter in bottom of a heavy medium size saucepan. Add drained rice, shaping it into the form of a cone. Drizzle remaining butter over top of rice.

Cover saucepan tightly. Place over very low heat until rice is just tender (about 7 to 20 minutes, depending on "fluffiness" desired). Toss rice lightly with a fork.

***Options** To make a Wild Rice Combo, add sautéed and seasoned sliced mushrooms (2 cups), parboiled raisins (³/₄ to 1 cup), Toasted Almonds (¹/₂ cup), and soya sauce (1¹/₂ tablespoons). (Ingredients and quantities may be added according to taste.)

For Chelo Rice with Pomegranate Pearls and Toasted Almonds, just before serving, toss 1 cup fresh pomegranate beads and ¹/₃ cup Toasted Almonds with 1 recipe of cooked Chelo Rice.

**Add as desired.

Doubly Dark Wild Rice

Serve Doubly Dark Wild Rice in small quantities as a garnish, an accompaniment, or in a stuffing for roast chicken or cornish hen.

Ingredients
¹/₂ cup wild rice, washed well

¹/₃ cup cold water

1 teaspoon dark beef bouillon cube, very finely crushed

(Makes ³/₄ cup)

To prepare Doubly Dark Wild Rice, place wild rice and cold water in a small saucepan; cover; bring to a boil over medium heat. Immediately reduce heat and simmer (covered) until some grains just begin to crack, and to show a bit of white interior (about 20 minutes). Remove from heat. If necessary, drain and discard any liquid.

Add crushed bouillon cube to drained wild rice; stir for several minutes until bouillon dissolves, and is very well blended into rice.

Garlic Butter

Use Garlic Butter to make garlic bread, or to add to freshly cooked vegetables, pasta, and rice.

Ingredients
1 cup soft butter

1 teaspoon fresh garlic, grated or crushed

2 tablespoons fresh parsley, finely chopped

(Makes 1 cup)

Cream all ingredients together. Place in an airtight container; refrigerate or freeze.

Orange Mustard Butter

Add Orange Mustard Butter to freshly cooked vegetables (including boiled potatoes), pasta, and rice.

Ingredients

$1/2$ cup soft butter
$1^1/4$ teaspoons French mustard
1 tablespoon orange peel, grated

(Makes $1/2$ cup)

Cream ingredients together thoroughly. Refrigerate or freeze in an airtight container.

Waffled Toast

Toast is the perfect accompaniment for dishes such as smoked salmon, caviar, and savoury mousses. For a more interesting presentation, I have come up with Waffled Toast. Although Waffled Toast is usually presented in triangular pieces, novel shapes may be suitable for particular occasions. If the Waffled Toast is served unbuttered, butter (plain or flavoured) may be offered at the table.

Ingredients

sliced bread (preferably white) as required
butter* as required

Remove crusts from bread.** If desired, butter bread on both sides.

Carefully arrange prepared slices on a pre-heated grill of waffle iron. (Pay particular attention to how bread is placed on grill in order to ensure that the resulting pattern is balanced.)

Close lid of waffle iron. Grill bread until golden brown (about $1^1/2$ to 2 minutes). Remove bread from waffle iron, transferring to wire cooling racks.

If necessary, cut into suitable pieces before serving.

*Optional

**Option

With sharp cookie cutters, cut out shapes (e.g. hearts, circles, maple leaves, animals) from bread slices.

Deluxe Brown Bread

This recipe incorporates all those tastes which I would like to find in one brown bread recipe. These include wholewheat flour, chopped orange rind, walnuts, brown sugar, plus a touch of ginger and anise seed. This is a slightly heavier bread, which makes it particularly suitable for preparing Bread Boxes or bowls.

Ingredients

1 teaspoon instant yeast
$1/2$ cup warm water
$1/4$ cup orange juice
$1^1/2$ cups all purpose flour
$1/2$ cup wholewheat flour
$1^1/2$ teaspoons salt
1 tablespoon brown sugar
$1/2$ teaspoon ginger powder
1 teaspoon anise seed
$2^1/2$ teaspoons orange rind, finely chopped
$2^1/2$ tablespoons walnuts, finely chopped
1 tablespoon margarine, soft
1 egg, beaten

*Sprinkle yeast over $1/4$ cup warm water; set aside for 5 to 10 minutes.

Combine remaining $1/4$ cup water with orange juice; set aside.

In a large bowl, combine all purpose and wholewheat flour, salt, sugar, ginger, anise seed, orange rind, and walnuts. Incorporate margarine with a fork. Using a wooden spoon, stir in yeast mixture and orange juice mixture.

Turn dough out onto a lightly floured surface; knead until smooth and elastic (about 15 minutes).

Shape dough into a ball. Place in a lightly greased bowl, turning once to grease surface of dough. Cover; let rise in a warm place until double in bulk (about 1 hour).

Punch down dough. Divide and shape dough as desired.

Place formed dough on a greased baking tray or into a well greased loaf pan. Cover; let rise in a warm place until double in bulk (about 90 minutes for 1 large loaf, or 40 minutes for 12 small rolls).

Brush with beaten egg. Bake at 190°C/375°F until done (about 40 to 50 minutes for one large loaf, or 20 minutes for a dozen small rolls).

*Option: A bread making machine (functioning on the "wholewheat" setting) may be used for this recipe. If bread of a particular shape or size is desired, remove dough from machine after the dough cycle, and continue as outlined in recipe.

Mini Pita Bread

Ingredients

$1^1/2$ cups flour*
$1/2$ teaspoon salt
$1/2$ tablespoon instant yeast
$1/2$ cup warm water

(Makes 70)

In a bowl, mix together flour, salt, and yeast. Gradually add water, combining water and dry ingredients (with one hand) to produce a pliable pita dough. (Add an extra drop of water if necessary.)

Turn dough out onto a lightly floured surface; knead until smooth and elastic (about 8 minutes or longer). (Draw in more flour if necessary.)

Place dough in a clean dry bowl; cover; let rise in a warm place until double in bulk.

Pre-heat oven to 240°C/475°F. Arrange heavy baking trays in upper third part of oven.

Roll dough out on a lightly floured surface to a thickness of 2 mm or $1/12$ inch, or use a pasta maker machine to roll dough.

Cut circles (diameter: 4 cm or $1^1/2$ inches) out of dough. Arrange dough circles on lightly floured baking trays; cover with a tea towel; let rise in a warm place for about 10 to 15 minutes.

Using a pancake flipper and working very quickly (within a few seconds), transfer as many dough circles as possible to hot trays located in oven. (Oven must not be allowed to cool.) Bake until Mini Pita Bread puffs up like inflated balloons** and is golden brown (about 2 minutes).

Promptly remove baked pita bread from oven, arranging immediately between clean damp tea towels to prevent bread from drying and to restore moisture.

Repeat process until all the bread is baked.

When Mini Pita Bread is cool, store in airtight plastic bags.***

*Option

For Wholewheat Mini Pita Bread, use 1 cup all purpose flour and $1/2$ cup wholewheat flour. Add about 1 extra tablespoon of water when mixing dough.

**A few mini breads may not puff; these usually can be pried or slit opened with the tip of a small sharp knife.

*** Pita bread may be stored in the freezer at this stage. It retains its quality for several weeks.

Garlic Bread

Ingredients

French bread or baguettes* as required

Garlic Butter (page 223) as required

Cut loaf of bread into slices (2 cm or $3/4$ inch thick). Lay out slices side by side so that bread may be easily reassembled into its original loaf.

Butter upper surface of each slice generously with Garlic Butter. Restore slices to their original positions to recreate loaf.

Wrap reassembled buttered loaf in aluminum foil (dull side out).** Heat in oven at 180^0C/350^0F until hot (about 15 to 20 minutes). Serve immediately.

*It is best to use French bread or baguettes; however, other types of bread may also be used.

**The Garlic Bread may be frozen at this point for up to several weeks. Remove from freezer at least 1 hour before required.

Marinade for Beef or Pork

Ingredients

For 1 kg of Meat

$1^1/2$ teaspoons fresh garlic, finely chopped

$1^1/2$ teaspoons fresh ginger root, finely chopped

$1/4$ teaspoon black peppercorns, crushed

$2/3$ cup red* wine

Rub meat with garlic, ginger, and pepper. Place in a glass baking dish; bathe with wine. Cover dish with plastic wrap. Place in refrigerator.

Marinate beef for up to 3 days, and pork for up to 36 hours, turning meat several times a day.

Remove meat from marinade, and drain well** before using.

*Option

White wine may also be used for pork.

**For convenience, beef and pork may be marinated and kept on hand in the freezer.

Marinade for Chicken

Ingredients

For 1 kg of Chicken

$1/2$ to 1 teaspoon* fresh garlic, grated

1 teaspoon fresh ginger root, grated

$1/3$ teaspoon black peppercorns, crushed

$2/3$ cup dry white wine**

Rub chicken with garlic, ginger, and pepper. Place in a glass baking dish; bathe with wine. Cover dish with plastic wrap. Place in refrigerator.

Marinate chicken for at least several hours (or up to 36 hours), turning occasionally.

Remove chicken from marinade, and drain well*** before using.

*Add quantity preferred.

****Option**

3 tablespoons lemon juice mixed with 1 tablespoon water may be used.

***For convenience, chicken may be marinated and kept on hand in the freezer.

Oriental Marinade

Ingredients

1 teaspoon fresh garlic, finely chopped

2 teaspoons fresh ginger root, finely chopped

1 teaspoon fresh mint, finely chopped

1 teaspoon lemon rind, grated

1 tablespoon red wine vinegar

1 tablespoon olive oil

$1/4$ cup honey

$1/3$ cup teriyaki sauce

$1/3$ cup oyster sauce

(Makes 1 cup)

Combine all marinade ingredients*. Pour over meat or fish; refrigerate for 4 hours or longer, turning meat or fish occasionally.

*Oriental Marinade may be prepared and kept on hand in the refrigerator for 1 week, or in the freezer for months.

Fish Poaching Bath

Ingredients
2 cups water

3/4 cup dry white wine

1/4 cup onion, sliced

1/4 cup carrot, sliced

1 teaspoon salt

1/4 teaspoon dried tarragon

1/2 teaspoon lemon zest

1/2 teaspoon fresh ginger root, finely chopped

1/2 teaspoon fresh garlic, crushed

1/2 teaspoon fresh dill, finely chopped

1 tablespoon fresh parsley, chopped

In a large deep skillet or electric frying pan, prepare poaching bath by combining all ingredients. Bring mixture to boil; cover; reduce heat and allow mixture to simmer for 5 minutes.

Carefully arrange fish in skillet. Bring poaching bath back to a boil; cover tightly and reduce heat. Allow fish to simmer very gently, turning fish occasionally to ensure even cooking. Poach fish until flesh flakes with a fork.

Remove fish from skillet; drain well.

Seasoned Flour

Ingredients
1 cup flour

1 teaspoon salt

1/2 teaspoon black peppercorns, crushed

1 1/2 teaspoons curry powder

1/2 teaspoon ground nutmeg

1/2 teaspoon garlic powder

1/2 teaspoon ginger powder

Combine ingredients together thoroughly.

Dust or coat desired product with Seasoned Flour mixture, shaking off any excess.

If appropriate, store any remaining Seasoned Flour in an airtight heavy plastic bag in freezer.

Pesto

Ingredients
1/4 cup toasted pine nuts

1/4 cup fresh (not bottled) Parmesan cheese, grated

1 cup fresh basil leaves, firmly packed

1/2 teaspoon fresh garlic, crushed

1 1/4 cups olive oil

(Makes 1 1/2 cups)

Blend pine nuts, cheese, basil, garlic, and half the oil (i.e. 5/8 cup) in a blender until smooth.

Gradually add the remaining oil in a thin stream while blender is operating. Blend until mixture is well combined.

Place in an airtight jar. Store in refrigerator for up to 2 weeks, or in freezer for 2 or 3 months.

Preserved Vine Leaves

Ingredients
1 tablespoon salt

12 cups boiling water

1/2 kg fresh vine leaves

Bring salt and water to a boil in a very large pot.

Add vine leaves, 12 at a time, pushing them down under surface of water with a wooden spoon. Bring water back to boil; cook for 5 minutes.

Remove vine leaves from cooking water; drain, separate, and allow to cool on large platters.

Remove cooking water from heat. Set aside to cool.

Carefully arrange vine leaves, in a flat position, one on top of the other, in a large airtight plastic container. Cover vine leaves completely with cooled salted cooking water. Place a small plate on surface of vine leaves to keep leaves submerged.

Refrigerate until required.*

*If refrigerated, Preserved Vine Leaves retain their quality for 1 month or longer.

Toasted Almonds*

Toasted Almonds are delicious in salads and stuffings, as well as a garnish for sweet or savoury dishes.

Ingredients
whole unblanched almonds as required

Working on a cutting board and using a sharp knife, individually cut unblanched almonds, in a vertical manner, into four slivers. Arrange slivered almonds, well separated, on a baking tray.

Place tray of slivered almonds in oven, 15 cm or 6 inches below a pre-heated broiler. Watch carefully and turn almonds frequently to ensure even toasting and colouring. Grill until nuts are golden brown, or until almost to the desired degree of toasting. Remove from oven immediately. (Almonds continue to roast slightly when removed from oven.)

Allow nuts to cool on baking tray. Store Toasted Almonds refrigerated in an airtight container.**

*Other nuts (e.g. pine nuts, hazelnuts) may be toasted in a similar manner.

**If refrigerated, Toasted Almonds retain their quality for months.

Toasted Coconut

Toasted Coconut is delicious in many recipes, or as a garnish. Shredded fresh coconut or dried commercial varieties, unsweetened or sweetened, all make wonderful Toasted Coconut. The choice of coconut is a matter of personal preference.

Ingredients
shredded, feathered, or
desiccated coconut as required

Spread coconut in a thin layer on a baking tray. Place in oven, 15 cm or 6 inches below a pre-heated broiler.

Watch carefully and turn coconut frequently to ensure even toasting and colouring. Grill until coconut is golden brown, or almost to the desired degree of toasting. Remove from oven immediately. (Coconut continues to roast slightly when removed from oven.)

Allow Toasted Coconut to cool on baking tray.

Store Toasted Coconut refrigerated in an airtight container.*

*If refrigerated, Toasted Coconut retains its quality for months.

Minted Coconut

Minted Coconut adds a final touch of colour and flavour to many recipes and presentations.

Ingredients
1 teaspoon water
$1/5$ teaspoon mint extract
$1/5$ teaspoon green food colouring
$1/2$ cup shredded, feathered, or desiccated coconut

(Makes $1/2$ cup)

Combine water, extract, and colouring in a jar (size: 250 ml or 8 oz) with a securely sealing lid.

Add coconut to liquid mixture in jar; close jar securely; shake vigorously until the coconut is uniform in colour.

Keep Minted Coconut in a well sealed jar. Store in refrigerator or freezer.*

*Minted Coconut retains its quality for several weeks in the refrigerator, or for months in the freezer.

Lady Fingers

Serve Lady Fingers* as biscuits, or use in such recipes as mousse cakes or Tiramisu.

Ingredients
$1/3$ cup flour, sifted
pinch of salt
2 eggs, separated
3 tablespoons sugar
$1/2$ teaspoon vanilla extract**

(Makes 30 traditional Lady Fingers 7 cm or 3 inches long and $2^1/2$ cm or 1 inch wide, or 40 thin round biscuits of diameter 5 cm or 2 inches)

If necessary***, line baking trays with parchment paper. Using a pencil, outline shapes of biscuits desired on parchment paper. Turn paper over to prevent pencil line from being transferred to biscuits; set aside.

Sift flour and salt together; set aside.

Whip egg yolks with 1 tablespoon sugar until creamy. Beat in vanilla extract**.

Beat egg whites until soft peaks begin to form; gradually add remaining 2 tablespoons sugar to produce a stiff meringue.

Using a rubber spatula, carefully fold meringue into egg yolk mixture. Gradually fold in flour and salt. (Makes about 2 cups batter.)

Spread Lady Finger batter into shapes traced on parchment paper, or pipe batter directly onto buttered and lightly floured baking trays.

Bake at 190°C/375°F, with oven door slightly ajar, until biscuits are golden brown and surface springs back to the touch (7 to 8 minutes for smaller biscuits, longer for traditional Lady Finger biscuits). Allow biscuits to cool for a few minutes before peeling away parchment paper or removing biscuits from baking trays.

*When making Lady Fingers for a particular recipe, prepare biscuits of a size, and perhaps shape, suitable for the container being used. This is particularly helpful when preparing Tiramisu in cups or bowls.

**Option
Add $1/2$ teaspoon mocha extract for coffee flavoured Lady Fingers. Coffee flavoured Lady Fingers are excellent for Tiramisu.

***The chef may require guidelines for the shape of the biscuits, or it may be necessary to spread the batter. However, if this is not the case, the batter may be piped directly onto buttered and lightly floured baking trays.

Avocado Sherbet

This is a basic sherbet recipe. To prepare other fruit sherbets, simply replace the avocado pulp with that of another appropriate fruit (e.g. mango). To make a creamier sherbet which maintains a distinct fruit flavour, add a little more whipping cream (i.e. up to an additional $1/4$ cup).

Ingredients
1 cup avocado pulp, puréed
1 teaspoon lime (or lemon) juice
$1/4$ teaspoon almond extract
$1/3$ cup sugar
$1/8$ teaspoon salt
$1/4$ teaspoon ginger powder
$1/2$ cup coconut milk
$1/4$ cup water
1 egg white
$1/4$ cup whipping cream, chilled

(Makes almost $1/2$ litre or 1 pint)

Mix together avocado purée, lime juice, and extract; set avocado mixture aside.

In a small heavy saucepan, combine sugar, salt, ginger, coconut milk, and water; simmer for 5 minutes; remove from heat.

Beat egg white until stiff. Gradually pour the hot sugar mixture into the beaten egg white while continuing to beat at high speed.

Fold avocado mixture into egg white mixture. Pour into a rectangular glass baking dish; cover with plastic wrap; place in freezer until crystals form around edges, but mixture is still mushy.

Whip chilled cream until firm peaks form. Remove mushy avocado mixture from freezer; break up mixture with a fork. Fold whipped cream into frozen crystals.

Pour creamy avocado mixture into a chilled rectangular glass baking dish; cover with plastic wrap; return to freezer. Freeze creamy avocado mixture until crystals begin to form around the edges of the baking pan. Remove from freezer.

Transfer partially frozen mixture to a chilled bowl (arranged in an ice bath); beat thoroughly with chilled beaters until mixture is smooth but not melted.

Place Avocado Sherbet in a chilled airtight plastic container, covering surface of sherbet closely with plastic wrap. Return immediately to freezer.

Before scooping and/or serving, allow sherbet to soften slightly in refrigerator.

Royal Icing

Besides decorating cookies and cakes with Royal Icing, I use it for making Painted Sugar Cubes. Pre-fabricated Royal Icing decorative numbers and designs may be prepared on wax paper, removed, and set aside for the appropriate occasion. Royal Icing is also an edible and long lasting adhesive for attaching Meringue Mushroom caps to their stems.

Ingredients
1 tablespoon egg white

$1/2$ cup icing sugar, sifted

$1/8$ teaspoon lemon juice

$1/8$ teaspoon extract (of choice)

$1/8$ teaspoon food colouring (of choice)

With a fork, whip egg white until foamy. With an electric beater on medium speed, gradually add sifted icing sugar to egg white.* Beat in lemon juice, food colouring, and extract as desired.**

Keep Royal Icing closely covered with plastic wrap.

Use in a variety of ways for decorating cakes and cookies, or for making pre-fabricated icing decorations***.

*Add more sugar (another $1/4$ cup) to make a stiffer icing (e.g. for pre-fabricated decorations).

**To make an icing that may be used for drawing (with a piping bag), add enough cold water to allow icing to fall in a steady stream from a spoon.

***Pre-fabricated icing decorations retain their quality for weeks if stored in an airtight container in a cool dry place. (Allow decorations to dry thoroughly before storing.)

White Chocolate Cream

Serve White Chocolate Cream with fruit, cake, pastry, or sweet crêpes. Use it as an icing, coulis, or an adhesive for holding elements in position. When used as an icing for cakes, remove the chocolate cream covered cakes from the refrigerator about 15 minutes before serving to allow the white chocolate icing to soften.

Ingredients
$1/4$ cup whipping cream

60 g or 2 oz white chocolate , chopped

(Makes $3/4$ cup)

Pour cream into a small heavy saucepan. Stirring regularly, bring cream to a boil over medium heat. Remove immediately from heat.

Add chocolate, stirring constantly until chocolate melts and mixture is smooth. Transfer mixture to a bowl.

Allow mixture to cool at room temperature until it begins to thicken (about 20 minutes). Arrange bowl with chocolate mixture in a second bowl of ice and water. Beat chocolate mixture, at high speed, over the ice bath for about 1 minute, or until mixture becomes thick and fluffy (resembling consistency of cake batter). If White Chocolate Cream is to be used later, refrigerate in an airtight container.*

*The White Chocolate Cream retains its quality for 2 weeks if properly refrigerated. Before using, allow chocolate cream to soften at room temperature.

Basic Novelty Craft Dough

Simple items such as Dough Napkin Rings can be made quickly and successfully. Dough baskets and trays of all sizes are particularly attractive; however, they are more challenging to make because cracking may occur after baking.

Ingredients
$2^1/2$ cups flour

pinch of salt

1 cup water

1 tablespoon oil

1 egg, beaten

Mix flour and salt together. Gradually add water.

Turn out dough on a clean dry surface; knead until dough is very soft and satiny. (Dough becomes less sticky. Do not add extra flour.)

Roll out dough on a floured surface; shape into desired forms or items.

Paint dough craft with beaten egg.

Bake at 190°C/375°F until golden brown.

Allow to cool. Set novelty dough objects aside to dry in a warm room for several days.

Store carefully to prevent breakage, in a cool dry place. If handled with care, novelty dough objects could last for years.

Flambé

Food flambéed at the table always adds a bit of magic to an occasion. Guests marvel at the length of time the flame lasts; however, there are a few tricks! First, I always use rum. Secondly, the rum and the container must both be hot. Thirdly, the surface area of the rum should be small, so that the rum is of sufficient depth to sustain a supply of fuel for the flame (while at the same time, only a limited amount of oxygen is allowed to access and gradually feed the flame).

If a sauce is served flaming in a bowl, it is best if the bowl is two-thirds to three-quarters full. The sauce bowl should have vertically straight sides which protect the flame from drafts and from being consumed too quickly.

When possible, I personally flambé individual dishes at the table with flaming rum which is presented separately on its own, in a small heated ramekin dish. With this "straight rum" technique, the flame lasts for the longest period of time.

Ingredient

white rum as required*

Pour rum in a very small covered saucepan. Place over medium high heat until it is "heard" to have come to a rapid simmer. Remove covered saucepan from (and away from) heat; only then, remove cover to check that rum is indeed hot and simmering.

Quickly and carefully pour simmering rum on surface of hot sauce in a heated container, or pour simmering rum directly into a heated small ramekin dish. Immediately ignite rum, and transfer it to the table. Dramatically, but carefully, spoon a little flaming sauce or rum over food. (When serving a flaming sauce, place sauce spoon directly, and deep, into sauce; remove spoon filled with sauce in a vertical fashion to avoid disturbing top layer of rum significantly, or mixing the rum with the sauce.)

*Usually ¼ to ⅓ cup rum is sufficient. If using the "straight rum" (poured into a heated ramekin dish) technique, allow ¼ cup rum arranged in a ⅓ cup size ramekin dish.

SALAD DRESSINGS

Herb Vinaigrette

Ingredients

1 cup salad oil

¼ cup white vinegar

2 tablespoons lemon juice

1⅓ tablespoons sugar

1½ teaspoons salt

1 tablespoon fresh dill, chopped

1 tablespoon fresh parsley, chopped

1 teaspoon black peppercorns, crushed

1 teaspoon powder mustard

1¼ teaspoons fresh garlic, crushed

(Makes 1⅓ cups)

Combine ingredients together well. Refrigerate in a well sealed bottle.*

Shake well before using. Serve with a wide variety of cold or hot salads. (Herb Vinaigrette may be served at any temperature.)

* If refrigerated, Herb Vinaigrette retains its quality for weeks. (It only gets better!)

Honey Mustard Mayonnaise

Ingredients

2 egg yolks

1 teaspoon powder mustard

½ teaspoon salt

1 teaspoon black peppercorns, crushed

1 teaspoon tarragon vinegar

½ cup olive oil

1 teaspoon lemon juice

½ cup salad oil

1 tablespoon liquid honey

2 tablespoons Dijon mustard

½ cup mayonnaise, commercial

(Makes 1¾ cup)

Using an electric beater set at medium speed, thoroughly combine egg yolks, powder mustard, salt, and pepper. Beat in vinegar.

At high speed, gradually add ¼ cup of the olive oil (1 teaspoon at a time).

Alternately add lemon juice and all remaining oil (¼ cup at a time) to form basic dressing mixture. (All remaining oil includes: ¼ cup olive oil, plus ½ cup salad oil.)

In a small bowl, blend together honey and Dijon mustard; beat into basic dressing mixture with electric beater.* Whisk mayonnaise into dressing to form smooth Honey Mustard Mayonnaise. Store refrigerated in a well sealed glass jar.**

Serve with salads, deep-fried foods, or as a dip. (Never heat Honey Mustard Mayonnaise.)

*If Honey Mustard Mayonnaise separates, pass it through a fine sieve; whisk with mayonnaise as outlined in recipe.

**If refrigerated, Honey Mustard Mayonnaise retains its quality for 1 month or longer.

Citus Peel Dressing

Ingredients

$^1/_4$ cup fresh orange rind, finely slivered

1 cup orange juice

2 tablespoons lemon juice

$^1/_4$ cup water

$^1/_4$ cup orange marmalade

2 teaspoons French mustard

1 teaspoon fresh ginger root, very finely chopped

(Makes about $^3/_4$ cup)

Simmer slivered orange rind in a saucepan with a little boiling water for 2 or 3 minutes. Drain cooked peel, and set aside. Discard liquid.

Combine remaining ingredients in saucepan over medium heat. Boil gently until sauce is reduced to half the original volume. Stir in the cooked orange peel. Store refrigerated in well sealed glass jar.*

Stir well before using. Serve Citrus Peel Dressing, hot or cold, with cooked vegetables, salads, chicken, or game.

*If refrigerated, Citrus Peel Dressing keeps well for about 1 week. It may be frozen for months.

Garlic Dressing

Ingredients

$1^1/_2$ teaspoons fresh garlic, crushed

1 egg

1 egg yolk

1 tablespoon lemon juice

1 cup oil

2 teaspoons Parmesan cheese, grated

$^1/_2$ teaspoon fresh garlic,* finely chopped

1 teaspoon liquid honey

$^1/_8$ teaspoon salt

(Makes $1^1/_3$ cups)

Place crushed garlic, egg, egg yolk, and lemon juice in a blender**. Blend until smooth.

Gradually add oil so that it flows in a thread-like manner. Blend mixture until dressing is thick.

Transfer dressing to a glass jar. Stir in Parmesan cheese, chopped garlic*, honey, and salt. Cover jar with an airtight lid. Store refrigerated.***

Serve Garlic Dressing drizzled over salad, grilled meat, or chicken. (Never heat Garlic Dressing.)

*Optional

**Option

An electric beater, operating on medium speed, may be used.

***If refrigerated, Garlic Dressing retains its quality for about 1 week. (It may not be frozen.)

Garlic Cheese Mayonnaise

Ingredients

1 cup mayonnaise, commercial

$^1/_4$ cup olive oil

3 tablespoons* Parmesan cheese, grated

1 tablespoon whole grain mustard

1 teaspoon Dijon mustard

1 teaspoon fresh garlic, finely chopped

$^1/_4$ teaspoon black peppercorns, crushed

1 egg yolk

(Makes $1^1/_4$ cups)

Mix all ingredients together in a blender to form a smooth mixture. Store refrigerated in a well sealed glass jar.**

Serve with salads, raw or cold vegetables, cold pasta or chicken, or as a dip. (Never heat Garlic Cheese Mayonnaise.)

*Add Parmesan cheese according to taste.

**If refrigerated, Garlic Cheese Mayonnaise retains its quality for 2 months.

Red Bell Pepper Mayonnaise

Ingredients

200 g or 7 oz fresh red bell peppers

$^1/_2$ teaspoon salt

2 tablespoons lemon juice

1 teaspoon French mustard

2 teaspoons fresh garlic, crushed

1 teaspoon fresh ginger root, finely chopped

2 egg yolks*

$1^1/_2$ cups oil*

$^1/_4$ cup basil, chopped

$^1/_8$ teaspoon fresh hot red chilli pepper, very finely chopped

pinch of white sugar

(Makes 2 cups)

Cut each red pepper into 6 pieces. Remove seeds and membranes. Grill under broiler or over hot charcoal with skin-side facing heat. When skin blisters and blackens, remove from heat. Peel away and discard skin.

Coarsely chop skinless roasted peppers. Place peppers in a blender; add salt; process to form a smooth purée. Remove purée from blender; set aside.

To make the mayonnaise*, combine lemon juice, mustard, garlic, ginger, and egg yolks in a blender; blend until smooth. With blender operating, gradually add oil so that it flows in a thread-like manner. Blend until mayonnaise thickens. (A mixer and bowl may also be used.)

Remove mayonnaise from blender; stir in red pepper purée, basil, and chilli. Add a pinch of sugar to enhance flavours. Store refrigerated in an airtight container.**

Serve with a wide variety of salads, grilled chicken, or veal. (Never heat Red Bell Pepper Mayonnaise.)

*Option If desired, to make Quick Red Bell Pepper Mayonnaise, commercial mayonnaise may be used as a base, omitting the egg yolks and oil. Simply add the roasted pepper purée, lemon juice, mustard, garlic, ginger, basil, and chilli pepper to 1³/₄ cups commercial mayonnaise. The final product is not as flavourful when first prepared; however, flavours are greatly enhanced if the mayonnaise is stored for a few days or 1 week. Quick Red Bell Pepper Mayonnaise retains its quality for a longer period of time (several weeks) than the regular version.

**If refrigerated, Red Bell Pepper Mayonnaise retains its quality for about 1 week. (It may not be frozen.)

Tahina Sauce

Ingredients

1 cup tahina (sesame seed paste)

3 tablespoons fresh lemon juice

²/₃ cup cold water

1 teaspoon fresh garlic, finely chopped

1¹/₄ teaspoons ground cumin

²/₃ teaspoon salt

pinch of sugar

1¹/₂ tablespoons virgin olive oil

¹/₂ cup fresh parsley, finely chopped

(Makes 2 cups)

Blend all ingredients together well to form a smooth mixture.*

Serve Tahina Sauce in a flat bowl. If desired, drizzle surface with additional olive oil, and garnish with more chopped parsley.

Tahina Sauce is excellent as a dip, particularly with pita bread.

*For a thinner sauce, add more olive oil.

Apricot Curry Mayonnaise

Ingredients

3 tablespoons apricot jam

1 teaspoon curry powder

1 cup mayonnaise, commercial

milk as required

(Makes about 1¹/₄ cups)

Stir apricot jam, curry powder, and mayonnaise together well. If necessary add a little milk, 1 teaspoon at a time, to produce a mayonnaise which forms soft peaks when dropped from a spoon. Store refrigerated in an airtight container.*

Serve particularly with deep-fried foods or as a dip. (Never heat Apricot Curry Mayonnaise.)

*If refrigerated, Apricot Curry Mayonnaise retains its quality for 2 months.

Ginger Mayonnaise

Ingredients

1 to 1¹/₂ tablespoons* fresh ginger root, very finely chopped

1 cup mayonnaise, commercial

1 to 2 teaspoons* sugar

milk as required

(Makes 1 cup)

Mix mayonnaise, ginger, and sugar together thoroughly, and according to taste. If necessary add a little milk, 1 teaspoon at a time, to produce a mayonnaise which forms soft peaks when dropped from a spoon. (Add more milk to produce a thinner mayonnaise for salads.) Store refrigerated in an airtight container.**

Serve with grilled or deep-fried foods, salads, savoury crêpes or pastry dishes, or as a dip. (Never heat Ginger Mayonnaise.)

*Add according to taste.

**If refrigerated, Ginger Mayonnaise retains its quality for 2 weeks.

Coriander Mayonnaise

Ingredients

1 cup mayonnaise, commercial

2 teaspoons fresh coriander, crushed

milk as required

(Makes 1 cup)

Mix mayonnaise and coriander together thoroughly. If necessary add a little milk, 1 teaspoon at a time, to produce a mayonnaise which forms soft peaks when dropped from a spoon. (Add more milk to produce a thinner mayonnaise for salads.) Store refrigerated in an airtight container.*

Serve with grilled or deep-fried foods, salads, vegetables, or as a dip. (Never heat Coriander Mayonnaise.)

*If refrigerated, Coriander Mayonnaise retains its quality for 2 weeks.

Hollandaise Mayonnaise

Ingredients

3 to 4 teaspoons French mustard

2 cups mayonnaise, commercial

milk as required

(Makes 2 cups)

Stir mustard and mayonnaise together well. Only if necessary add a little milk, 1 teaspoon at a time, to produce a mayonnaise which forms soft peaks when dropped from a spoon.

Store refrigerated in an airtight container.*

Serve Hollandaise Mayonnaise particularly with eggs, vegetables, savoury crêpes, and pastry. (Never heat Hollandaise Mayonnaise.)

*If refrigerated, Hollandaise Mayonnaise retains its quality for 2 months.

Horseradish Mayonnaise

Ingredients

1 tablespoon Horseradish relish

1 cup mayonnaise, commercial

milk as required

(Makes 1 cup)

Stir horseradish relish and mayonnaise together well. If necessary add a little milk, 1 teaspoon at a time, to produce a mayonnaise which forms soft peaks when dropped from a spoon. Store refrigerated in an airtight container.*

Serve Horseradish Mayonnaise with fish and beef. (Never heat Horseradish Mayonnaise.)

*If refrigerated, Horseradish Mayonnaise retains its quality for 2 months.

SAVOURY SAUCES

Basic White Sauce*

Ingredients

1 teaspoon medium flavoured chicken bouillon cube, crushed

2 tablespoons hot water

$2/3$ cup whole milk

$1/3$ cup evaporated milk

1 to $1^1/2$ tablespoons* flour

$1/2$ teaspoon salt

$1/8$ teaspoon white pepper

other herbs and spices** as desired

cream as desired

(Makes 1 cup)

In a small heavy saucepan, dissolve crushed bouillon cube in hot water.

Combine whole milk and evaporated milk in a bowl; whisk in flour to form a smooth mixture. Sieve flour mixture into a small heavy saucepan. Whisk constantly over medium low heat until sauce thickens and bubbles.

Add salt and pepper. Add herbs and other spices as desired. Adjust seasoning to taste. Whisk in a little cream if desired.*** Remove from heat.

Use White Sauce for a variety of recipes (e.g. other sauces, soups, savoury mousses). (This sauce may be frozen.)

*Option
The quantity of flour used may be adjusted depending on the consistency of sauce desired. Use about $3^1/2$ tablespoons flour to prepare a Thick White Sauce, suitable for making stuffings or croquette type of dishes.

**These may include fresh garlic, ginger, tarragon, curry, and saffron.

***If not using sauce immediately, cover surface closely with wax paper until sauce cools.

Curry Sauce

Ingredients

2 tablespoons butter

$1/4$ cup shallots, chopped

1 tablespoon flour*

$1/4$ teaspoon ground cumin

1 teaspoon curry powder

$1/2$ teaspoon salt

1 cup whole milk

$1/2$ cup evaporated milk

cream as desired

(Makes $1^1/2$ cups)

Melt butter in a small heavy saucepan; add shallots, and stir over medium heat until tender.

Blend in flour, cumin, curry powder, and salt; cook for about 1 minute.

Gradually add whole milk and evaporated milk, whisking constantly to form a smooth mixture. Continue whisking until sauce bubbles and thickens.* Reduce heat to low. Stir in a little cream if desired.**

Serve with poultry, particularly roasted poultry. (Sauce may be frozen.)

*If a thicker sauce is desired, whisk a little more flour with a minimum amount of water. Whisk flour mixture into sauce; stir constantly until sauce bubbles and thickens.

**If not using sauce immediately, cover surface closely with wax paper until sauce cools.

Saffron Sauce

Ingredients

$1/16$ teaspoon saffron threads, very finely chopped

3 tablespoons hot water

1 teaspoon medium flavoured chicken bouillon cube, crushed

$1/2$ cup evaporated milk

1 tablespoon flour*

$1/2$ cup whole milk

$1/2$ teaspoon fresh ginger root, grated

$1/2$ teaspoon fresh garlic, crushed

$1/4$ teaspoon ground nutmeg

$1/4$ teaspoon salt

$1/8$ teaspoon black peppercorns, crushed

$1/2$ teaspoon French mustard

$1^1/2$ teaspoons brandy

cream as desired

(Makes 1 cup)

Soak saffron in 1 tablespoon hot water for about 5 minutes.

Dissolve crushed bouillon cube in remaining 2 tablespoons hot water.

Heat evaporated milk in a small heavy saucepan over medium heat.

In a small bowl, whisk flour into whole milk until smooth. Pour flour mixture through a sieve into hot evaporated milk over medium heat, whisking constantly. Add bouillon and saffron mixtures, ginger, garlic, and nutmeg; whisk constantly until sauce bubbles and thickens.* Season with salt and pepper.

Reduce heat to warm; stir in mustard and brandy. Add a little cream and adjust seasoning if desired.**

Serve with seafood, fish, chicken, pasta, crêpes, and vegetables. (Sauce may be frozen.)

*If a thicker sauce is desired, whisk a little more flour with a minimum amount of water. Whisk flour mixture into sauce; stir constantly until sauce bubbles and thickens.

**If not using sauce immediately, cover surface closely with wax paper until sauce cools.

Watercress Sauce

Ingredients

280 g or 10 oz fresh watercress* leaves

1 teaspoon medium flavoured chicken bouillon cube, crushed

2 tablespoons hot water

1/2 cup dry white wine

3 tablespoons dry vermouth

2 tablespoons shallots, finely chopped

3/4 cup whipping cream

pinch of dried tarragon

1/2 cup cold butter

salt to taste

pepper to taste

(Makes 2 cups)

To blanch watercress leaves, drop leaves into a large pot of boiling salted water; bring back to a boil. Drain immediately, discard water; quickly transfer leaves to a pan of ice water; allow leaves to cool. Drain fairly well.

Place leaves in a food processor; blend to form a purée. Set watercress purée aside.

Dissolve chicken bouillon cube in hot water; set aside.

Cut cold butter into 1 cm or 1/3 inch cubes; refrigerate. Combine wine, vermouth, and shallots in a small saucepan. Bring shallot mixture to a boil over medium heat. Without lowering heat, allow mixture to boil for 3 minutes, reducing volume to about 1/3

cup. Strain liquid into another small heavy saucepan, discarding shallot pulp.

Add chicken bouillon mixture, cream, and tarragon to strained liquid in saucepan. Cook over medium heat until mixture almost reaches a boil; immediately remove from heat.

Whisk cold butter, one cube at a time, into mixture. If necessary, place saucepan over very low heat; carefully allow butter to just melt, producing a creamy sauce; promptly remove from heat. (Mixture must not become oily.) Stir in watercress purée; add salt and pepper according to taste.

Before serving, carefully reheat sauce over just hot (not yet simmering) water.

Serve Watercress Sauce with fish, seafood, chicken, pasta, savoury crêpes, tofu, and egg dishes. (Do not freeze sauce.)

*Option
To make a basic White Wine Sauce, omit the watercress and butter from the recipe.

Caper Cream Sauce

Ingredients

1/2 cup fresh shallots, finely chopped

1 tablespoon butter

1 1/2 tablespoons flour

1 1/2 teaspoons dark beef bouillon cube, crushed

3/4 cup boiling water

1/2 cup white wine

1 teaspoon wine vinegar

1/4 cup whipping cream

1 to 2 tablespoons capers (very well drained)

salt to taste

crushed black peppercorns to taste

(Makes 1 1/2 cups)

In a small heavy saucepan, sauté shallots in butter until golden brown. Blend in flour; cook for about 1 minute.

Dissolve beef bouillon cube in boiling water; add to saucepan, whisking constantly to form a smooth mixture. Whisk in wine and vinegar; cover; simmer gently for 15 minutes, stirring occasionally.

Pour contents of saucepan into blender; purée well; strain.

Pour strained purée into top of double boiler; add cream, salt, and pepper; heat carefully. (If cream does not blend in smoothly, return sauce to blender; process for about 10 seconds.) Add capers as desired.

Reheat sauce over medium low heat.*

Serve sauce with veal, lamb, beef, pork, or white fleshed fish such as swordfish. (Sauce may be frozen.)

*If a thicker sauce is desired, whisk a little more flour with a minimum amount of water. Whisk flour mixture into sauce; stir constantly until sauce bubbles and thickens.

If not using sauce immediately, cover surface closely with wax paper until sauce cools.

Red Bell Pepper Sauce

Ingredients

400 g or 14 oz fresh red bell peppers

4 cloves garlic (large)

1/2 teaspoon dried thyme

pinch to 1/3 teaspoon* black peppercorns, freshly crushed

2 tablespoons olive oil

1/2 teaspoon medium flavoured chicken bouillon cube, crushed

1/2 cup hot water

1/8 teaspoon fresh hot red chilli pepper, very finely chopped**

1/3 to 1/2 teaspoon salt

1 teaspoon vinegar

1 teaspoon sherry

(Makes 2 cups)

Cut peppers into quarters. Remove and discard seeds and membranes.

In a baking dish, toss together bell peppers, garlic, thyme, black pepper, and oil. Cover dish with aluminum foil (dull side out).

Bake pepper mixture, covered, at 180°C/350°F until bell peppers are tender (about 45 minutes).

Place contents of baking dish in a blender. (Do not peel roasted peppers.) Add all remaining ingredients; blend until smooth.

Transfer Red Bell Pepper Sauce to a small heavy saucepan; bring to a boil.

Adjust seasoning if necessary. Allow sauce to rest over warm heat for about 15 minutes to develop flavours.

Serve with chicken, pasta, or savoury pastry dishes. (Sauce may be frozen.)

*Add quantity desired.
**Optional

Brandy Cream Sauce

Ingredients

1 teaspoon fresh garlic, finely chopped
1 tablespoon butter
1¹/₂ tablespoons flour
1¹/₂ teaspoons medium flavoured chicken bouillon cubes, crushed
³/₄ cup boiling water
2 tablespoons dry white wine
1 teaspoon French mustard
¹/₄ cup whipping cream
1 tablespoon brandy

(Makes 1 cup)

Sauté garlic in melted butter in a small heavy saucepan over medium heat; blend in flour. Dissolve crushed bouillon cube in hot water.

Add bouillon mixture, wine, and mustard to saucepan over medium heat, whisking constantly to blend well. Bring sauce to a boil.* Reduce heat to low. Stir cream into sauce, heating carefully. When sauce begins to bubble, remove immediately from heat. Stir in brandy.** Reheat sauce over medium low heat.

Serve with chicken, fish, seafood, pork, veal, and pasta. (Sauce may be frozen.)

*If a thicker sauce is desired, whisk a little more flour with a minimum amount of water. Whisk flour mixture into sauce; stir constantly until sauce bubbles and thickens.

**If not using sauce immediately, cover surface closely with wax paper until sauce cools.

Tomato Brandy Cream Sauce

Ingredients

1 recipe Brandy Cream Sauce
1 tablespoon tomato sauce

(Makes 1 cup)

Prepare Brandy Cream Sauce as outlined in recipe, adding tomato sauce along with brandy (when sauce is cooked and has been removed from heat).

Reheat sauce over low heat.

Serve with chicken, fish, seafood, veal, and pasta. (Sauce may be frozen.)

Red Wine Mustard Sauce

Ingredients

1 tablespoon butter or margarine
1¹/₂ to 2 tablespoons flour*
1¹/₂ teaspoons dark beef bouillon cubes, well crushed
1 cup hot water
¹/₂ cup dry red wine
1 teaspoon French mustard

(Makes 1¹/₄ cups)

Melt butter in a small heavy saucepan. Blend in flour; stir over high heat until flour browns; remove from heat.

Dissolve beef cubes in water. Whisk beef bouillon mixture and wine into saucepan; blend well. Continue to whisk mixture constantly over high heat until sauce boils.

Reduce heat to medium. Allow sauce to boil rapidly, uncovered and stirring occasionally, for about 5 minutes until sauce thickens.* Stir in mustard.**

Serve with beef, lamb, pork, veal, or game. (Sauce may be frozen.)

*If a thicker sauce is desired, whisk a little more flour with a minimum amount of water. Whisk flour mixture into sauce; stir constantly until sauce bubbles and thickens.

**If not using sauce immediately, cover surface closely with wax paper until sauce cools.

Green Peppercorn Sauce

Ingredients

2 tablespoons butter
2 to 4 tablespoons* flour
1 tablespoon dark beef bouillon cubes, crushed
1 cup hot water
1 cup dry white or red wine**
1 teaspoon sugar
1 teaspoon Dijon mustard
1¹/₂ to 3 teaspoons green peppercorns (preserved in brine), drained
2 tablespoons whipping cream***

(Makes 2 cups)

Melt butter in a small heavy saucepan over medium heat. Add flour*, blending well into melted butter.

Dissolve crushed bouillon cubes in hot water. Add bouillon mixture, wine, sugar, and mustard to saucepan, whisking constantly to blend well and until sauce bubbles. Stir in peppercorns according to taste. Reduce heat; simmer for 3 minutes.

Stir cream into sauce; remove from heat. If not using sauce immediately, cover surface closely with wax paper until sauce cools. Reheat sauce over medium low heat.

Serve Green Peppercorn Sauce with beef, lamb, chicken, veal, pork, game, or white fleshed fish such as swordfish. (Sauce may be frozen.)

*The quantity of flour used depends on the consistency desired for the sauce. Use 1/4 cup (i.e. 4 tablespoons) flour to produce a thick sauce such as that required for Lamb Stroganoff.

**Red wine produces a sauce with a mellower flavour and richer colour which is more suitable for serving with red meats. Green Peppercorn Sauce prepared with white wine is better for veal, pork, poultry, or white fleshed fish.

***Optional
Whipping cream gives the sauce a milder flavour and creamier colour.

Whisky Parsley Sauce

2 teaspoons dark beef bouillon cubes, well crushed
1 cup hot water
2 tablespoons butter
$1^1/_3$ tablespoons flour
$1^1/_2$ tablespoons fresh parsley, chopped
$^1/_2$ cup whipping cream
1 tablespoon whisky*
$^1/_2$ teaspoon lemon juice*

(Makes $1^1/_2$ cups)

Dissolve crushed bouillon cubes in hot water.

Melt butter in a saucepan over medium heat. Add flour, blending well with melted butter.

Add bouillon mixture to saucepan, whisking constantly until smooth. Continue whisking until sauce bubbles.** Reduce heat to simmer.

Blend parsley and cream into sauce. If desired, stir in whisky (according to taste), and lemon juice.***

Serve with beef, lamb, veal, game, and chicken. (Sauce may be frozen.)

*Optional
**If a thicker sauce is desired, whisk a little more flour with a minimum amount of water. Whisk flour mixture into sauce; stir constantly until sauce bubbles and thickens.

***If not using sauce immediately, cover surface closely with wax paper until sauce cools. Reheat sauce over medium low heat.

Newburg Sauce

2 tablespoons butter
2 tablespoons flour
$^1/_4$ teaspoon ginger powder
$^1/_4$ teaspoon paprika
$^1/_8$ teaspoon garlic powder
pinch of ground nutmeg
pinch of dried dill weed
$^1/_4$ teaspoon salt
1 cup whole milk
$^1/_2$ cup whipping cream
1 can crab meat, undrained
(can size: 170 g or 6 oz)
2 tablespoons dry sherry

(Makes 2 cups)

Melt butter in a small heavy saucepan over medium heat. Combine flour, spices, and salt; blend into melted butter.

Add milk, whisking constantly to form a smooth mixture. Continue whisking until mixture begins to thicken. Reduce heat to medium low; add cream, whisking constantly until sauce bubbles and thickens. Remove sauce from heat.

Drain liquid from crab meat into sauce. Remove and discard any pieces of shell from crab meat. Separate crab meat into flakes; blend crab meat into sauce. Stir in sherry. Adjust seasoning if necessary. Carefully reheat sauce over low heat.*

* If not using sauce immediately, cover surface closely with wax paper until sauce cools.

Orange Cranberry Sauce

Ingredients
1 cup cranberry sauce
1 tablespoon orange marmalade, preferably coarse cut
1 teaspoon orange peel, grated
1 teaspoon orange peel, finely slivered

(Makes 1 cup)

Mix all the ingredients together well. Refrigerate in an airtight container until required.*

Serve with poultry, game, pork, and veal.

*If refrigerated, Orange Cranberry Sauce retains its quality for 2 weeks or longer.

DESSERT SAUCES

Ginger Sour Cream

Ingredients
1 cup sour cream
1 teaspoon ginger powder
1 tablespoon ginger marmalade
2 tablespoons* sugar
$1^1/_2$ teaspoons candied ginger, finely chopped

(Makes 1 cup)

Mix all ingredients together until smooth.** Place sauce in an airtight container; refrigerate.***

Serve with fruit, scones, tea biscuits, crêpes, coffee breads, and cakes.

*Add more sugar if desired. (Adjust sweetness of sauce, depending on its use or personal taste preference.)

**If a thinner sauce is required, add evaporated milk, 1 teaspoon at a time, to create desired consistency.

***If refrigerated, Ginger Sour Cream retains its quality for 2 weeks.

Butterscotch Sauce Supreme

Ingredients
¹/₂ cup butter

¹/₄ cup corn syrup

³/₄ cup brown sugar, well packed

1¹/₃ cups whipping cream

(Makes 2¹/₂ cups)

Melt butter in a small heavy saucepan over medium low heat.

Add syrup and sugar. Stir constantly to dissolve sugar without allowing mixture to boil. Reduce heat to barely simmer.

Without stirring, let syrupy mixture simmer, uncovered, for 2 minutes. Remove from heat.

Stir in cream. If Butterscotch Sauce Supreme is not to be used immediately, store refrigerated in an airtight container.*

Butterscotch Sauce Supreme may be served at any temperature depending on the consistency desired. It is best served at room temperature or barely warm.

Serve with ice cream, crêpes, waffles, French toast, some fruits, and desserts.

*If refrigerated, Butterscotch Sauce Supreme retains its quality for at least 2 weeks. The sauce may also be frozen.

Quick Fruit Sauce

This sauce is also great as a coulis for desserts. Almost any jam may be used. The choice depends on the colour as well as the flavour desired. I prefer sugarless varieties of jam, adding a little liqueur which complements the flavour of the jam. Sometimes, only a few drops of water, rather than a liqueur, are added. However, only enough liqueur or water (or a combination of the two) is added carefully to give the sauce the consistency desired.

Quick Strawberry* Sauce

1 cup strawberry jam*

1 tablespoon orange* flavoured liqueur (or water)

1 teaspoon lemon (or lime) peel**, grated

¹/₄ teaspoon ground cinnamon (or ginger powder)**

(Makes 1 cup)

Blend ingredients together. Refrigerate in an airtight container***.

Serve as a coulis or as a sauce for ice cream, scones, tea biscuits, crêpes, or desserts.

*Options

Other jams and liqueurs may be used.

**Optional

***If refrigerated, Quick Fruit Sauce retains its quality for 2 to 3 weeks.

RECIPE INDEX

GENERAL INDEX